SPEAK FOR YOURSELF

AN INTRODUCTION TO PUBLIC SPEAKING

D0947634

SPEAK FOR YOURSELF

AN INTRODUCTION TO PUBLIC SPEAKING

FOURTH EDITION

James H. Byrns
Diablo Valley College

Boston, Massachusetts   Burn Ridge, Illinois   Dubuque, Iowa
Madison, Wisconin   New York, New York   San Franciso, Californa
St. Louis, Missouri

McGraw-Hill

*A Division of The **McGraw·Hill** Companies*

SPEAK FOR YOURSELF
An Introduction to Public Speaking

Interior photos courtesy of Diablo Valley College and Los Medanos College. Reprinted by permission.

This book is printed on acid-free paper.

4 5 6 7 8 9 0 DOC DOC   0

ISBN 0-07-009632-5

This book was set in Times Roman by The Clarinda Company.
The editors were Marjorie Byers, Fran Marino, and Valerie Raymond;
the production supervisior was Kathryn Porzio.
The cover was designed by Karen K. Quigley.
Project supervision was done by Tage Publishing Service, Inc.
R. R. Donnelley & Sons Company was printer and binder.

Cover Photo: David Young-Wolff/PhotoEdit.

Library of Congress Cataloging-in-Publication Data

Byrns, James H., (date)
    Speak for yourself: an introduction to public speaking / James H.
Byrns. — 4th ed.
        p.   cm.
    Includes bibliographical references and index.
    ISBN 0-07-009632-5
    1. Public speaking.   I. Title.
PN4121.B96   1997
808.5′1—dc20   96-19071

ABOUT
THE AUTHOR

JAMES H. BYRNS is a professor of speech communication at Diablo Valley College, a large two-year college (22,000 enrollment) in Pleasant Hill, California located in the East Bay of San Francisco. He received his B.A. and M.A. degrees from California State University, Sacramento. He has served as an officer and president of various professional organizations including the Bay Area Speech Teachers (San Francisco Bay Area), the California Communication Association, and on various organizing committees and special interest sections of the Western States Communication Association, and the Speech Communication Association of America. He has also been a member of the National Association of Training and Development (NSTD).

He chaired the Communications Development Committee that conducted surveys of training needs of large organizations and developed a series of communication workshops for business and professional groups.

He is a consultant and conducts communication workshops for large organizations. His clients include MCI, AT&T, Coopers & Lybrand, and Levi Strauss & Co.

To Kathy
for your inspiration and love

CONTENTS

PREFACE

Public speaking is an integral part of the student's college experience and future professional life and success. In today's Information Age, students speak more, not less, to more diverse audiences on-the-job, in the community, politically, and in the banquet hall. New settings for speaking, such as teleconferencing, videoconferencing, and team presentations, place even greater demands on communicating effectively.

At its heart, public speaking is about ethics, and students are immediately encouraged to discover and articulate their values and beliefs and make them the basis of their communications. Authenticity and integrity are the foundations of effective public speaking.

Speak for Yourself encourages students to view public speaking as a means of empowering others. When speakers communicate ethically and substantively they enhance listeners' lives. When speakers show an audience how to complete a new task or do one more efficiently, communicate an idea that enlightens, motivate listeners to behave in a beneficial manner, or inspire people to do good, they are building listeners' confidence by giving them information that helps them grow and succeed.

To that end, *Speak for Yourself* focuses on mastering the fundamentals of communication with a special emphasis on audience analysis, organization, and critical thinking. Selecting quality information has been added to this list. T. S. Eliot said, "Where is the knowledge we have lost in information?" Students must be able to distinguish between entertainment and information if they are to create real meaning and speak with credibility.

As in previous editions *Speak for Yourself* makes a conscious effort to be gender–neutral and culturally inclusive, not as ends in themselves but as means to an end. The goal is not to create artificial distinctions or new stereotypes. The better we understand and the more we respect each other's needs and aspirations, the more effectively we can communicate.

The fundamentals of public speaking are presented in a lively and entertaining style. The text does not talk down to students or belabor key concepts. Indeed, *Speak for Yourself* lives up to the principles it espouses: important ideas clearly and enthusiastically presented. Communication comes to life.

As always, *Speak for Yourself* is uncompromising in its approach to credibility, rational analysis, the ethics of communication, and quality information, themes that resonate throughout the text.

Speak for Yourself has been significantly revised. A new chapter on reasoning has been added, "Reasoning and Critical Analysis." Coverage of important ideas has been expanded—such as the principles of public speaking, credibility, ethics, critical thinking, persuasion, evidence, discovering the central idea, and selecting quality information. Chapter 14 has been rewritten to expand the coverage of ethics, credibility, and emotional proofs.

Important concepts are introduced early in the text and reinforced in subsequent chapters. The subject of ethics, for example, is introduced in Chapter 1 and then covered extensively in Chapters 2, 3, 5, 7, 13, 14, and 15. Similar patterns have been designed for other principles such as audience analysis, credibility, and selecting quality information.

More than a hundred new, vivid, and entertaining examples from contemporary speeches bring the concepts to life and make reading enjoyable. Numerous new learning aids and activities reinforce important concepts and processes. For example, a unique formula helps students discover and phrase the specific purposes and central ideas for their speeches.

FEATURES OF THE FOURTH EDITION

New chapter:

- A new chapter, Chapter 15, "Reasoning and Critical Analysis," shows students how to use evidence to build and strengthen their arguments. Four important types of arguments are extensively discussed along with sample outlines. Six common types of fallacies are discussed along with examples.

New material:

- Chapter 14, "Speaking to Persuade," has been rewritten. The "Ethics of Persuasion" has been expanded, explaining why ethical persuasion is crucial to success. Specific guidelines are presented. Many examples are used in support. The discussion of logos, pathos, and ethos uses real-life examples and guidelines for strengthening these important appeals. An exciting new sample speech helps students learn how inductive reasoning and emotion are used to persuade.
- A unique approach to public speaking, called "ARRCS," is introduced in Chapter 1. ARRCS is an audience-based approach to public speaking

that stands for "Getting Attention, Establishing Rapport, Showing Relevance, Building Confidence, and Proving Satisfaction." This approach gives the student important principles for preparing speeches and measuring their effectiveness.

- "Using the Library," in Chapter 5, has been updated so students can easily use computer and electronic databases and other sources of information. A section on selecting quality information helps students choose the strongest sources for their presentations. A unique table helps students distinguish between reliable and less reliable information.
- Numerous new, unique learning aids add to the many already contained in the text. In Chapter 4, a "Specific Purpose/Central Idea Formula" helps students learn how to discover and phrase the specific purpose and central idea, a problem for many students. A "logic tree" in Chapter 15 helps students understand how arguments are developed and presented in a speech.

ORGANIZATION OF THE TEXT

The fourth edition adds a new chapter, Chapter 15, "Reasoning and Critical Analysis," to aid students in building and testing their arguments and to avoid erroneous thinking.

Part One, "Introduction to Public Speaking," establishes the philosophy of the text and the importance of listening in the public speaking process.

Chapter 1, "Introduction to Public Speaking," is a complete overview of the public speaking process. It defines the role of public speaking in the Information Age and describes the scope of public speaking, including banquet speaking, political speaking, on-the-job speaking, ceremonial speaking, and community speaking. It introduces the principles of public speaking— "ARRCS"—that make the audience the centerpiece for preparation and delivery, and emphasizes the importance of credibility to public speaking. Public speaking is presented as a skill to be embraced, not feared.

Chapter 2, "Listening," presents a unique six-step model for listening in the classroom and actual public speaking situations. It shows the student how to listen critically and for meaning. It lays the groundwork for critical analysis and speech organization by discussing the anatomy of a message— goal, central idea, main points, and evidence—and how to listen for them in a speech. It presents guidelines for presenting constructive feedback.

Part Two, "Preparing the Message," presents the steps of planning and preparing a speech.

Chapter 3, "Analyzing the Audience and Setting," places the audience at the center of the preparation process. Five steps for defining the target audience, along with exercises, are presented for students to apply to their classroom speeches and real-world audiences.

Chapter 4, "Selecting a Topic and Purpose," presents various methods for choosing a speech topic. Students learn how to narrow down and formulate a specific purpose and central idea. A unique formula is presented for helping students refine their objectives and ideas.

Chapter 5, "Gathering Information," simplifies the research process and makes it enjoyable. Every relevant source of information for personal interviews to computer databases and electronic search strategies is covered in detail. Students learn how to discover and select quality information.

Chapter 6, "Arranging the Body of the Speech," is the first of three chapters on outlining a speech. Students learn how to discover, select, phrase, arrange, and highlight main points in a speech. This is a key chapter on critical analysis; students learn to think logically and focus on communicating ideas.

Chapter 7, "Supporting the Main Points: Telling and Doing," is the first of two chapters on the use of supporting information. It shows how to use verbal support and activities to amplify and prove ideas, and gives students vivid and entertaining examples of supporting materials to make their ideas stand out. Special emphasis is given to statistics and testimony and how to communicate them clearly, credibly, and memorably. Extensive coverage is given to planning structured activities and leading audiences through them.

Chapter 8, "Supporting Main Points: Visual Aids," provides comprehensive coverage—with creative and entertaining illustrations—of types of visual aids, selecting the appropriate medium, and preparing and presenting visual support.

Chapter 9, "Opening and Closing the Speech," is a thorough discussion of introductions and conclusions with many examples from contemporary speeches. The focus is on achieving objectives for the introduction and conclusion, such as establishing rapport and reinforcing ideas.

Chapter 10, "Outlining Your Speech," shows students how to pull the parts of their speech together in one final outline form. Students learn to select an outline form, add subpoints, coordinate the opening and closing, and add finishing touches. The chapter builds to a complete speech outline from its parts. It also details methods for using speaking notes, including note cards, page outlines, and Post-it™ Notes.

Part Three, "Presenting the Speech," covers wording the speech and nonverbal communication.

Chapter 11, "Using Language in Public Speaking," guides the student in the effective use of language. The chapter encourages students to choose language that is clear, specific, vivid, and appropriate for the audience, and shows how to eliminate clutter. It has many examples from contemporary speeches and includes exercises and activities for improving language skills and using personalized language.

Chapter 12, "Delivery," focuses on credibility and authenticity as the basis of speaking and gives specific techniques for improving delivery. It shows students how to build enthusiasm and confidence, and gives tips for handling nervousness. Body language is emphasized with exercises to develop an open and natural speaking style. Also covered are team presentations, how to handle interference, and how to adapt to audience feedback.

Part Four, "Preparing Different Types of Speeches," shows how to plan and deliver speeches to inform and persuade as well as special-occasion speaking.

Chapter 13, "Speaking to Inform," emphasizes the value of communicating information effectively—empowering others—and the consequences of ineffective speaking. The chapter discusses four types of informative speeches and how to organize them. It gives eight principles for communicating information, supplies examples, including a sample informative speech about CPR with a manuscript, outline, and commentary.

Chapter 14, "Speaking to Persuade," emphasizes ethics, credibility, and reasoning as the basis of persuasion. The chapter covers different types of persuasive speeches and strategies for presenting them, sample outlines, and guidelines for ethical persuasion with extensive coverage of building credibility, and the appropriate use of emotional appeals. The many examples for contemporary speeches include a sample persuasive speech about "bomb-making literature" with a manuscript, outline, and commentary.

Chapter 15, "Reasoning and Critical Analysis," extensively discusses evidence and how to use it logically and persuasively in a presentation. Different types of arguments are discussed including reasoning with facts, reasoning from premises, reasoning from cause, and reasoning by analogy. Common fallacies are discussed in detail along with examples.

Chapter 16, "Speaking for Special Occasions," shows students how to prepare and deliver special presentations such as impromptu speeches, answering informational and challenging questions, introductions, after-dinner speaking, and acceptance and commemorative speeches with extensive coverage of the use of humor and many sample speeches.

The Appendix contains contemporary speeches by a diverse group of professional people:

"How to Talk to Anyone, Anytime, Anywhere," by Larry King, host, *Larry King Live.*

Acceptance Speech, by Supreme Court Justice Ruth Bader Ginsburg.

"I Am Not a Candidate," by General Colin Powell, retired Chairman of the Joint Chiefs of Staff.

ACKNOWLEDGMENTS

Writing a book is a team effort and I have many people to thank. First, I am grateful to the many reviewers whose excellent comments shaped both the organization and content of the book. They are Renie S. Braswell, Mayland Community College; James Como, York College; Steven A. Rollman, James Madison University; Paula Thomas, Washington State Community College; and Kevin Twohey, Diablo Valley College. A special thank you to Betty Bortz, for her help writing the section on using the library, and to Brett Dowell for his drawings and artwork. At McGraw-Hill, thanks to Fran Marino and Marge Byers, and at Tage, Tony Caruso.

James H. Byrns

SPEAK FOR YOURSELF

AN INTRODUCTION TO PUBLIC SPEAKING

INTRODUCTION TO PUBLIC SPEAKING AND LISTENING

1

INTRODUCTION TO PUBLIC SPEAKING

In 1960 President John F. Kennedy addressed a crowd at the Houston Space Center. During the course of that speech he made a prediction that scientists around the world dismissed as a pipe dream. He announced NASA's goal of landing a man on the moon within the decade. At that time the technology to accomplish the feat existed only in the minds of science fiction writers, the American space program was lagging far behind Soviet efforts, and the cost was absolutely prohibitive. Almost everyone believed that it was impossible—except Kennedy. The public statement of his vision galvanized the American scientific community to seek solution after solution, dismantling the seemingly endless series of roadblocks that stood between them and their goal, until, on July 22, 1969, nearly six years after Kennedy's death, Neil Armstrong became the first human to set foot on the moon.

This is one of thousands of potent examples of the power of public speaking. Through the simple act of speaking, President Kennedy was able to define a crucial national goal, and focus the energies of the nation on it. At its heart, public speaking is an act of public definition. Public speaking serves to express belief and intention.

Effective speakers are valued in all societies, whether literate or nonliterate, for a single reason: they are able to convey the ideas of the society. Using their voices, they stand out. They move and inspire others. They empower others. They articulate concepts and define issues in ways that help people learn and succeed.

President Clinton feels strongly on this issue. It is his view that at the core of the American economy and American competiveness in the future will be people whom he calls "symbolic analysts," that is, individuals who think in abstract symbols and are able to manipulate those symbols in order to communicate their meaning and value to others.[1] He believes that the focus will shift away from institutions and organizations toward individuals and their abilities to manipulate ideas and solve problems in the abstract, and then communicate those ideas to others so that the abstract becomes the real. The demand for good speakers, for effective communicators, will only grow and grow. It is our goal to help you become an effective speaker.

THE SCOPE OF PUBLIC SPEAKING

Each day millions of speeches are given that influence thoughts, actions, decision making, and learning. From the president addressing the nation to a homeowner speaking out against a new development in his community, public speaking affects the world in which we live and work. Let's discuss some of the important ways you will use public speaking.

Banquet Speaking

A speaker with special expertise or experience is invited to address the group about a subject of interest to them. For example, the American Management Association may invite an authority on sexual harassment to address their convention. The local Kiwanis Club may invite an expert on small business to address their weekly luncheon meeting. One authority estimates 100,000 banquet speeches are given daily.[2]

These speeches are highly prepared and usually given by very experienced and professional speakers. The topics are informative, sometimes persuasive, and must be entertaining. Many speakers are famous people like General Colin Powell and Margaret Thatcher, former Prime Minister of England, who command $60,000 for a single presentation. Former Secretary of State Henry Kissinger receives $40,000 for a 45-minute speech, lunch included. Professional lecturers or less well known speakers may command fees ranging from several hundred dollars into the low thousands for a single speech.[3] These speakers are sponsored by hundreds of speakers' bureaus throughout the country. The National Speaker's Association alone has 3,000 members.[4]

On-the-Job Speaking

On-the-job speaking is the broadest category of speaking and is directly related to performance and productivity. Job-related presentations include formal speeches as well as lectures, briefings, reports, and many unplanned or spontaneous addresses. They include a teacher or professor lecturing, a manager persuading a group of employees to cut costs, or an account executive giving a multimillion-dollar sales presentation. Attorneys arguing in the courtroom are speaking on the job.

Today, many presentations are given using teleconferencing technology. This type of communication requires clear and concise use of language so that business can be handled quickly and efficiently. Team presentations are becoming increasingly popular.[5] People working in small groups give team presentations directly to management and customers. These kinds of speeches require careful planning and coordination so that the whole team knows who is going to say what, and for how long.

On-the-job speaking is results-oriented and places great emphasis on informing and persuading. The presentation of information must be clear so that ideas and processes can be easily absorbed. Much employee learning, productivity, and motivation depend on effective communication. It must also be persuasive and empathetic because people can no longer be told what to do; they must be convinced that a particular policy or vision is worthy of acceptance. The performance of many supervisorial, management, and professional people is based on their ability to communicate.

On-the-job speaking is considered so important that it is a requisite skill for promotion and advancement.[6] Most large companies have trainers who specialize in teaching public speaking skills to their employees.[7] There are thousands of speakers' bureaus and organizations for professionals who want to upgrade their communication skills. The Toastmasters Club alone has more than 150,000 members worldwide. Speech training is a required course for most teacher certification programs. Most colleges and universities offer extensive public speaking courses to students and professionals.

Political Speaking

Political speaking is the most deliberate of all speaking. Many politicians have abandoned the traditional standards of debate and oratory and practice a highly sophisticated and manipulative form of communication designed to conceal real beliefs and highlight personal image. The political scene is dominated by political handlers and consultants who use television techniques to communicate their message and help their clients retain power. According to Christopher Matthews, Washington journalist, ". . . 99% of what you get from Washington is crafted for your consumption. . . . Everything is a creation of political pros so that you will like the candidate."[8]

Political speaking has become a commercial. Robert MacNeil, journalist and former cohost of the *MacNeil-Lehrer News Hour,* describes political communication this way: "They've (politicians) gone for any way that will get themselves elected and they've borrowed all the techniques of television and Madison Avenue and everything else, and they've made the choice of an election no more important than the choice of a toothpaste or a cereal or buying a new car."[9]

Political speakers in many instances no longer present coherent messages. The content of political speaking is made up, according to syndicated columnist Bob Green, of short catchy phrases, eight to twelve seconds in length, designed to be picked up by television. Meaningful discourse based

Credibility is the basis of effective speaking.

on substantive ideas and eloquence has been abandoned in the age of television. Here is how Green describes the process:

> They (politicians) have begun to speak almost exclusively in those cute little bursts expressly written to be picked up by television producers—predigested 8 to 12 second nuggets that don't resemble anything an actual person would ever say during a real-world conversation.
>
> This goes on even on the floor of Congress; this goes on especially on the floor of Congress. If there are men and women in Congress who routinely deliver the staid, logical, one-thought-building-on-another speeches of American life past, they are a secret to the citizenry.[10]

This form of political speaking has been rejected by a great majority of voters who in the words of pollster Louis Harris, "have lost respect for those who govern."[11] People need and want ethics and honesty brought back into political speaking and they need and want communication they can understand.

Ceremonial Speaking

Ceremonial speaking includes speaking for a wide range of occasions: commemorations, after-dinner speaking, introductions, presentations, and acceptance speeches. We've all attended celebrations where speakers have honored the achievements of others such as award ceremonies, graduations, banquets; Fourth of July celebrations; Veterans Day; and Memorial Day. On these occasions for ceremonial speaking, these speeches are designed to inspire, motivate, entertain, acknowledge achievements, and praise.

Community Speaking

The speeches that constitute community speaking are given at thousands of community meetings daily. Parents speak out on issues and problems that affect their children. Should the high school allow condoms to be sold on campus? What subjects should be taught in a sex education curriculum? How can students be protected from violence in schools and the increasing threat from firearms? How should limited school funds be allocated? These issues bring parents to school board and PTA meetings proposing solutions, seeking answers, and demanding changes.

Citizens speak out when events threaten their community. Will a developer's plans for new housing stretch the limits of the fire department in an emergency? Will the presence of an adult bookstore reduce traffic for surrounding businesses and set a bad example for children walking to school? Where in the community should the new waste disposal plant be located?

Citizens must be able to express their ideas and concerns clearly and persuasively and be able to rally others to their cause. In many instances, they are opposed by professionals such as lawyers, representatives of special interest groups, and experts who are experienced speakers and debaters and can skillfully articulate their positions. The well known national group Mothers Against Drunk Driving (MADD) that has fought for stricter penalties for drunk drivers was started by a single mother after her daughter was killed by a drunk driver who received only a slap on the wrist. The taxpayer revolt in California in the late seventies was started by citizens outraged by the inequities in the tax system that was driving people from their homes because they could not pay their property taxes.

Banquet, on-the-job, political, and ceremonial speaking are just some of the many types of speaking. Legal speaking and preaching are others. You will give many of these kinds of presentations. In the course of your career you will be in positions of authority and responsibility in which others will depend on your ability to communicate clearly and confidently. As a citizen you will speak out on issues that affect you, your family, community, and well-being. Your success will depend on your ability to speak effectively.

Let's now discuss in detail the speech communication process, a model that explains the dynamics of public speaking. This process describes the key steps in public speaking and how they work together. Understanding it will improve your ability to prepare and deliver speeches.

THE SPEECH COMMUNICATION PROCESS

Speaking is more than just a person talking to a group. Speech initiates a communication process that links the speaker and listener in both verbal and nonverbal ways. Understanding how this process works improves your preparation and delivery skills because you will recognize the critical factors at work in a presentation. The important elements of the communication process are the speaker, message, listener, channel, feedback, context, and interference (Figure 1-1).

Speaker

The speaker initiates the process by preparing a speech for a specific audience. The speaker analyzes the audience, formulates a specific purpose, gathers and organizes the information, rehearses, and delivers the speech in a knowledgeable and confident manner.

Message

The message is the speaker's vehicle for communicating her ideas to the audience. The message is determined by the speaker's goal, audience analysis and occasion, and may be to inform, to persuade, or entertain. The main ideas are arranged so they stand out and are strongly supported with evidence and visuals to make them clear and interesting.

FIGURE 1-1
The speech communication process.

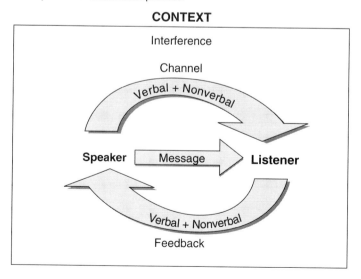

Channel

Words, voice, body language, and visual aids are the channels you use to convey the message. (Your CD player is a channel for sending music.) You want to use these channels effectively so your message is presented clearly and effectively.

Listener

This is the person or audience for whom the message is intended. If the speech is to be effective, the listener must be involved and capable of understanding. Lack of interest or concentration and poor listening skills will cause the process to break down and make the speech ineffective.

In turn the speaker must understand the audience and make every effort to meet their expectations and tie the speech to their wants, needs, and problems. Former president Ronald Reagan was called "the great communicator" because he understood his audience and spoke directly to them.

Feedback

Feedback is the listener's response to the speaker during the presentation. Feedback influences the direction, progress, and quality of the message. Being attentive, showing interest through facial expression, and posture encourage the speaker to communicate effectively. Faking attention, showing disinterest, or just plain rudeness prevent effective communication and can even stop communication altogether.

Context

The context is the occasion and setting for the speech. Every speech occurs for a reason and happens under certain conditions. The Kiwanis Club wants to hear a speech about the status of the economy at its monthly meeting in the banquet room at the local Lyon's restaurant. The President of the United States addresses the nation on television while seated at his desk in the Oval Office. Your speeches will be delivered in the classroom to your peers. You adapt your speech to these conditions and resources.

Interference

Interference is any element that disrupts the process. Interference is like a computer virus and can attack at any step in the process. The speaker may use technical language the audience can't understand. The speaker may not accurately analyze the audience and not speak to their expectations. The audience may have poor listening skills and not grasp important ideas.

The effectiveness of your speaking will depend on how well you manage these seven elements of the speech communication process. A breakdown in even one area will reduce your effectiveness as a speaker. But if you understand this process and how the steps interact, you are on your way to mastering effective speech communication.

BECOMING AN EFFECTIVE PRESENTER

Emerson said, "The man is only half himself, the other half is his expression." Effective speaking involves more than just learning rules, processes, and techniques. It involves the whole person. When you speak, you're telling the audience who you are. It's not a part of you talking, it's all of you—your values, experience, knowledge, and beliefs. It has been said that the speaker is the message. That is why the game playing and manipulation of political speaking is so disconcerting; it is the language of concealment. Such speakers use speech to disguise ideas and meaning—that is, themselves—rather than using it to express themselves openly and clearly so an audience can be enlightened and make intelligent decisions. Ann Richards, former governor of Texas, talks about how public speaking is an expression of self:

> Speaking in public is a very personal piece of business. Giving a good speech, especially one with some passion and emotion, you're revealing a lot about yourself. . . . It's sort of like Lady Godiva riding down Main Street without clothes on. Or stepping up on a scale and getting weighed.[12]

Speaking is also a means of self-discovery. Through communication you define who you are. Susan Faludi, a writer and a leader in the feminist movement, sees public speaking not only as a tool for change but a means by which we establish our identity. When we express our ideas we not only reveal our thoughts, we define who we are:

> Until you translate personal words on a page into public connections with other people, you aren't really part of a political movement. I hadn't declared my independence until I was willing to declare it out loud. I knew public speaking was important to reform public life—but I hadn't realized the transformative effect it could have on the speaker herself. Women need to be heard not to just change the world but to change themselves.[13]

Our goal is to help you communicate the whole person. Let's discuss some steps that can help you become an effective public speaker.

Use the Principles of Communication to Build Your Speech

As a speaker your objective is to achieve the greatest possible impact from your presentation. You want a high degree of audience involvement, a positive and highly credible relationship, and feedback that your speech has been a valuable source of information. How can you achieve these objectives? You can attain them by getting the attention of the audience, establishing rapport, making your subject relevant, giving the audience confidence, and by emphasizing the benefits of your presentation. Let's discuss these important communication principles (Figure 1-2).[14]

Get the Attention of the Audience Your first objective is to get the audience focused on you and your subject. Audiences are not ready to be informed or persuaded until they are mentally prepared to listen. There are internal and external forces competing for their attention. The room may be stuffy, some members of the audience may be hungry, some may be talking among themselves, some people may be facing pressing business following your presentation. Your goal is to reach the audience with a provocative and/or entertaining statement or action that gets their attention and prepares them for the message to follow. This is a fundamental principle of public speaking and one you should apply skillfully.

Establish Rapport With the Audience Audiences are motivated to listen to speakers they like and with whom they feel comfortable. Showing genuine sincerity and interest in the audience through a smile, eye contact, and being poised and relaxed helps establish rapport. Making personal references about members of the audience or achievements of the audience helps establish bonds of association. General Colin Powell has great rapport with audiences. He is described as "congenial," "confident," and "a very easy man to like."[15] Establishing bonds of friendship with the audience must be authentic. Faking rapport will backfire by turning the audience off.

FIGURE 1-2
Principles of public speaking.

	Principles of Public Speaking		
	STEP	**DESCRIPTION**	**AUDIENCE RESPONSE**
A	ATTENTION	Get and hold attention.	"I want to listen."
R	RAPPORT	Connect personally with the audience.	"I like the speaker."
R	RELEVANCE	Persuade audience to listen. Tie topic to needs, values, and experience of listener.	"This topic is beneficial and worth listening to."
C	CONFIDENCE	Give audience confidence in you and your message by speaking honestly and clearly.	"I trust the speaker and understand the message."
S	SATISFACTION	Demonstrate success. Show how the speech benefits the audience.	"I learned valuable information/new skills."

Make Your Topic Relevant   The blunt reality is people listen to subjects that address their needs and concerns. In the Information Age people are exposed to thousands of messages daily but only listen to those handful that address their interests. You must put your audience under a microscope and discover their motivations, problems, attitudes, and any other psychological issues and show how your speech addresses them in a meaningful way. If your topic is child safety and you're speaking to the local Chamber of Commerce, then you must show how your topic helps them achieve important objectives. Successful speakers do this. If you do not demonstrate the relevance of your topic, the audience will not listen.

Give Your Audience Confidence   Audiences are motivated to listen to speakers they perceive to be credible and whose message they understand. Audiences believe speakers they trust. A speaker with integrity and knowledge reduces resistance to the message and creates synergy with the listeners. Clearly presented speeches inspire and motivate because knowledge empowers people. Confusion is reduced or eliminated. Ideas crystalize. Arguments come into focus. Options unfold. The audience has information that helps them understand events or make intelligent decisions.

Give Your Audience a Feeling of Satisfaction   Audiences are excited when a speech fulfills or exceeds their expectations. Their time has been well spent and they have received valuable information. Reinforce these results. Specifically and precisely demonstrate how your speech benefits the audience in the workplace, at home, in school, or in daily life. If you informed an audience of parents how to discipline their children while maintaining their self-esteem, show them specifically how your speech helped them do it. Compare what the audience knew about the skill before the speech to what they know at the end. Show the audience the concrete results of your speech.

Prepare Your Speeches Effectively

Good preparation helps you skillfully integrate the principles of communication into your message and manage the speech communication process. The following steps have proven effective in preparing successful speeches. You may have already used many of these steps although probably in a less systematic way. The steps include: (1) analyzing the audience and setting, (2) selecting a topic and formulating a specific purpose, (3) gathering information, (4) organizing the information, (5) wording the presentation, (6) rehearsing the speech, and (7) getting feedback about the speech (Figure 1-3). Let's discuss each of these steps.

LANGUAGE	REHEARSAL	FEEDBACK
GATHER INFORMATION	SPECIFIC PURPOSE + CENTRAL IDEA	ORGANIZE INFORMATION
	AUDIENCE ANALYSIS	

FIGURE 1-3
Speech preparation process.

Analyze Audience and Setting   Your first and most important priority is to analyze the audience and learn about the setting so you can adapt your topic and the message to the audience and the physical environment of the presentation. You want to build your speech on the audience's interests and concerns and to create a message that is easily understood and engaging.

Select a Topic and Formulate a Specific Purpose   Select a topic you are knowledgeable about and interested in and adapt it for a specific audience. You narrow the topic and formulate a clearly phrased goal that can be accomplished in the allotted time. Being able to adapt a message to a specific time frame is a fundamental speaking skill and disciplines you to focus on the important ideas you want to present.

Gather Information   You select the information for your speech. It may come from your experience and knowledge or research from quality sources or a combination of both sources. The impact of your speech will be partly determined by the information you use in your speech.

Organize the Information   You select and arrange the main ideas in the body of your speech so they stand out during the presentation. The main points are the focus of any speech and the content is built around them. You structure the whole speech—the way it is to be delivered—into the sequence of introduction, body, and conclusion, so that the information flows smoothly to the audience.

Word the Presentation   You use clear and concrete language to present the speech so the audience can grasp the information easily and with a minimum of confusion.

Rehearse the Speech   You rehearse the speech a sufficient number of times so you are comfortable with the information and can deliver it with confidence to the audience.

Get Feedback About Your Speech Be receptive to feedback about your performance so you can improve your skills and develop your natural style of speaking. Even experienced speakers seek feedback about their presentations so they can continue to improve.

Whether you have spoken once or a thousand times, you use these steps to prepare and deliver your speech. The more you apply and practice them, the greater your skills will improve.

Build Your Credibility

Some people take the narrow view that public speaking is primarily a matter of learning voice and body techniques. If they perform slick gestures, wear "power clothing," and utter popular cliches or catchy sound bites, they will be successful. Image and style replace substance as the basis of communication. Television, for example, places great emphasis on personality, on how a person looks and acts. Real knowledge and character are secondary and, in many cases, disregarded altogether. Former television evangelists Jimmy Swaggart and Jim Bakker had style but little character.

Audiences believe speakers they respect and trust. These are speakers who through their communication show strength and conviction. They speak honestly and directly. They know their subjects and speak intelligently about them. Mother Teresa doesn't have polished delivery skills and doesn't need them. Her character speaks louder than her words. President Harry Truman was often criticized by the press for his blunt style, but was respected and admired by the people because he had great character. Historian David McCullough described Truman's character this way:

> Certainly his lack of artifice is terribly appealing to us today. But more than anything else, it is the fact that he stood for something. You might not have agreed with where he stood, but you knew where he stood. There was substance, and there was principle. We knew, we saw, that he was willing to risk his political hide for his principles.[16]

Building credibility means speaking from principle—that is, building your communication on your personal beliefs and a solid base of integrity, goodwill, and knowledge. Then you speak with power and conviction. Even when audiences disagree or dislike you, they will respect what you say. What you are communicates far more eloquently than what you say or do. For Martin Luther King, "character" was the measure of a person. Here are some guidelines for developing your credibility:

1 Clarify your personal principles. Write out the values and beliefs on which you base your life. In short, know who you are so that you have a solid ethical center for making decisions.

2 Translate these values into a code of personal behavior. Ask yourself: How do I use these principles to relate and communicate to others?

3 Apply these principles to the preparation and delivery of your speech. The guidelines you make for yourself might include speaking on subjects about which you have conviction and knowledge, using information from reliable sources, and being open and natural when speaking.

To some, these guidelines may sound naive and run counter to a culture that focuses on personality, relativism, and situational ethics. Those artificial approaches may have short-run success but in the long run will fail because

Develop a solid knowledge base for your presentations.

they are based on expediency, not solid principles. Journalist Cal Thomas remarks on the importance of having solid values:

> When we look around us, our values and convictions sometimes seem fragile and tenuous, like a small flame in a strong wind. In reality, these laws have all the certainity of physical laws.[17]

Develop a Solid Knowledge Base for Your Presentations

Einstein observed, "The significant problems we face cannot be solved at the same level of thinking we were at when we created them." We live in a complex, challenging, and rapidly changing world—we must cope with illiteracy, environmental problems, racism, changing employment patterns, and global competition. We must bring our thinking to a level that will allow us to confront these problems and communicate them intelligently.

We must be open to new ideas. We must not allow ourselves to be trapped in shallow political stereotypes and special interest pleadings that narrow and oversimplify critical issues or conceal important ones. We must carefully select sources of information that help us rationally analyze issues and make intelligent decisions because much of the media has become unreliable as a source of quality information. David Broder, the distinguished journalist of the *Washington Post* believes journalistic ethics is the number one problem facing the industry today. He states, ". . . the sad thing is so much of the media is headed . . . toward the trivialization of substance and the substitution of sensationalized junk journalism."[18] The result is an increasingly distorted picture of issues and society. We must equip ourselves with substantive information and use it to develop the ideas we communicate to others.

Set Personal Learning Goals

People are motivated to learn and learn best when they have a need for the information. A person promoted to a manager's position requiring speaking skills may enroll in a company's public speaking course or an organization like Toastmasters to gain skills and experience. Not to do so would limit that person's ability to manage others.

As a student of public speaking you need to be clear about what you hope to learn from this class and why. Although you may be inexperienced and unsure what your learning goals are, finding a stake in the learning process will enhance your ability to master the skills and principles of effective speaking. When you take ownership, you learn faster and with greater impact. Here are some ideas to help you.

1 Set learning objectives. Write down two learning objectives for improving your communication. What do you want to achieve as a result of the class? Here are some examples:

> I want to build confidence so I will feel less nervous when I speak.

> I want to organize my thoughts better so I don't ramble when I speak.

Write these objectives down and put them in a prominent place so you can refer to them easily. As you gain experience and receive feedback, your goals may change. Rewrite them to reflect your knowledge and new insights. Limit your goals to two, as more may overload you.

2 Gain experience. Take every opportunity to speak, in and out of the classroom. The more experience you get, the faster your confidence will grow. Join the college's speech team where you can gain valuable experience preparing and delivering different types of speeches. If you belong to a club, get in positions where you can speak. Give oral reports in your other classes. All these experiences will pay off handsomely for you.

3 Welcome feedback. In fact, encourage feedback. Feedback helps you develop your own style and build confidence. Find out what you do well and build on that. Learn how you can improve.

LEARNING PUBLIC SPEAKING

Whether you have spoken once or a thousand times, nervousness is a distraction. But it is not fatal or catastrophic. Put nervousness in perspective by understanding that public speaking is a learned skill that involves a unique way of communicating, and that any nervousness that you experience is natural. As you learn more about public speaking, you will begin to feel more comfortable about your nervousness and even find it beneficial.

Public speaking is a deliberative type of communication. You have an idea, plan a speech around it, and then deliver it to an audience, often without interruption. This is an unusual way of communicating. In typical communication, conversation is spontaneous give-and-take with each party guiding the other through the message. Public speaking is different. You determine the goal, prepare the message, and carry the burden of delivery.

Learning these skills is challenging and sometimes unnerving. Instinctively we want or need more audience feedback to guide us through the process; this is because we learned to communicate with lots of feedback, and in most situations still communicate that way. What is important is to work with your emotions in a way that enhances the development of your public speaking skills.

Understand That Learning Is an Emotional Process

Learning is not just a physical and intellectual process. When you begin to learn a new skill, you initiate a process that involves the emotions. Whether you're learning to ski, play tennis, or speak Russian, the beginning steps involve feelings of awkwardness or discomfort. As you gain experience and grasp the fundamentals, you begin to relax, improve your skills, and gain confidence.

A similar process occurs in public speaking. There is an initial feeling of resistance or awkwardness, but as you gain experience and insights you begin to take control and build confidence. Here is how that process might work for you in your public speaking class (Figure 1-4):

1 *Resistance.* Fear of the unknown. Moving into uncharted territory. Reaction might be "Maybe I'll put public speaking off until next semester."

2 *Uncertainty.* Feelings of awkwardness and discomfort. Unsure if path is correct. Your reaction might be "Practicing eye contact sure feels strange."

3 *Recognition.* The principles of communication begin to make sense. Reaction might be "Not so bad as I thought." "Organizing the main points really did help my speech."

4 *Application.* Begin to use principles of communication in preparing and delivering speech. You've built confidence now. Your reaction might be "Not bad. I can get pretty good if I work at it."

5 *Integration.* You have integrated the principles into your behavior. You now use the principles instinctively. New skill has been acquired. Reaction: "This is a piece of cake."

As you learn public speaking you will move through these stages. The higher you go the more confident you will become because you are integrating public speaking into your behavior.

FIGURE 1-4
Emotional steps of learning.

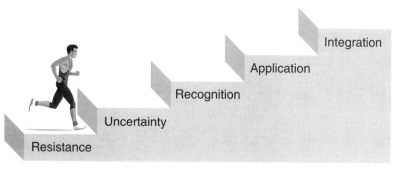

SUMMARY

Public speaking enhances your personal and career effectiveness. Effective speakers are valued because they help others succeed and lead others to successful results. Important types of public speaking include banquet speaking, on-the-job speaking, political speaking, ceremonial speaking, and community speaking. The speech communication process involves a speaker, message, channel, listener, feedback, context, and interference. Becoming an effective speaker includes mastering the principles of public speaking, preparing your speeches effectively, building your credibility, developing a solid knowledge base, and setting personal learning goals. Learning public speaking involves understanding the uniqueness of public speaking and understanding that learning is an emotional process with distinct stages that you pass through as you gain skills.

PROBES

1 Briefly describe the scope of speaking.
2 What are some of the career benefits of effective speaking?
3 Why are effective speakers held in high regard?
4 How does on-the-job speaking differ from political speaking?
5 List the elements of the speech communication process.
6 Briefly describe the principles of public speaking.
7 How do you build your credibility?
8 What is a learning objective?
9 Briefly describe the uniqueness of public speaking.
10 Briefly describe the emotional steps involved in learning.
11 Briefly describe the speech preparation process.

APPLICATIONS

1 Interview people with effective communication skills. How have these skills helped them be effective? How have these skills helped them build confidence?
2 What opportunities exist for you to speak on family and community issues?
3 Identify a person you know with high credibility. What are this person's strengths?
4 Complete the exercise on developing your credibility. How will you communicate with others based on this analysis?
5 Write down two learning goals. Modify them as you gain experience and knowledge about public speaking.
6 Write down the emotional steps of learning. Keep track of your progress as you move up the scale.
7 Identify the principles of public speaking in the next speech you listen to.

NOTES

1 Christopher Matthews, "The Brave New World of Clintonomics," *The San Francisco Sunday Examiner/Chronicle,* November 22, 1992, p. A17. See also, Robert Reich, *The Work of Nations* (Knopf: New York, 1991).

2 Elinor Donahue, "The Eight Fold Path to Better Speeches," *Vital Speeches,* Vol. 61, August 15, 1995, p. 670.

3 Phyllis Berman and Lisa Sanders, "As Henry Kissinger Said the Other Night at Dinner," *Forbes,* Vol. 153, June 6, 1994, p. 56.

4 Terry Toczynski, "Orators Turn Talking into Business," *Contra Costa Business Times,* January 30, 1989, p. 8.

5 Marie Flatley, "Team Presenting Skills: Essential Tools," *Business Education Forum,* Vol. 45, November 11, 1990, pp. 19–21.

6 Anonymous, "Critical Link between Presentation Skills, Upward Mobility," *Supervision,* Vol. 52, October 1991, pp. 24–25.

7 Lloyd E. Corder, "Survey Report of Presentation Skills Training in Fortune 500 Industrial Companies," *Research Report,* 1989, 16 pp.; James C. Bennett and Robert J. Olney, "Executive Priorities for Effective Communication in an Information Society," *Journal of Business Communication,* Vol. 23, September 1986, pp. 13–22.

8 Christopher Matthews, "A View From Washington," *The Commonwealth,* Vol. 87, June 4, 1993, p. 362. See also, Kathleen Jamison, *Eloquence in the Electronic Age* (Oxford University Press, New York, 1988), and Carol Blair, "The Decay of Political Eloquence," *USA Today,* March 1992, Vol. 120, p. 87.

9 Transcript, "Fifteen Years of MacNeil/Lehrer," PBS special hosted by David Gergen and Mark Shields, pp. 6–7.

10 Bob Green, "The Lost Art of the Political Speech," *San Francisco Chronicle,* April 24, 1992, p. C24.

11 Louis Harris, "This Strange and Significant Political Year," speech delivered before The Commonwealth Club of California, July 10, 1992, p. 450.

12 Ann Richards, *Straight From the Heart: My Life in Politics and Other Places* (Simon and Schuster: New York, 1989), pp. 11–12.

13 Susan Faludi, "Speak for Yourself," *New York Times Magazine,* January 26, 1992, Vol. 41, p. 10.

14 Principles adapted from J. M. Keller, "Development and Use of the ARCS Model of Instructional Design," *Journal of Instructional Development,* Vol. 10, 1987, pp. 2–10. See also Ann Bainbridge Frymier and Gary M. Shulman, "What's in It for Me?: Increasing Content Relevance to Enhance Students' Motivation," *Communication Education,* Vol. 44, January 1995, pp. 40–50.

15 David Halberstam, "There Is Something Noble to It," *Parade,* September 17, 1995, p. 4.

16 David McCullough, "Truman," speech delivered before The Commonwealth Club of California, July 14, 1992, p. 467.

17 Cal Thomas, "The Sixties Are Dead: Long Live the Nineties," *Imprimis,* Vol. 24, January 1995, p. 6.

18 David Broder, "Junk Journalism Outshines Depth," *The Washington Post,* February 23, 1994, p. A17.

2

LISTENING

EMPOWERING OTHERS: GIVING EFFECTIVE FEEDBACK

Elements of Evaluation

Try the following listening experiment in your next one-on-one conversation. Listen attentively to your partner for about two minutes. Encourage the speaker to express him-/or herself freely by making good eye contact, concentrating on the message, and making positive verbal statements. Note your listener's response to your active listening behavior.

Next, switch from being an involved listener to being an indifferent one. Avoid eye contact, glance at your watch, rummage through your backpack, read a newspaper. Do this for about two minutes. How did the speaker react?

Your different listening behaviors probably resulted in dramatically different reactions from the speaker. During the first part of your experiment the speaker probably felt relaxed and spoke openly and confidently. During the second part the listener probably became defensive, inhibited, and maybe even frustrated and angry.

The point of the exercise is to show that listening greatly impacts the communication process. How you listen influences the progress and outcome of the speech and can even prevent communication. Listening also affects the speaker's confidence and self-esteem. There must be an involved listener for communication to happen.

THE IMPORTANCE OF LISTENING

Effective listening is a valuable communication skill. We spend over 50 percent of our time listening, often in situations in which our performance is tied to listening (Figure 2-1).[1] For some professionals, such as managers and executives, the figure is even higher, 64 percent.[2] As a student the quality of your work is often tied to how well you follow verbal instructions, comprehend the main ideas of lectures, and take notes. Many surveys of professional groups rank listening as the most important communication skill.[3] Why is listening such an important communication skill?

Effective listening improves your speaking. You learn to focus on the audience and work harder to discover and understand wants and needs. It improves your relationships and gives you control of the communication process because you know how to listen and apply what you hear. The

FIGURE 2-1
Time spent in different types of communication.

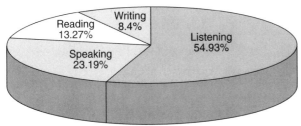

experiment at the beginning of the chapter demonstrated the power you have as a listener. Effective listening improves your credibility because people trust those who listen to them.

Effective listening is a skill just as effective public speaking is a skill. The average person listens at only about 25 percent efficiency. Listening instruction can double that figure.[4] In this chapter, we will discuss how we listen, types of listening, improving listening skills, and how to respond effectively.

HOW WE LISTEN

The accuracy of our listening is influenced by how we interpret information and how we like information presented to us. Let's discuss how we listen and personal listening styles.

The Listening Process

Listening isn't just hearing. It is a process of interpretation and response similar to the speech communication process discussed in Chapter 1. Although it seems instantaneous, listening involves a series of steps that determine what we listen to and how we interpret information. Listening is divided into four steps: (1) sensing, (2) interpretation, (3) evaluation, and (4) responding (Figure 2-2).[5]

FIGURE 2-2
The listening process.

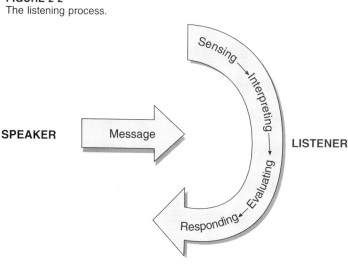

Sensing   We give attention to the speaker and message. This is fundamental. If a listener does not give her or his attention to the message, the process cannot begin. That is why, in public speaking, getting the attention of the audience is the opening step. If you do not have their attention, the audience will not listen.

Interpreting   Here, you apply your own meaning to the message. We filter information through our personal experience, knowledge, motivation, and emotion. If the speaker is using unfamiliar language, you may have problems understanding the meaning. A teenager and senior citizen would have very different interpretations of rap or heavy metal lyrics.

This is why we must be very careful to ensure that our interpretation is accurate—because we are listening through our own subjective lens. We need to interpret accurately before we judge. Bob Woodward, a Pulitzer Prize-winning journalist, criticizes the press on this very issue. He says much investigative reporting and the desire to be ahead of the story "has led to a lot of impatient reporting. Too often these days, it leads us to write from ignorance."[6] Many reporters jump to conclusions and don't get the whole story. Suppose you are very strongly pro choice and the speaker is advocating a pro life position. You automatically interpret the speech as stupid and false, and you tune out.

Evaluating   Here, you determine the value of the message. You agree or disagree, accept or reject. The key is to determine meaning before you reach this stage. You weigh the evidence or information and determine its importance to your goals and objectives. You may discard the information or record it for future use. If while listening to a lecture you decide a particular idea will be on a test, you will give it greater value than information that you will not be tested on.

Responding   During and following the speech we give the speaker verbal and nonverbal feedback. During the speech you may yawn, smile, nod, take notes, make eye contact, or laugh at a joke, all different ways of manifesting your reaction to the speech. As we saw in the little experiment, our nonverbal feedback has significant impact on the speaker. Following the speech we may make comments regarding content, ask questions, seek clarification, or debate ideas. Responding is showing and telling the speaker our reaction to the speech. Analyzing this process of sensing, interpreting, evaluating, and responding may help us understand our listening behavior and where we can improve our listening skills. Being inattentive may cause you to miss important information. Jumping the gun on assigning meaning may lead you to false conclusions. We may discard important information. Inappropriate responses may mislead the speaker.

Listening Style[7]

The way information is presented influences how we listen. Some people prefer to be shown rather than just told. Others prefer hands-on experience over being shown. When a message is presented using channels preferred by the listener, the listener grasps the information faster and more easily. When the channel is incompatible, listening is more difficult. Four important listening styles include:

Verbal: Likes language and well-structured lecture.

Feeling: Likes to interact and become emotionally involved in topic.

Visual: Likes to observe and prefers pictures, drawings, video, and film.

Active: Likes hands-on exercises and practice, self-paced projects.

Learning about listening styles helps us better understand why we interpret information differently. If we are visually oriented and the speech is straight lecture, we may have to work harder to maintain attention and accurately interpret meaning. That is why, as we shall see in Chapter 7, a multichannel approach to content is the most effective. It appeals to all the listening styles.

TYPES OF LISTENING

We listen for a variety of reasons. Sometimes we listen to get information, such as directions or important ideas from a lecture. Sometimes we listen critically when others are trying to persuade us—for example, a politician or member of a special interest group. Sometimes we just listen to have fun and be entertained. By identifying the occasion we can adapt our listening behavior to get the maximum benefit. Let's focus on three of the important reasons we listen: to understand, to evaluate, and to empathize.

Listening to Understand

We listen to understand and gather information. Your primary goal as a student is to gather, understand, and retain information. Professionals spend a majority of their time listening in briefings, meetings, and conferences, gathering information they will use to make decisions. In business and industry employees routinely attend workshops and seminars to upgrade their skills. This kind of listening is becoming more and more important as rapid change makes yesterday's concepts obsolete, and new knowledge and new ways of thinking are continually required. Listening skills can help you retain more information and improve your performance.

When you listen to understand, your goal is to discover the central theme and major points of a presentation. You are interested in the facts insofar as they reveal the main points or ideas. When you listen to a lecture, look for the main ideas and take notes to enhance recall. Many business and professional people carry laptop computers on which they record notes for later use.

Listening to Evaluate

We listen critically when the speaker's intention is to influence our thinking and actions. Many times we are in situations in which a speaker is trying to persuade us to believe or act in a certain way. Your congressperson may try to convince you that eliminating school district boundaries and allowing parents to send their children to the school of their choice will improve the quality of education. A high-tech salesperson may attempt to convince a management group to purchase his company's mainframe computer.

When we listen critically we weigh the evidence and its sources and the speaker's reasoning. Were the arguments logical? Were they well-supported? We judge the speaker's character, asking ourselves: Is this person knowledgeable, trustworthy, and sincere? Can this person be believed? How does this message benefit us? What motivation is the speaker appealing to? Does the speaker understand my wants and needs? What motives is this person appealing to? Based on these kinds of criteria we make a decision as to the value of the message or concept.

Listening to Empathize

Empathic listening is often associated with one-on-one communication, when a listener is attempting to understand the feelings and concerns of another. Applied to public speaking it means discovering the audience's psychological and motivational links to your topic so you can appeal to them in your presentation. Does the audience feel compassion, fear, hope, or anger? For example, if your topic is sexual harassment, there may be people in the audience who have experienced it and feel angry and humiliated. Addressing those feelings would pull the audience deeper into your speech. Listening to empathize will be discussed further in Chapter 3.

IMPROVING YOUR LISTENING SKILLS

The majority of our time communicating is spent listening. Yet most people receive little if any training on how to listen effectively. As a result they don't know how to listen to, not to speak of what to listen for, in a message. These poor listening habits limit their efficiency and performance (Figure 2-3).

Ten Worst Listening Habits

1. Declaring topic uninteresting: "I'll never use this information."
2. Hooked on style over substance: "He *looks* convincing."
3. Getting the facts instead of the ideas: "Just give me the facts."
4. Outlining mania: "Hey, can you wait while I get it down?"
5. Surrendering to complex material: "It's way over my head."
6. Faking it: "Oh, I think its a great idea! I think."
7. Emotional overreaction: "What a jerk!"
8. Becoming overstimulated by ideas: "Let's see, $E=MC^2$ and multivariate applications plus theory of functions..."
9. Succumbing to distractions: "Pardon me, what was that you said?"
10. Jumping to conclusions: "Oh, that's not what you meant!"

FIGURE 2-3
Ten worst listening habits.

Effective listening is a skill. A good listener focuses on ideas like a heat-seeking missile zeroing in on a target. Good listeners listen with attention and concentration and encourage open expression of thoughts and feelings by the speaker. They give short verbal responses that clarify remarks and help keep the speaker on target. They take control of the communication process without dominating it.

In this section we will discuss steps for improving your listening skills: (1) Take the initiative. (2) Align yourself with the speaker's goal. (3) Focus on meaning. (4) Concentrate. (5) Take good notes. (6) Make sure your interpretation is accurate (Figure 2-4).

Take the Initiative

A French proverb says, "The spoken word belongs half to those who speak, and half to those who hear." As we have seen, listening is not a passive function. You are jointly responsible for the success of a message, and how you behave determines the progress, direction, and quality of the presentation.

Become a co-leader with the speaker in making the communication effective. Here is a description of how one executive takes the initiative when meeting an associate in her office:

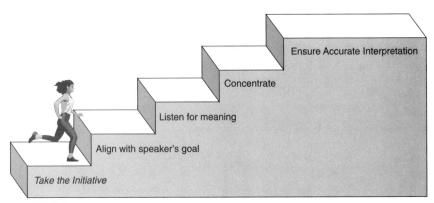

FIGURE 2-4
Steps for improving listening skills.

When the associate enters, she closes the reports she's working on and puts them away. She stands up, moves around her desk, and greets the visitor with a smile and strong handshake and invites him to sit down. She takes a seat next to him so they can talk directly without any obstacles between them. She gives the speaker 100 percent of her attention.

Take the initiative when you listen. Have paper and pencil ready to take notes. Face the speaker and make steady eye contact. Be relaxed and attentive. Maintain an open position. Lean toward the speaker. Respond in a reassuring manner and tone. Encourage the speaker to talk by nodding agreement and making acknowledging statements such as "Yes, I understand" and "Please continue."

If there is an opportunity to speak during the presentation, make comments that show your grasp of the material. Expand an idea. Give an example. Relate a remark to your personal experience. In short, take the lead as a listener. Figure 2-5 shows an active listening profile. How do you rate? What are your strengths and weaknesses?

Your classroom offers you an excellent opportunity to begin practicing these listening skills. You will begin developing habits that increase your ability to grasp information quickly and build your credibility.

Align Yourself with the Speaker's Goal

What is the speaker's objective? To inform? Persuade? Relieve tension? Entertain? Discover the speaker's goal and assume the appropriate listening role. If the speaker is persuading, become the critic. If she is informing, become the learner. This approach helps both you and the speaker achieve your objectives. You are on the same wavelength. A good skier uses gravity to gain speed and the contour of the hill to navigate the descent. A ballroom

During a listening situation:	Most of the time	Often	Seldom	Never
Nonverbal Responses				
I maintain eye contact with speaker				
I show interest through body position				
I give appropriate nonverbal responses				
I give appropriate vocal responses				
I avoid figeting				
Verbal Responses				
I share relevant comments				
I pick up on ideas and expand on them				
I ask relevant questions				
I share relevant personal experience				
I respectfully correct inaccuracies				

FIGURE 2-5
Active listening profile.

dancer dips with her partner when he stumbles to keep him from falling, and guides him back into the rhythm of the dance. You do the same thing when you align with the speaker.

Alignment doesn't mean you agree with the speaker; it means putting yourself in the appropriate mental state to understand and support the speaker. A jury, for instance, should adopt a critical but fair attitude, so that the lawyers for both sides can present the strongest case for their respective clients. You want to do the same thing with the speaker.

Alignment helps reduce resistance when listening and puts you "in sync" with the speaker and occasion. As you listen, practice alignment and see how your listening improves. Ask yourself: What is the listener's goal? Then assume the compatible listening posture.

Focus on Meaning

Your single most important objective is to listen for meaning! Among the Sufis, a Moslem mystic sect originating in Persia, certain people were trained in acute listening skills and were called Fair Witnesses. They were trained to listen objectively for meaning. They attended council meetings and public discussions and listened with great concentration and objectivity to everything that was said. When disputes or misunderstandings occurred, everyone would turn to the Fair Witness, who would then impartially restate or summarize what everyone had said so the matter could be resolved.

Meaning is determined by discovering the speaker's central theme and main points and by accurately interpreting body language. Think of yourself as a cryptologist, a person who deciphers secret codes—or maybe as a Sherlock Holmes, who, through brilliant deduction and keen observation, grasps meaning long before a person has finished talking. Here are some tips for discovering meaning.

Discover the Central Idea   Bill Gates, founder of Microsoft and the boy wonder of software, calls communication an IQ share. "A speech is an idea share." The speaker takes an idea, builds a speech around it, and communicates it to an audience (Figure 2-6). That idea is what we want to identify as we listen. Often it can be stated in a single short sentence. In a speech about CPR the speaker's theme may be "CPR is easy to learn and saves lives." Or in a speech persuading the audience to vote, it may be "Your vote can make a difference." Sometimes the central idea is stated explicitly in a speech; often it is not and must be inferred from the content. In the following example, the speaker states the central idea of the speech in the introduction:

Specific purpose:	To persuade the audience to ban smoking in public places.
Introduction:	I am not a crusader. I do not generally demand or assert my rights, but this issue is about the quality of health and life for all who have not chosen to

FIGURE 2-6
Grasp the central idea.

pollute their bodies with tobacco. Public education and the demand for respect for nonsmokers has not worked.

Central idea: Well-defined, enforceable laws must be enacted to protect the health of children, the sick, and non-smokers.

When the central idea is not stated, you must infer it by listening carefully to the speech, especially the main points. If the speech is well crafted, it should emerge fairly early. Unfortunately, many people are not very good communicators and ferreting out the central idea can be challenging. Some speakers—including many politicians—are masters of concealment. Syndicated columnist Richard Reeves says, "One of the most distressing things about modern politicians is that even if you grant that they believe what they say, they do not often say what they believe—and never say what they feel."

Listening for the central idea helps you quickly grasp the speaker's meaning and respond appropriately even when the message is cluttered, confusing, and disorganized. In the classic dark comedy *Dr. Strangelove,* a renegade general unleashes a squadron of B-52s for a nuclear attack on what was the former Soviet Union. As the film continues, he commits suicide and leaves a rambling, incoherent message explaining his actions. The president's advisers tell him they are having difficulty trying to understand the message. The president replies that there is nothing to understand; the general was insane. The president grasped the general's central idea.

Become proficient in listening for the central idea. Practice as you listen to classroom speeches, your professors' lectures, and public speeches.

Discover the Main Points   Listen for ideas, not facts. The main points are the ideas on which the speech was built and the vital information you want to understand. They reveal the speaker's thinking and strategy and give you a deeper understanding of the message. For example, if a speaker wants you to believe that capital punishment is justified, then identifying the reasons for that position helps you evaluate the speech. In the following example, the speaker explains a main point:

> In 13 years, 44 percent of all jobs will require the highest levels of education. That has profound implications for all of us. What we used to do for the college-bound we have to do for a broader range of young people. Our competitiveness, economic growth, quality of life, and standard of living will depend on paying attention to the educational reform effort and trying to upgrade the quality of life for all young people.[8]

The necessity of improving the quality of life for all young people is the speaker's main point and the concept he wants you to grasp or believe.

Discovering the main points reveals a speaker's persuasive strategy. Once you know what the main points are, you can tell how the speaker has planned to inform or persuade you. If the speaker is giving you a series of benefits, you know she is appealing motivationally. If the main points are in a problem/solution sequence, you can analyze how effectively the solution matches the problem. Main points will be discussed in depth in Chapter 6.

Observe Body Language   Meaning is determined by the speaker's nonverbal behavior as well as verbal. How a person gestures, moves, and dresses can all give clues to meaning. Tone and inflection can reveal feeling. Some scholars claim that body language accounts for 55 percent of meaning; voice, 38 percent; and words, only 7 percent. Nonverbal behavior influences a message in a number of ways:

Complements:	A speaker's body language mirrors the verbal message. A speaker says, "I have three major points to cover," and holds up three fingers.
Highlights:	The speaker's body language reinforces or strengthens the spoken word. The speaker says, "I am delighted to be here," as her face lights up in a smile.
Replaces:	A gesture or movement communicates without words. The speaker puts her finger over her lips to signal silence.
Contradicts:	The words give one meaning and the body language another. The speaker talks about her enthusiasm and then yawns. When this occurs, the audience believes the body language.

Louis Nizer, a famous trial lawyer, tells how the nonverbal cues of witnesses convey meaning:

Time and again, I have seen a witness discredited by the manner of his testifying rather than what he said. A witness, on cross examination, who glances at his counsel as if pleading for help, turns red, pauses, and then hesitantly replies, "I don't remember," well may give the jury the impression that his answer is an evasion.

Jurors usually watch every mannerism of the witness, every inflection of voice, every reaction under stress. Witnesses who scissor their legs at certain questions; or look up at the ceiling for help at some inconsequential question although they have been untroubled by difficult ones; or become unduly emphatic, abandoning previous equanimity; or assertive though their eyes register doubt; or substitute nastiness for indignation; or pretend they didn't hear the question to stall for time; or are affectedly obsequious; or pass their hands over their mouths before answering a question, in a gesture which might mean, "I wish

I didn't have to say what I am about to say," (particularly if repeated whenever the same sensitive subject matter is posed) . . . may forfeit the jury's confidence.[9]

How would you interpret the following body language?

Folded arms
Speaks in monotone
Wrinkled shirt
Avoids eye contact
Slumped shoulders
Slouches over podium
Constantly looks at watch

Concentrate

Karen L. Porat has said, "The most priceless gift we can give another human being is our undivided attention." Concentration is challenging. Attention spans are short and the natural tendency is to want to talk. A topic may be complex and the speaker boring. There may be internal and external forces competing for your attention: your thoughts may be on the new person you're dating Saturday night or on a big party, or there may be people talking next to you or a loud noise outside the window.

The solution is to make concentration a skill, to gain the ability to tune out distractions and maintain focus. You do this when you listen to someone speaking on a subject you like or need to hear about. Good trial lawyers concentrate. They have the ability to follow an opponent's line of argument, a witness's testimony, and the jury's reaction to evidence, and then to respond with rebuttal, objections, or clarification. Business meetings require concentration because strategy is formulated and decisions made that will affect productivity. Figure 2-7 shows what a high level of concentration looks like. Concentration dips periodically but remains at a high level. Here are some hints for improving your concentration:

1 Find value or areas of interest in the presentation. You are listening to the speech for a reason. Find an idea or process that can help you.

2 Focus on one listening objective at a time. Maybe your first objective is to discover the central idea and then the main points.

3 Focus on what is going on in the room. Don't think about what you might have for lunch, or what you are going to do this coming weekend.

Practice concentrating during your classmates' speeches and your professors' lectures. Make a game of it and see how quickly you can discover the central idea and main points. Give yourself a reward. Search for useful information or areas of interest such as potential test questions that keep you

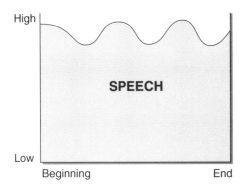

FIGURE 2-7
Effective concentration level.

tuned in. Your ability to concentrate will increase quickly if you take the time to practice.

Take Good Notes

Good note taking keeps your memory fresh. Remember, retention drops off significantly without reinforcement.

There are a number of ways of taking notes. You may use the traditional linear method of recording the information, identifying main points and subpoints with Roman numerals and capital A's and B's (Figure 2-8). You might use a visual display method in which the main points are listed side by side and subpoints listed underneath (Figure 2-9). A single glance reveals each of the major points. Write the main ideas and supporting material in short phrases, short concise sentences, or using key words. Avoid outline mania; your job is to concentrate on the speaker. A template for these note-taking methods can be created on a computer and printed out for later use.

Another method of note taking is mind-mapping. Mind-mapping organizes information visually and the result resembles a map (Figure 2-10).[10] To make a mind-map, start in the middle of the paper with the topic and work outward in all directions. Using key words and images, you create an organized diagram of the speech. Many practitioners of this note-taking form use colored pens and draw three-dimensional shapes, pictures, and diagrams to embellish the data. This aids recall.

Mind-maps help you organize and recall information because you can see information in pictorial form. If you use color and images, stronger associations can be made. Try it.

Speaker: Joanne Jones
Specific purpose: Convince us to walk for health
Central idea: Walking has many health benefits

   I. Lowers cholesterol level
      A. Dr. Bill Castelli, dir. of Framingham Heart Project
         Studied research: walking reduces bad cholesterol levels
  II. Increases longevity
      A. Dr. Ken Cooper, dir. Dallas Aerobic Res. Institute
         Tested 13,000 people over 20 yrs.
         People who walked regularly had 75% lower death rate than those who didn't walk.
         Moderate walking reduces death rate by 50%.
  III. Strengthens immune system
      A. Loma Linda Univ. experiment: one group walked regularly, control group did not.
           Results: walkers 50% less illness
                   increase in disease-fighting antibodies
  IV. Other benefits:
      A. Weight loss
      B. Less stress
      C. Greater creativity

FIGURE 2-8
Linear method of outlining.

FIGURE 2-9
Visual display outline.

MAIN POINTS	I. Lowers Cholesterol Levels	II. Improves Longevity	III. Strengthens Immune System	IV. Other Benefits
Subpoints	A. Dr.Bill Castelli, dir. of Framingham Heart Project: Studied research. Conclusion: Walking reduces base cholesterol levels.	A. Dr. Ken Cooper, Dallas Aerobic Res. Institute. 13,000 people over 20 yrs. Walkers 75% lower death rate then nonwalkers. Moderate walking, 50% less death.	A. Loma Linda Univ. Experiment: Regular walkers 50% less illness, increase in antibodies.	A. Weight loss. B. Less stress. C. Greater creativity.

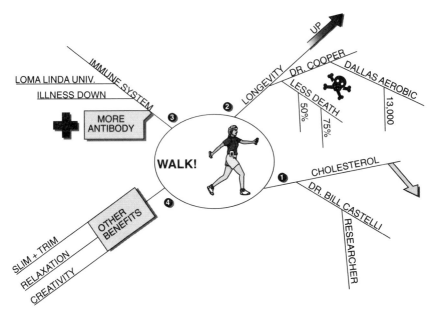

FIGURE 2-10
Mind-mapping outline form.

Make Sure Your Interpretation Is Accurate

There are a number of things you can do to ensure that you have accurately interpreted the speaker's remarks: paraphrase, ask questions, and summarize.

Paraphrasing   You repeat, in your own words, the idea expressed by the speaker. You want to be concise and objective. Your goal is to make sure you have grasped the speaker's idea. You might say: "Your point is that poverty breeds crime. Is that correct?" You have given your interpretation of the speaker's remarks in a short sentence.

Read the following passage and paraphrase it in a short sentence.

> The current system of financing elections for the U.S. Congress is unfair. It's unfair because private campaign contributions can be used to obtain influence, or create the appearance of influence, over government decisionmakers. And it's unfair because congressional incumbents have such an extraordinary advantage over challengers in raising campaign contributions that we are actually losing our ability to have real congressional elections.[11]

The main point is "The current system for financing elections is unfair." That was a main point the speaker wanted you to get.

Summarizing Summaries are like paraphrases, but they are longer because they cover more ground. You might summarize a whole argument, the main points, or the message itself. Here is an example of how one listener summarized the main points to verify his interpretation:

> Your position is that television advertising directed at children should be banned because it manipulates children's needs and wants, encourages them to eat food that is not nutritious, and models unrealistic behavior.

Questioning Questions help clarify meaning. You may ask the speaker to give an example to clarify a fact or concept. You might ask the speaker to define a key word. You could give a hypothetical example and ask the speaker if this matches his meaning. Your job is not to debate but to clarify meaning. Here are some examples:

You used the phrase "presentation software" in your speech. What do you mean?

Please give me an example of what you mean by "deficit reduction."

How can your plan help my situation?

Effective feedback empowers others.

EMPOWERING OTHERS: GIVING EFFECTIVE FEEDBACK

Helping others succeed and improve is one of our most important goals. Coaches show athletes how to improve their strokes or passing, blocking, and hitting. Managers give performance evaluations and on-the-job feedback to help employees succeed. Professors and teachers give evaluations to help students improve performance.

You may feel uncomfortable giving feedback. You may be afraid to hurt someone's feelings or lack confidence in giving feedback. You may not know how to give feedback. These are all honest concerns that will be overcome when you learn how to give feedback. Remember, evaluation is instructional and supportive communication; it is not debate, manipulation, or deceit. Remember too that people who give effective feedback are respected and admired because they help others. Here are some guidelines for giving effective feedback.

Praise First   Management guru Ken Blanchard recommends you praise before correcting. Observe what a speaker does well and praise that behavior before making corrective comments. That makes sense because a speaker's pluses will often far exceed the minuses.

Positive feedback might sound like this:

Your main points really stood out. You used a preview and listed the main points on a chart. The acronym BASS helped me remember the sequence. You used transitions between the points and that helped me follow the main divisions of the speech.

Here's another example:

Your eye contact improved as the speech progressed. In the beginning you looked mostly at the right side of the audience, but you caught yourself doing that and began looking at the whole audience.

Focus on the positive and be specific. This builds self-esteem, confidence, and enthusiasm for future speeches.

When Correcting, Think in Terms of Options   When helping a speaker make changes, speak in terms of options. Don't say, "That was awful" or "You made a mistake" or "The visual was confusing"; state the problem in objective terms and give a solution. Read the following response.

Problem: The speaker's visual was cluttered and confusing.

Solution: I would recommend you make two visual aids, one listing

the ingredients and the other, the minimum daily requirements. That would make it easier for the audience to grasp
the information.

Options stimulate and foster creative thinking. They give the speaker
ideas for improving communication.

Limit "Change" Feedback   Limit your feedback to one or two specific
points the speaker can focus on for the next presentation. To expect more is
unrealistic considering all of the preparation requirements for speaking.
More feedback will overload the speaker and possibly create more problems
than it solves, such as creating the impression the speech was ineffective.

Be Specific   Be descriptive and avoid generalities. Saying "I thought it
was a good speech" is of little value unless supported with specific details
describing the good qualities. Define what you mean by "good." Specific
language deals with: How much? How often? When? Where? Compared to
what?

Here is an example of descriptive language used in feedback:

You used many "ums" and "ahs" *(what)* throughout the speech *(where).* I
stopped counting them after 15 *(how much).* For your next speech try and
reduce them by half *(how much).* Make it a goal. When you rehearse,
record each session and count how many "ums" you use. If you practice
before a live audience, have them count the number of "ums" and "ahs."

In the following example, the listener uses specific language to praise a
speaker's demonstration:

Your demonstration of proper posture *(what)* was very helpful and thorough. You showed us proper posture and contrasted it with poor posture
(comparing), and told us the three steps on how to attain it.

Avoid Emotional Language   What kind of effect do you think the following words would have on a speaker's learning and confidence: phony,
weak, poor, lousy, stupid, wrong?

The effect would be negative and counterproductive. Wouldn't it be better to say:

What do you think of this idea?
Look at the audience when you show visuals.
A problem/solution arrangement would strengthen your arguments.
The idea to use a model was creative; position the demonstration to max-
imize the view.

Avoid words that degrade and demotivate. Focus on observable actions and describe them objectively.

Elements of Evaluation

Speeches can be evaluated in a number of ways. One is by results. Did the speaker achieve her objective? A high-tech salesperson giving a multimillion-dollar sales presentation can measure success by whether she gets the sale. George Bush's speech accepting the Republican nomination for President in 1988 was considered a make-or-break event for him. He was 17 points behind in the polls and labeled a "wimp" by the popular press. The speech established him as a viable and credible candidate and was considered the turning point of the election campaign.

Classroom speeches are learning vehicles and often cannot be evaluated strictly on results. Perhaps the most effective way to evaluate classroom speeches is to break them down into their component parts and see how effectively they employed communication principles. Elements of evaluation include audience analysis, delivery, organization, supporting material, and language.

Delivery   You focus on body language and voice. Was the speaker natural and credible? Was the speech well rehearsed? Was there good eye contact? Were there distracting physical or vocal mannerisms? Was there good volume and pacing?

Organization   Did the main points stand out and were they logically arranged? Were the specific purpose and central idea clear to the audience? Did the introduction capture the attention of the audience and did the conclusion effectively wrap up the speech and reinforce the central idea?

Supporting Information   Were the main points completely developed using language, visual aids, and activities? Did the speech hold the attention of the audience? Were a variety of language devices used? Were the visuals skillfully prepared and clearly presented? Were the activities well thought out and well executed?

Language   Was the language clear and specific and easy to understand? Was it appropriate? Did the speaker use slang or jargon that interfered with meaning?

Audience Analysis   Did the speaker accurately gauge the interest and knowledge level of the audience? Did the speaker address the expectations of the audience? Did the speaker empathize with the audience?

Each one of these categories helps you evaluate a speech. Figure 2-11 shows a sample evaluation form you might use to respond to classroom speeches. Your instructor may suggest alternatives as well as emphasize different criteria.

FIGURE 2-11
Speech evaluation form.

Speaker: _____

Topic: _____

Goal: _____

Rating scale: Excellent 5, Good 4, Average 3, Fair 2, Poor 1

Content:

Introduction

____ Got attention

____ Established relevance

____ Established credibility

____ Stated goal

____ Previewed main point

Body

____ Main points clear

____ Main points logically arranged

____ Stated goal

____ Tell

____ Show

____ Do

____ Transitions and summaries

Conclusion

____ Summary

____ Stated concrete results

____ Call for action

____ Unified speech

Delivery:

Body

____ Natural style

____ Controlled nervousness

____ Maintained good eye contact

____ Well-rehearsed

____ Natural gestures

____ Proper appearance

Voice

____ Proper rate

____ Good volume

____ Enunciated words clearly

Language

____ Clear and concrete

____ Appropriate

Audience analysis

____ Met audience expectations

____ Clear picture of target audience

____ Spoke at appropriate level of understanding

Speaker's strengths:

One recommendation for improvement:

Comments:

SUMMARY

Listening is an important part of the communication process. We listen by sensing, interpreting, evaluating, and responding. We have different learning styles that include thinking, feeling, watching, and doing. Three important types of listening are listening to understand, to evaluate, and to empathize. Improving listening skills involves taking the initiative, aligning yourself with the speaker's goal, focusing on meaning, concentrating, taking good notes, and making sure your interpretation is accurate. When you give effective feedback, you give praise, give options, limit feedback, use specific language, and avoid emotional triggers. Elements of evaluation include audience analysis, delivery, organization, supporting information, and language.

PROBES

1 Why does a listener have veto power over a speech?
2 What are the four steps of the listening process?
3 What is listening style? Briefly describe the four types of listening styles.
4 Briefly describe the types of listening.
5 What does it mean to align with a speaker?
6 What are three ways to make sure that your interpretation is accurate?
7 List five ways of giving feedback.
8 List six ways to improve your listening.
9 Briefly describe three ways of listening for meaning.
10 Briefly describe four ways body language influences the meaning of a message.
11 Why is grasping the central idea important to listening effectively?

APPLICATIONS

1 Examine Figure 2-3, the list of the ten worst listening habits. How many apply to you? What are the top three? What can you do to improve them? Be specific.
2 Attend a public speech unrelated to the college and use the elements of evaluation to critique the speech. Do you see any differences between the classroom speeches and the occasion you attended? Watch a speech on C-SPAN and do a similar evaluation.
3 Rate yourself on the Personal Listening Profile. What are your strengths? What areas do you need to improve?
4 Try the note-taking methods discussed in the chapter: linear, visual display, and mind-mapping. Which one do you prefer?
5 For one week, practice listening only for the central idea in the speeches you hear. Write down the central idea. Limit yourself to one short, concise statement. Do the same thing with the main points.
6 Evaluate your ability to concentrate. Practice using the methods discussed in the chapter to improve your concentration.

NOTES

1 Andrew Wolvin and Carolyn Gwynn Coakley, *Listening* (Wm. C. Brown: Dubuque, IA, 1992), pp. 19–21.

2 Ibid., p. 20.

3 Patricia Buhler, "Managing in the 90's: The Other Component of Communication—Listening," *Supervision,* Vol. 5, May 1992, pp. 19–20; Clay S. Willington, "Oral Communication for a Career in Business," *The Bulletin of the Association for Business Communication,* Vol. 52, June 1989, pp. 8–12; George E. Tuttle, "A Study of Listening across Three Situational Variables," paper presented at the Ninth Annual Meeting of the International Listening Association, Scottsdale, Arizona, March 2, 1988.

4 Jack E. Hulbert, "Barriers to Effective Listening," *The Bulletin of the Association for Business Communication,* Vol. 52, June 1989, p. 5.

5 Adapted from Lyman K. Steil, Larry L. Barker, and Kittie W. Watson, *Effective Listening* (Addison-Wesley: Reading, MA, 1983), Chap. 2, pp. 9–33.

6 Paul Taylor, "Watergate Spawned Cynicism, Attack on Presidential Power," *San Ramon Valley Times,* June 19, 1992, p. 19A.

7 This section adapted from David A. Kolb, *Experience as the Source of Learning and Development* (Prentice-Hall: Englewood Cliffs, NJ, 1984), pp. 20–95. See also Bernice McCarthy, *The 4 Mat System* (Excel: Barrington, IL, 1987), pp. 1–66.

8 John Sculley, "Preparing America for the 21st Century," *The Commonwealth,* Vol. 49, November 13, 1987, p. 542.

9 Louis Nizer, *The Implosion Conspiracy* (Fawcett: Greenwich, CT, 1973), pp. 16–17.

10 Tony Buzan, *Use Both Sides of Your Brain* (Penguin: New York, 1989), pp. 89–110.

11 Fred Wertheimer, "It's Time to Restore the Health of Our Democracy," *The Commonwealth,* Vol. 27, July 8, 1991, p. 474.

PREPARING THE MESSAGE

3

ANALYZING THE AUDIENCE
AND SETTING

CHAPTER OUTLINE

THE PROCESS OF AUDIENCE ANALYSIS
Define the Audience's Expectations
Draw a Factual Picture of the Audience
Measure the Audience's Knowledge about the Topic
Measure the Audience's Attitude toward the Topic
Discover the Audience's Psychological Links to Your Topic
Define the Target Audience
FAMILIARIZE YOURSELF WITH THE SETTING

On November 13, 1979 Ronald Reagan spoke to the nation announcing his candidacy for president. The speech was vilified by the press and the television networks and ridiculed by some members of his own party. One Reagan supporter called it "mostly mush." However, the speech was warmly received by the American people, the audience for whom Reagan had prepared and delivered the presentation. According to Lou Cannon, a Reagan biographer, "Reagan's target was neither the movement conservatives nor the national press. His audience, as usual, was the millions of Americans watching television. . . ." Reagan's goal was ". . . to establish bonds of association, and of trust, with his audience" and he did it successfully.[1] Reagan's approach is a powerful example of effective audience analysis.

President Ronald Reagan was called "the great communicator" because he had the unique ability to target his audience and speak to them in a personal way. Your success will also hinge on understanding the audience. The goal of audience analysis is to develop a profile of the audience that guides your preparation and delivery. When you do an audience analysis, you put your audience under a microscope and uncover their problems, motivations, aspirations, so you can speak to those issues.

Think how easy it is to talk to your best friend. You understand your friend's aspirations and problems, and maybe even know his or her intimate secrets. You know what motivates your friend. As a result you know how to talk to him or her, what buttons to push to get your friend's attention, how to make your point clear and meaningful. Make your audience your best friend. It will simplify preparation, build your confidence, and impress your audience.

THE PROCESS OF AUDIENCE ANALYSIS

Audience analysis is the process of identifying the audience to whom you will be speaking. The audience is an important resource and ally for your presentation. They bring expectations, attitudes, experiences, and motivations that help you organize and select information. The more you include these issues in your speech, the greater the impact of your presentation. You want the audience to say, "Those are important issues," "The speaker has hit the nail on the head," "The speaker is speaking for me," "That is a crucial problem." The following approaches can help you understand your audience.

Define the Audience's Expectations

Public speaking is driven by goals. When you are asked to speak, the audience has certain expectations: they are looking to solve a problem; they want to learn a new skill; they want to make a decision on an important issue. A group of employees may want to know about a new company policy, and how it affects their status. A group of parents have gathered to learn specific skills for building self-esteem in their children. A current affairs organization meets a local representative to get her views on new legislation that will affect the audience's lifestyle. The audience is there for a reason, and it is your job to define that reason and speak to it directly.

Pinpoint the audience's expectations. What do they want to walk away with at the end of your speech? What do they want to know and why do they want to know it? An experienced speaker would interview the program chairperson and possibly two or three members of the future audience to discover the group's goals. Here is an example of how one speaker wrote out the objectives of the audience:

Audience's Expectations:

> My audience is the PTA. They want to know what drug prevention programs the police department is using in schools and how they are working. They are interested in the information because they are considering initiating a drug prevention program in their school.

He then converted those group goals into a goal statement for the speech:

> My Objectives:
>
> To describe to the audience the drug prevention program used by the police department, including its philosophy, steps of the process, implementation, and success rate.

In the following example the speaker was asked to address the Columbus (Ohio) Rotary. She framed her remarks based on the interests and expectations of the audience.

> Good afternoon. It's a pleasure to be here to talk about care and education for young children. In the next few minutes we'll look at change—"from the Lone Ranger, to Power Rangers," because these mythical heroes represent very different eras—from the days when a lone fighter battled forces of evil—to today's high-tech team, the Power Rangers.[2]

Discover the audience's expectations.

Expectations of classroom audiences are sometimes difficult to pinpoint because they have not gathered for a specific speech. Nevertheless, you want to practice this important principle of audience analysis. Suppose your topic is AIDS. What should be the thrust of your speech? Causes? Prevention? Scope of the problem? You could interview a couple of your classmates and ask them for areas they would like to see emphasized. Or maybe contact the campus health center and interview a counselor on student concerns about AIDS. Expectations might be expressed this way:

Audience's Expectations:

Students are concerned that they may be vulnerable to AIDS and want ideas on how to help them avoid contracting the disease.

My Objectives:

To describe the spread of AIDS among college students, some of the causes, and specific solutions for avoiding contracting the disease.

Write out the goals of the audience—and be specific. This will help you focus your thinking.

Draw a Factual Picture of the Audience

Putting together a factual picture of the audience, called demographic analysis, increases your understanding of the audience and helps you select and adapt content. This is similar to the process political pollsters use to gather information about the groups they target. They develop a profile of a group—age, sex, income, occupation, ethnic diversity—and from this data develop content and communication strategies. If a particular population is composed of middle-class, culturally diverse people, the message would be different than if the population were inner-city and predominantly black.

Experienced speakers gather facts about their audience, looking for significant features that will help them find and select content. Maggie Kuhn, founder of the Gray Panthers, gets as much factual information—such as mission, size, professions, expertise—as she can about her audience before preparing her speeches.[3] If the majority of your audience were professional women, then you would select examples and illustrations relevant to them. Ross Perot, when he ran for president in 1992, described some of the characteristics of his audience in one of his campaign speeches:

Well, now that we have gotten things kind of stirred up . . . all the professionals are saying, "Who are these people?" Well, let me tell you who these people are. . . . These are people who love their country. . . . These are people who work hard, who play by the rules, who live in the center of the field of ethical behavior—they try to do the right thing. These are people who are active in their schools and their communities. These are people who serve in the armed forces of the United States.[4]

Some key factual data include age analysis, sex breakdown, educational level, occupational type, ethnic diversity, and group affiliation.

Age Analysis Age helps you to draw conclusions about how to approach subjects and to select content such as examples and stories. People understand information based on their experience. A senior citizen who lived through or served in World War II or the Korean war may view government defense expenditures very differently from a college senior who has only seen television coverage of American troops serving in Bosnia. Senior citizens may react very emotionally to discussions about trimming Medicare benefits, while young career-track professionals may be indifferent to the topic. You would prepare very different speeches for each group. In the following example, the speaker adapted the speech to the age of his audience:

> How can we, the older generation, do that (leave a large national debt) to our children? Do we assume that they will have an easier time than we did? Does it seem to us that our children have an easier time purchasing their first home, furnishing it, and having the resources to educate and raise their children? I can tell you the younger generation is having a real hard time making ends meet.[5]

Sex Gender makes a difference. Sex roles have changed and are evolving at a rapid pace. As women break down the stereotypes and barriers to professional and personal development, speakers, especially males, must be sensitive to these changes not only in content but delivery as well. Sexist examples, language, or humor, as well as condescending attitudes, need to be eliminated. In the following example, Kathleen B. Cooper, Chief Economist at Exxon, describes in a speech before the Distinguished Women Leaders of Dallas some of the barriers she faced in her career:

> Over the years, of course, there have been hurdles. There are those who listened to my soft Southern accent and assumed that I was soft inside as well. There are those who tried to intimidate me but found I would not flinch. There are those who dismissed me because my academic credentials were not Ivy League. They simply did not understand what is instilled in someone who juggles motherhood, career, and college. That something does not show on any transcript.[6]

Take an honest look at your attitudes and see if you hold beliefs that may result in offending or turning others off. Treat everyone with respect and dignity.

Education   Educational level influences how information is presented. A group of MBAs would be approached quite differently from an audience of blue-collar workers, or a group of high school dropouts. A corporate trainer speaking on job safety would select different content if she were speaking to a group of assembly-line workers than a group of managers. She would select anecdotes and role plays for the workers and research studies, statistics, and sophisticated graphs for the managers. In persuasion, an educated group would require evidence and sound reasoning whereas a less educated audience may require more emotional appeals. Here is how one speaker alluded to the educational level of his audience in his speech:

> I am particularly pleased to be speaking to engineers, architects, scientists, businesspersons, educators, politicans, etc., this evening; for you are the important people who can solve our educational problems—that is, if you have the courage to do so.[7]

Occupation   What the audience does for a living can give you helpful hints for selecting information. Many speeches are given to professional groups such as accountants, financial planners, chemical engineers, doctors, and nurses. They have special interests, problems, and issues relevant to their groups that can be used as a guide to adapting material. Here is how one speaker, himself a lawyer, addressed an audience of lawyers:

> We, as lawyers, are entrusted with great privileges—and with those privileges go obligations. We are empowered by society—and therefore ensure its progress. The concept of the practice of law solely for private gain is contrary to the ideals thrust upon us by our profession.[8]

If the audience is made up of people from different professions, you might look for large subgroups such as small business owners, like merchants; managers from companies; or professionals, like doctors and lawyers. If you have large subgroups, you can select and adapt material for them.

Ethnic and Cultural Diversity   Audiences are becoming more ethnically and culturally diverse. *Workforce 2000: Work and Workers for the 21st Century* predicts that by the year 2000 almost 61 percent of the new workers will be women and 29 percent will be minorities.[9] By the year 2000 California is expected to be the first state with the majority of its student population, kindergarten through high school, being ethnic and racial minorities.

You need to be aware of these differences but at the same time avoid stereotyping. The key to communicating effectively with culturally diverse audiences is to understand your own attitudes and work to overcome your conscious and unconscious stereotypes. One goal is to see people as individuals and to focus on their needs as people, not has whites, blacks, Asians, or hispanics. The other is to ensure that your presentation does not contain language or examples that is offensive. Here is how Farah M. Walters, CEO, addressed the issue of diversity before a management conference on diversity:

> The challenges that we face today in terms of building effective, diverse work forces, are . . . clear and . . . significant.
>
> We can either successfully anticipate those changes, effectively diversify, and become winners . . . or we can ignore the future, and build canals, and end up relics.
>
> It is my fervent hope that within my lifetime we will all be competing on a level playing field, no longer needing to treat people differently, no longer being treated differently . . . and that successfully managed diversity will be so much the norm that there no longer will be the need to hold a conference such as this.[10]

Group Affiliations   Group membership can often suggest values, needs, and attitudes. A person may join the local Chamber of Commerce to promote her business, meet others with similar interests, or participate in community activities. A person may join the college ski team for social and financial reasons. Whatever the reason, a person's membership is a reflection of some value or need. One of the best ways to find out is to ask the chairperson or members some of the group values so you can adapt or incorporate them into the speech. Here is how Suzanne Winters addressed the issue of group affiliation in a group of science teachers:

> I am honored and delighted to join you today at the beginning of an experience over the next couple of days which will stimulate your minds and motivate you to take back to your principals, your peers and classrooms the excitement of discovery. . . . I'd like to talk about discovery of the qualities that make up character and how we as scientists and educators can apply those characteristics toward our missions.[11]

Factual Analysis in the Classroom   Use the demographic model to analyze your class audience. Figure 3-1 contains a form for determining the demographic characteristics of your audience. As a practice exercise, analyze the following classroom audience:

Size: 29
Age: 18 to 42
Sex: Majority of women
College level: Mixed; freshmen, sophomores, juniors, seniors
Job: All work, great majority part-time
Ethnic diversity: Mixed

Age: Range from _____ to _____

         Average _____

         % younger _____ % middle age _____ % older _____

Sex: % male _____ % female _____

College % freshman _____ % sophomore _____ % junior _____

  year: % senior _____ % graduate _____

Job: % working _____ % not working _____

Ethnic diversity: % White _____ % African American _____

                    % Hispanic _____ % Asian _____

Group affiliations: % campus clubs _____

                    % religious organizations _____

Significant features:

Implications for speech:

FIGURE 3-1
Classroom audience demographic breakdown.

Group affiliations: Some belong to campus sports clubs, various religious
                                groups
Significant features:

Implications for speech:

Factual analysis by itself is incomplete. It needs to be combined with other information to give a clear picture of the audience.

Measure the Audience's Knowledge about Your Topic

You need a starting point from which to begin talking about a topic. If the audience knows little about your subject and you begin talking about it at an advanced level, the audience will not understand your speech. Gauging the audience's level of understanding of your topic helps you start at the appropriate level.

Simply asking pertinent questions about the audience's knowledge of the topic can produce guidelines for designing the message. For instance, if your speech is to inform, you might ask: How much does the audience know about the subject? Nothing? Little? A lot? Do they have the necessary background to understand it? From these and similar questions, you determine the level at which to prepare your presentation. For example, before delivering a speech explaining how a jet engine works, a speaker concluded that the audience had little technical knowledge. He therefore began with a demonstration in which he blew up a balloon and then let the air out of it to show that released compression can generate energy. Similarly, a field representative explaining to a client how to use a new copying machine would not explain all the technical details of how the machine actually does its job; instead, the rep would concentrate on which buttons to push and where to feed in new paper.

Another way of measuring the audience's knowledge is to take a survey. Even a random sample of four or five students may help you determine how to develop your topic. Needs assessment instruments are often used by businesses and government agencies to determine skill and knowledge levels so that new information is presented at the appropriate level. Figure 3-2 shows a sample survey form. Answers to the three questions would give you a starting point to begin discussing electric cars.

Interview people, like teachers, professors, or corporate trainers, who give information on a regular basis and ask them how they determine the discussion level for a topic. As a rule of thumb, don't overestimate the audience's knowledge about a topic. It is better to reinforce than to risk not communicating. Also, don't assume the audience has extensive knowledge about your topic just because you do. What may be routine knowledge to you may be unknown to others.

Measure the Audience's Attitude toward the Topic

Knowing the audience's attitude toward your subject helps you determine where the thrust of the persuasive effort needs to be. An indifferent audience

FIGURE 3-2
Sample survey.

1. Have you heard about the electric-powered car?
   a. Yes ☐
   b. No ☐

2. If yes, have you:
   a. Read about it   Yes ☐   No ☐
   b. Studied it   Yes ☐   No ☐
   c. Talked about it Yes ☐   No ☐

3. How would you classify your knowledge of electric-powered cars?
   a. No knowledge   ☐
   b. Superficial knowledge ☐
   c. Extensive knowledge   ☐

will require a different approach than an interested one. If the majority of employees dislike a new incentive plan and the manager chooses to advocate its benefits, the speech will fail because it doesn't address the workers' prevailing attitude. The speaker's goal is unrealistic and off-target.

Attitudes may be divided into five categories: favorable, interested, indifferent, unfavorable, hostile (Figure 3-3). Each predisposition represents increasing resistance to the preceding one and requires a different strategy:

Favorable:	The audience agrees with your views on your topic.
Strategy:	Reinforcement of perceptions.
Interested:	Intrigued by your viewpoint on your topic and will consider adopting it.
Strategy:	Emphasize the evidential soundness of your viewpoint and use new arguments in support.
Indifferent:	Don't see the need or relevance of what you are espousing.
Strategy:	Prove how your subject affects their well-being.
Unfavorable:	The audience is opposed.
Strategy:	Acknowledge the objections, attempt to minimize them, and then argue your case.
Hostile:	The audience strongly dislikes your viewpoint on your topic.
Strategy:	Choose another topic.

Your objective is to move the audience up the scale. If the audience is "indifferent," your objective is to move them to "interest." You do this by showing them how their well-being is affected by what you advocate. If your audience is "interested," you attempt to move them to "favorable" by presenting sound evidence. To attempt to jump from "unfavorable" to "favorable" in one speech may be unrealistic; it is a radical shift considering the audience's state of mind.

Dan Rather, CBS News anchor, in a speech before the Radio and Television News Directors Association criticized the industry for its absence of standards, a position not shared by the audience. He asked, "How goes the

FIGURE 3-3
Attitude categories.

Favorable	Interested	Indifferent	Unfavorable	Hostile

battle for quality, for truth, and justice, for programs worthy of the best within ourselves and the audience?" His answer was "Not very well." He went on to say ". . . . we have allowed this great instrument, this resource, this weapon for good, to be squandered and cheapened. About this, the best among us hang their heads in embarrassment, even shame."[12] Rather's speech was not well received by the audience.

Rather attempted to change an attitude the audience was incapable of changing or unwilling to change. They may have been unfavorable or even hostile, and he was appealing to indifference. The goal of the speech didn't match the attitude of the audience.

One method of measuring your audience's attitude is to conduct a survey similar to the one on measuring knowledge and record your results on a form like the one shown in Figures 3-4 and 3-5. You might survey the whole class or every other student to get a representative sample. You might use a scale, with extremes on the ends—do you strongly agree or strongly disagree— and spaces in between to reflect less extreme attitudes. Phrase your question carefully so it elicits accurate responses, and then record the results on the scale.

Suppose your topic was to persuade the audience that "women should be allowed in combat" and you wanted to know the audience's attitude toward your topic. You might ask "Should women be allowed in combat?" and then ask the interviewees to respond on your scale. The responses could then be tabulated and would give you a good idea of where the audience stands on the issue. If most of the responses are clustered in the middle, then your goal is to generate interest because people are indifferent (Figure 3-5). If most of the responses fall toward agreement, then your goal is to use evidence to reinforce the audience's interest and move the responses to "favorable." If the responses fall toward "disagreement," then your goal is to minimize the objections and use evidence to move them left to a more neutral position.

Discover the Audience's Psychological Links to Your Topic

Audiences listen when a message benefits them. The speech may help them solve a problem, achieve a personal goal, or expand their knowledge and skills. By relating your topic to the motivations of the audience, you generate interest. Some important motivations are:

FIGURE 3-4
Form for recording results of attitude survey.

| Strongly Agree | _____ | _____ | _____ | _____ | _____ | Strongly Disagree |

Should women be allowed in combat?					
		xxx	xxxx	xx	x
Strongly Agree	x	xxxx	xxxxx	xxx	xxx	Strongly Disagree

FIGURE 3-5
Survey results.

1 To achieve well-being
2 To increase self-esteem
3 To help others
4 To gain independence
5 To be entertained
6 To gain knowledge
7 To feel safe
8 To seek truth
9 To have companionship
10 To feel competent

In the following example, General Colin Powell appealed to the audience's motivation to help others:

> We should sacrifice for one another, care about one another, never be satisfied when anybody in this group is suffering and we can do something about it. That's what we've been missing. That's what's causing this angst in our public consciousness, the sense that we've lost the ability to care and sacrifice for each other, that we're too busy taking advantage of one another, that we're not sharing with those in our community who are least fortunate. We've lost the sense of shame, we've lost the sense of outrage. . . . America is a place that I believe in the depths of my heart was given to us by a divine providence that made us the stewards of this place. Our responsibility is to make sure that there are other youngsters who have the same kind of faith and hope that a young Colin Powell had forty years ago when I was growing up.[13]

Abraham Maslow, the eminent psychologist, organized human motivation into five categories and in an hierarchical order (Figure 3-6). The ones at the top are the most desirable but the least often satisfied. Maslow's classification helps you target motivations, and appeal to those most important to other people. Here is how one speaker tied his speech to Maslow's concept of self-actualization, experiencing one's capabilities at the highest level:

> Therefore the most important responsibility we have as black people is to *succeed,* to succeed in spite of racism, to succeed in spite of drugs, to succeed in spite of the odds against us. Our ancestors succeeded in the face of even greater

	Degree of Satisfaction	
Self-Actualization	10%	(Development of capabilities)
Esteem	40%	(Self-respect, recognition)
Social acceptance and belonging	50%	(Family, friendship)
Security	70%	(Stability, order)
Physiological	85%	(Food, sleep, shelter)

SOURCE: *Abraham H. Maslow,* Motivation and Personality, *2nd ed. (New York: Harper & Row, 1970), p. 54.*

FIGURE 3-6
Maslow's categories of needs.

odds—it is our turn now, we are much better prepared. We must not, we cannot and we will not fail them.[14]

As you prepare your speeches, ask yourself: What primary motivations connect my subject with the audience? This approach can help you begin thinking about the audience's motivations and how to link those motivations to your topic.

Adapt your speech to the needs of the audience.

Empathy can help you find other psychological links to the audience. Put yourself in the shoes of the audience and attempt to see how your subject relates to their wants and needs, values, anxieties, and emotions. In a speech advocating the fingerprinting of children, the speaker explained how this process helped identify abducted children, every parent's nightmare. By taking the audience's perspective, you can select and adapt content. In the following example, Governor John Engler uses empathy to discuss the problem of education in public schools:

> In my travels around the state these past weeks and months, I've been listening. And I keep hearing people talk about the need for "real change" in our schools. Last week there were rallies outside this capitol in which the crowd called for "real change" again.
>
> I agree—we need real change. And real change means not just more politics, but more principle. Not just talking about putting kids first, but doing it. Not just paying for a world-class education, but delivering one. Not just caving in to special interests, but standing up to them. Because let's get something straight from the start: There is only one special interest in this state—our kids. And our kids deserve better![15]

As a student yourself, you share many feelings with your audience of fellow students. *The Chronicle of Higher Education* reports that students are overwhelmingly optimistic about their personal and societal goals. Seventy percent want high-paying jobs and 70 percent want socially responsible professions.[16] Fifty percent of all students do volunteer or service work. More students are choosing majors that meet social and environmental concerns, such as psychology, social work, and sociology.[17]

These characteristics represent many of the feelings and attitudes of your classroom audience. You may refer to them as you prepare your speeches. Here is how one student used empathy in her speech urging the audience to help the homeless:

> Helping homeless children gives you the opportunity to express yourself. I'm not talking about donating money but giving your time and talents to help others. I sew, so I can mend any old clothes that are donated. I know many of you have other skills that could be used to make, repair, or paint old toys. Some of you can repair and build shelters. St. Anthony's Shelter needs people to paint the building and servers for the food lines.

Define the Target Audience

When an audience is small, two to four people, every member can be reached because you can accurately measure their expectations, attitudes, and motivations and appeal directly to them in the speech. For example, a manager presenting a proposal to three peers could analyze their organizational and personal concerns and prepare a highly focused presentation addressing them (Figure 3-7).

	AUDIENCE ISSUES	Ann Gee	John Jones	Mary Romero
J O B I S S U E S	FINANCE			X
	MANUFAC-TURING	X		
	HUMAN RESOURCES		X	
P E R S O N A L	ATTITUDE: POSITIVE	X		
	NEUTRAL		X	
	NEGATIVE			X

FIGURE 3-7
Audience analysis profile for small audience (2-4 people).

As an audience grows in size, it becomes unrealistic to expect to reach every member of the audience. Not everyone will have the same goals, attitudes, motivations, and knowledge about the topic. Some people will disagree no matter how powerful the appeal. Some members have closed minds and will not listen. Still others may have poor listening skills and not be able to grasp important ideas. That does not negate your efforts to understand the audience, but it puts a premium on directing your remarks to the reachable audience, the target audience (Figure 3-8).

Your speech can't be all things to all people. A teacher will always have children in the classroom who, for whatever reason, are undermotivated or immature. She doesn't ignore these children, but her teaching must be targeted to the majority of students who benefit from the instruction. As we've noted before, former President Ronald Reagan was very skillful at defining his target audience. When President Reagan spoke he wasn't speaking to a large, undifferentiated mass. He distilled the American audience down into a single, highly defined image and spoke directly to that group. He created a target audience for his remarks, just as you need to do for your speeches.

You define the target audience by analyzing the information about your audience. Suppose your topic is to persuade the audience to practice safe

FIGURE 3-8
Target audience graphic.

sex. This excludes the married, monogamous students, those who already practice it, and those who out of personal or religious conviction choose celibacy until marriage. This leaves those who are interested, indifferent, and possibly unfavorable to the topic as your core audience, and you would prepare your arguments for that group. You would still try to include all members by making references to their attitudes, and you would urge the ones most likely to practice safe sex to counsel friends and family, but your main arguments would be directed at those at great risk. You should write a description of your target audience as in the following example:

> My target audience is those members of the audience who do not practice safe sex. They are the ones who are indifferent to the risks they are taking; the "It can't happen to me" crowd. I will use statistics to show the increasing dangers college students face when they are indiscrete and give real-life examples of students just like them who were careless and contracted the HIV virus. This information will also be helpful to other members of the audience in talking to their friends and peers.

Figure 3-9 shows a form you can use to develop a profile of your target audience.

FAMILIARIZE YOURSELF WITH THE SETTING

A trial lawyer reminiscing about his first courtroom experience recalled that having received his B.A. and his law degree and passed the bar examination that permitted him to practice law, he had with a great flourish and much excitement retained his first client and eagerly awaited his first day in court. When that day arrived, he rushed with great anticipation to the courtroom with his client, only to discover he didn't know where to place

1. Audience expectations:

2. Demographic Analysis:
   Significant features:

		College		Ethnic		Group
❑ Age	❑ Sex	❑ Year	❑ Job	❑ Diversity		❑ Affiliations

3. Knowledge level: ❑ Low   ❑ Medium ❑ High

4. Predominant attitude:

   ❑ Favorable   ❑ Interested   ❑ Indifferent   ❑ Unfavorable   ❑ Hostile

5. Motivational Target:

		Social		
❑ Self/Actualization	❑ Esteem	❑ Acceptance	❑ Security	❑ Physiological

6. Summary of target audience:

FIGURE 3-9
Target audience profile.

his briefs, where to stand when presenting his case, or when and how to address the judge. Greatly humbled, he sought a private conference with the judge.

Experienced presenters familiarize themselves with the setting for the speech and often visit the location before their presentation. Public speeches are given in many different settings and under very different circumstances. The setting may be an outdoor rally or a luncheon meeting of the local Chamber of Commerce. The audience may be sitting at a table, desks, chairs, or on the lawn. A lectern may or may not be available, microphones may or may not be used, the room may be large or small, the audience may be permitted to drink or eat during the speech, you may be sharing a platform with other speakers or you may be the only speaker. Flip charts or overhead projectors may need to be ordered. Any of these conditions is possible, and you should be prepared for each of them.

The key question to ask about the setting is, how does it influence the message? Suppose you are planning an important demonstration or activity that will require the audience to rearrange their seats. You discover in analyzing the setting that the audience will be seated theater-style in chairs bolted to the floor. You will have to adapt the activity to that seating arrangement or select another activity. If you were unaware of these conditions before the presentation, you may have had to skip an important part of your presentation.

The classroom is a good place to experience different environments for a message. How will the audience be seated? In rows, in a circle, in a semi-circle? Will audiovisual equipment need to be ordered? Will display stands for visual aids be available? How long will it take to set up for your speech? Can your props be easily handled? At what point in the agenda will you be speaking? All of these factors can and will influence the response to a message.

Many experienced speakers carry "emergency kits" with them to speeches. Many times the equipment and material needed to deliver a speech, such as colored markers, tacks, masking tape, scissors, and a stapler, is unavailable. Experienced speakers bring these items with them. You should do the same for your classroom speeches.

Being prepared for the setting is an important aspect of presenting. And just as a single technical flaw in a play or movie can tarnish an otherwise excellent production, a miscalculation or oversight about the setting can impair an otherwise effective presentation. Don't make the mistake that the young lawyer made; know your setting.

SUMMARY

Audience analysis is the process of discovering pertinent data about the audience that can be used in the message. Steps of the process include defining audience expectations, drawing a factual picture of the audience, measuring the audience's knowledge about the topic, measuring the audience's attitude toward the topic, discovering the audience's psychological links to the topic, and defining the target audience. Familiarizing yourself with the setting is another important part of message preparation.

PROBES

1 Why is defining audience expectations important?
2 How do you discover audience expectations?
3 What is demographic analysis? What are key factual categories about an audience?
4 Why is measuring the audience's knowledge about your topic important?
5 Why is understanding the audience's attitude toward your topic important?
6 Briefly explain how you would determine the audience's psychological links to your speech.
7 Briefly explain how the setting can influence a speech. Give two examples.
8 How does motivational theory apply to audience analysis?
9 Briefly describe the idea of the target audience.
10 Briefly describe Maslow's hierarchy of needs.

APPLICATIONS

1 Conduct a demographic analysis of your class audience. What salient features can you discover? How can these characteristics be used to adapt your speeches?

2 In what ways can the needs and wants of your classroom audience be incorporated into your speech?

3 Briefly explain how you would analyze the following audiences:
  a. A group of businesspeople interested in improving their communication skills
  b. A group of parents concerned about the safety of their children walking to school
  c. A disgruntled group of union workers threatening to strike

4 Describe the setting of your classroom speeches. Look for such characteristics as the resources available to you and the arrangement of the audience.

5 Prepare a one-minute persuasive speech about abortion if your audience's attitude is indifference. What if their attitude is unfavorable. How do those attitudes influence your approach?

6 Prepare a one-minute speech urging a group of parents of high school students to support installing a condom dispensor in the bathrooms. What if the audience is a group of high school students?

NOTES

1 Lou Cannon, *Reagan* (G. P. Putnam's Sons: New York, 1982), pp. 241–242.

2 Diane Bennett, "From the Lone Ranger to Power Rangers," *Vital Speeches,* Vol. 61, February 1, 1995, p. 251.

3 Victoria L. DeFrancisco and Marvin D. Jensen, *Women's Voices in Our Time* (Waveland Press: Prospect Heights, IL, 1994), p. 232.

4 Jerry Roberts, "Perot Rally at Capitol," *San Francisco Chronicle,* June 19, 1992, p. A20.

5 George Marotta, "Bureaucracy: The National Debt," *Vital Speeches,* Vol. 58, June 1, 1992, p. 499.

6 Kathleen B. Cooper, "What Do I Recommend for Young Women?" *Vital Speeches,* Vol. 61, November 15, 1994, p. 84.

7 Benjamin H. Alexander, "The Importance of Education in Today's America," *Vital Speeches,* Vol. 61, April 15, 1995, p. 403.

8 William S. Sessions, "Fundamental Changes in the Legal System: Professional Priorities," *Vital Speeches,* Vol. 58, January 15, 1992, p. 196.

9 Beverly Geber, "Managing Diversity," *Training,* Vol. 27, July 1990, pp. 23–30; William A. Henry, "Beyond the Melting Pot," *The Nation,* April 9, 1990, pp. 28–35; Audrey Edwards, "The Enlightened Manager: How to Treat All Your Employees Fairly," *Working Woman,* January 1991, pp. 45–51; Linda Beamer, "Learning Intercultural Communication Competence," *Journal of Business Communication,* Vol. 29, 1992, pp. 285–295; Dr. Joan Bowen, President, Industrial Council of California, "The Cultural Renaissance: A Cultural Diversity Experience," speech delivered at Diablo Valley College, January 15, 1991.

10 Farah M. Walters, "Successfully Managing Diversity," *Vital Speeches,* Vol. 51, June 1, 1995, p. 500.

11 Suzanne Winters, "The Dynamics of Discovery," *Vital Speeches,* Vol. 61, November 15, 1994, p. 441.

12 Dan Rather, "Call It Courage," *Vital Speeches,* Vol. 60, September 15, 1993, p. 79.

13 *U.S. News and World Report,* "The Man to Watch," August 21, 1995, p. 22.

14 George C. Fraser, "Ten Trends That Are Changing Black America," *Vital Speeches,* Vol. 50, April 15, 1994, p. 411.

15 John Engler, "Our Kids Deserve Better," *Vital Speeches,* Vol. 50, November 15, 1993, p. 72.

16 Arthur Levine and Deborah Hirsch, "Student Activism and Optimism Return to Campus," *The Chronicle of Higher Education,* November 7, 1990, p. 48.

17 Susan Dodge, "More Students Choose Academic Majors That Meet Social and Environmental Concerns," *The Chronicle of Higher Education,* December 5, 1990, p. 1.

4

SELECTING A TOPIC AND PURPOSE

When individuals are called upon to speak, they usually have specialized knowledge about or recognized skills related to a topic the audience wants to know about: Julia Child talks about cooking; John Madden, about football; Carl Sagan, about science. An engineer working on a special project may be asked to give a status report about it at the next managers' meeting. The representative of a special interest group may be asked to present her controversial views before a public group. Thus, speech topics originate from the knowledge and experience of the speaker and the interests of the audience.

The same is true of speeches you give in the classroom. You want to speak about subjects you are knowledgeable about and that will be of interest to the audience.

METHODS OF SELECTING A TOPIC

As a new student in a public speaking course, you may feel that the range of topics on which you are qualified to speak is limited and that you know little if anything about the interests of the audience, your classmates. These are legitimate problems. But as you will see, you have an abundance of experience, interests, and knowledge that will help you select topics and prepare speeches that will be interesting and valuable to the audience. Let's look at some methods for discovering topics for your speeches.

Speak from Your Experience

Whether you have spoken in public once or a thousand times, you still communicate from your own experience and knowledge. You are the source of your topics. While you may not have the in-depth experience of a professional who has worked at a job for years, you have sufficient experience to speak on any number of topics. You have skills, past experience, interests, and hobbies that, when looked at as sources of possible speech topics, have great potential. Here is a sample list of personal experiences and the speech topics that could be based upon them:

Sue is an amateur cartoonist. Her topic: How to draw cartoons.
Gary is an amateur juggler. His topic: The basics of juggling.
John surfs the net. His topic: How the internet works.
Becki is a member of the Ski Patrol. Her topic: Ski safety.
Joan works at a preschool. Her topic: Working with children.
Rick is on the basketball team. His topic: How to shoot free throws.

In each of these examples, the topic originates from the experience of the speaker.

Choose Topics about Which You Are Knowledgeable

Speaking on topics about which you are knowledgeable increases your confidence and credibility. Because your experience with a subject is personal, you can prepare and present a speech in a more comfortable style. That is preferable to doing extensive research on a topic about which you know little. Your presentation might lack authenticity, and you could end up sounding stiff and perhaps phony.

You have gained knowledge from a variety of sources that can help you select topics for a speech. Past activities, jobs, hobbies, or courses may have given you extensive knowledge about specific topics. Maybe you took a course in marketing and could prepare a speech about subliminal advertising. Maybe your work as a camp counselor could lead to a topic about organizing activities to build children's self-esteem. Perhaps you've studied the solar system as a hobby. You could discuss any number of topics in that subject area: planets, stars, galaxies, black holes, and so forth. Here are some examples of how students' knowledge was turned into topics:

Mitzi worked with marine mammals at a sea ranch and decided to give a speech on how whales and dolphins are trained.

Bill worked on a political campaign for a local congressional representative and used that knowledge to speak on political strategy.

Margaret did extensive research and wrote a number of papers on the issue of gun control and selected that topic for her presentation.

Choose Topics in Which You Are Interested

Cal Ripken, Jr., Michael Jordan, Barbara Walters, and Robin Williams all have one significant characteristic in common, their enthusiasm for their work. Ralph Waldo Emerson once said, "Nothing great was ever achieved without enthusiasm." Enthusiasm creates enthusiasm. When a speaker is excited to talk about a subject, the work of research and planning, not to mention the presentation itself, seems less like a chore and more like a pleasure. Moreover, a speaker's enthusiasm about a topic is infectious and transfers to the audience.

What subjects excite you? A particular sport? A particular career? Your faith? An academic subject or theory? A current event? A hobby? Here are some examples of how enthusiasm for a subject generates topics for a speech:

Joan has taken ballet lessons for fourteen years and spoke on how ballet dancers rehearse for performances.

Tanya is a skydiving enthusiast and spoke on the process of jumping from an airplane.

Larry is a triathlete and spoke on the rigors of preparing for a competition.

Mike is a student of the Bible and spoke on how the scripture can help people better understand their lives.

Choose Topics You Feel Strongly About

Great historical events and social changes have happened as a result of people having strong convictions and speaking passionately about them. Thomas Jefferson's advocacy of civil rights and civil liberties resulted in those principles becoming the cornerstone of the Constitution. Martin Luther King, Jr., spoke eloquently about equality and led the fight against racial discrimination. Betty Friedan was an early leader and eloquent spokesperson for the women's rights movement of the last three decades. Having conviction about your topic makes preparation and delivery enjoyable. Your delivery is strong and forceful because you are speaking from deep within yourself. Your conviction motivates audiences to listen and increases your credibility.

Select topics about which you feel passionate. If you feel deeply concerned about child abuse, the plight of disabled people, or abortion, you should speak about these topics. There may be philosophical issues or solutions to problems about which you feel strongly. Individual liberty, the importance of personal responsibility, or the need for using one's potential may be subjects you feel compelled to address in a speech. Here are some examples of how personal convictions became speech topics:

Glenn believed passionately that dolphins would become an endangered species if current methods of fishing were not changed and encouraged the audience to boycott companies that profit from the slaughter of dolphins.

Joan believes that television advertising targeting children is wrong and urged the audience to boycott companies that sponsor children's programs.

Sarah believes that battered women are not adaquately protected by the law and that stronger legislation is needed for their safety.

How to Discover Topics for Speeches

Perhaps the simplest method of finding topics for speeches is to inventory your knowledge and experience. Some areas to explore are:

1 Jobs, past and present
2 Sports you participate in
3 Skills you have
4 Hobbies you pursue
5 Places you've visited
6 Unique personal experiences
7 Academic knowledge
8 Contemporary issues: local, state, national, and international

Figure 4-1 illustrates the number and range of topics one student discovered by examining her personal history. Mary Johnson's list revealed not

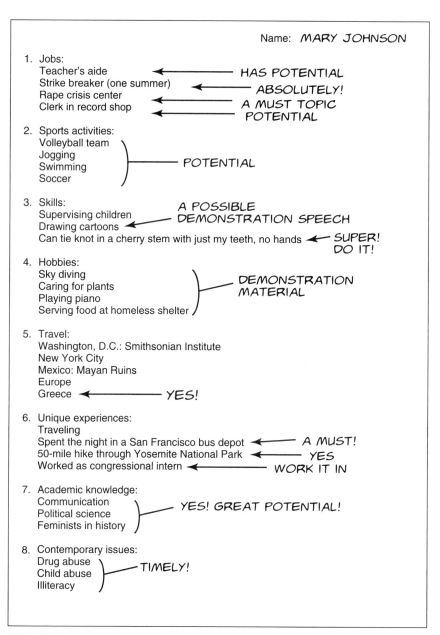

FIGURE 4-1
Inventory of knowledge and experience.

only specific topics that could serve as the basis for speeches but many potential subjects as well. For example, each of her travel experiences could be developed into several specific topics, and her academic knowledge provides many additional possibilities.

Rapid association, even brainstorming, is one way to discover the variety of subjects within yourself. Meet with a classmate or two someplace where you won't be disturbed and brainstorm for topics. Start with a general topic of interest and spontaneously associate subjects with it and write them down. Don't worry about being too specific. Do not disregard any topic. Even the most remote item may be the catalyst for a speech. The following list of subjects came from a single brainstorming session between two students:

Television	Space station
Effects of television	Favorite movies
Sex and violence on television	Child pornography
Advertising on television	Violent crime
Television news	Prisons
Public television	Police brutality
Information highway	Handguns
Communications satellite	Drugs
Space shuttle	Victims' rights

Another way of finding speech topics is to ask yourself what kinds of subjects you talk about on a daily basis. Do you find yourself talking about current events? A favorite course? A part-time job? One student came up with the following list of topics by noting the subjects of his daily conversations:

Relationship with parents	Characteristics of bad teachers
Affirmative action	Defining personal values
Career opportunities	Interviewing for a job
Marriage and family	Practicing Christian values
High-paying summer jobs	Educational reform
Raising children	Internet
Building self-esteem	Political correctness
Improving study habits	AIDS prevention
Deciding on college major	Physical fitness
Shortcuts to scheduling classes	Term limits

Reading newspapers and magazines can help you find subjects and reinforce your interest in topics that you may decide to speak on.

If you are still stumped for a topic, peruse *10,000 Ideas for Term Papers, Projects, Reports and Speeches* (Kathyrn Lamm, Arco). Topics include children, environment, media, sex, aging, and many more.

In summary, your experience, knowledge, interests, concerns, brainstorming, reading, and subjects of daily conversation can help you find topics for speeches.

TAKING OWNERSHIP OF YOUR TOPIC

Whatever topic you select, take ownership of it. Effective speakers are successful because the topic is "theirs." It belongs to them. They believe in it. The topic is an expression of their knowledge, experience, values, and beliefs—a part of them. With it they can convey important information to the audience.

Classroom speeches should be treated the same way. Even though you are speaking in a learning environment, you should "own" your topic. Treat it with care and turn it into an act of self expression. Whether your topic is describing a mountain bike or explaining how to make grandma's great chocolate chip cookies, prepare and present the best speech you can.

SELECTING A TOPIC FOR A SPECIFIC AUDIENCE

Effective speakers understand that while their topic may be exciting to them, they must also make it relevant to the audience. They use sound audience analysis to adapt their topic to the needs, interests, and expectations of the audience. A consultant asked to speak about cultural diversity to a group of managers will work to relate that subject to improving morale and performance in the workplace because managers are concerned about productivity. Here is an example of how one speaker adapted her knowledge about nutrition to a particular audience.

> Jane Williams is a dietician who specializes in sports nutrition. She was asked to speak about nutrition to a group of college athletes. Possible topics included history of nutrition, types of nutrition, malnutrition, etc. However, the audience was interested in knowing how their diet could be used to enhance their athletic performance. So Jane selected the topic "Diets to Improve Athletic Performance." She adapted the topic to the interests of the audience.

Tailor your topic to the audience. One way is to match your topic to their needs and interests as Jane Williams did in the previous example. List your topic in one column and your audience's interests, based on your audience analysis, in the next column. Next, look for the connections.

Your topic	Audience interests	Speech topic
Career opportunities	Career goals Prestige Financial security	How to select a career that pays well and leads to self-fullment
Volunteer time to youth groups	Helping others Learning supervisory skills Learning communication skills	Volunteering to youth groups helps others and improves management skills

Your topics, career opportunities and volunteering time has been related to important career objectives of the audience.

NARROWING YOUR TOPIC

After you have selected a topic and related it to a specific audience, you will probably find that it is still too broad or imprecise to serve as the basis for a speech. You need to determine your overall objective and then phrase a specific purpose so you have a clear and logical basis for preparing your speech. A child psychologist, asked to speak before a group of parents about building self-esteem in children, might first decide if, for example, he is going to advocate a specific method for building self-esteem or offer them some information about several different methods. Then he must formulate his specific purpose for the presentation. After choosing a topic, the next step is to narrow the topic and mold it into a statement that can be covered in the allotted time.

Determining the General Purpose

Determining the general purpose of your speech helps you focus on the overall objective of your presentation. Three general purposes of speech-making are speaking to inform, speaking to persuade, and speaking for special occasions.

Speaking to Inform   One of the important reasons that we communicate is to exchange information. Professors, teachers, managers, coaches, supervisors, executives, and administrators spend a large percentage of their time imparting information. The purpose of speaking to inform is to increase the listeners' skills, knowledge or to clarify ambiguous or complex data for them. For example, a lawyer defines sexual harassment in the workplace to a group of managers to help them understand and prevent the problem. A computer technician explains to a client's employees how to use new computer hardware. If you were giving an informative speech to your class, you might discuss skydiving techniques, describe the space shuttle, or explain the AIDS virus.

Speaking to Persuade   A second important reason we communicate is to convince others to accept our point of view. If you have ever tried to talk a police officer out of giving you a ticket for speeding or a professor into changing a grade, then you have spoken to persuade. The goal of persuasion is to change the beliefs, attitudes, or behavior of the audience. The key word here is "change." You want to change the audience's perception of a subject or their way of doing something. A professional athlete may attempt to persuade a group of teenagers that using drugs is harmful and life-threatening. A supervisor in a factory may need to persuade employees of the importance of following inconvenient safety measures when operating dangerous equipment. If you belong to an organization that aids the homeless, you might want to persuade your class to donate food and clothing.

Speaking for a Special Occasion   Public speaking has a host of other uses, including introducing a speaker, accepting or presenting an award, making an after-dinner speech, and commemorating achievements. These types of speeches have emotional goals. The coach gives her team a pep talk after the second period of a tight game hoping to motivate them to victory. A colleague accepting an award describes the hard work and sacrifice that led to his success. Colleagues present light and entertaining stories when "roasting" an associate. A veteran describes bravery under fire at a Memorial Day celebration.

Formulating the Specific Purpose

After selecting a topic, relating it to the audience, and determining the general purpose, the next step is to mold it into a statement that can be adequately developed in the allotted time. Phrasing a topic to serve as the goal of the speech is called "formulating the specific purpose."

The specific purpose is the statement of your goal for the speech. It states in an accurate and precise way what you want your presentation to accomplish.

Specific purpose:	To persuade the audience to have a complete physical examination annually.
Specific purpose:	To describe to the audience how the AIDS virus attacks the body.

The importance of a clear and realistic specific purpose cannot be overestimated. Steven Covey, leadership trainer, says the most important principle

Carefully phrase your specific purpose.

of planning is to "begin with the end in mind." Goal setting helps you make decisions about selecting main points, supporting material, and the areas of emphasis that will make that goal a reality. Mountain climbers don't begin climbing without a plan. They look at where they want to go and work back from there to the starting point. They look at what is the best way to reach their destination and then establish a plan to attain their objective. Know where you are going. Let's discuss the steps to follow in order to formulate a workable specific purpose.

Limit Your Goal to One Idea   Your speech should have a single purpose. Multiple purposes are confusing for the audience and difficult to develop.

Multiple purpose: To explain to the audience tips on photographs, judging photographs, and selling good photographs.

Single purpose: To explain to the audience how to take good photographs.

The first statement contains three separate goals: (1) how to take good photographs, (2) how to evaluate photographs, and (3) how to sell good photographs. It would be unrealistic to attempt to cover all three goals in a single speech. The second statement has only one goal and could be completely developed in a single presentation.

Use Clear, Specific Language to State Your Specific Purpose Use clear and specific words to phrase the specific purpose. This statement guides the development of a speech and tells the audience the goal of your presentation.

Confusing: To persuade the audience about women's role.

Clear: To persuade the audience that women should have more leadership positions in the college's administration.

The first statement could be about any role related to women: women in industry, women in politics, women in space, and so forth. No role is specified. The second statement is easily understood. It identifies the leadership role you feel women should have and where it should be exercised.

You should also define any words in the specific purpose that may be ambiguous to the audience.

Ambiguous: To persuade the audience that criminal laws are too liberal.

Precise: To persuade the audience that the sentences given to convicted felons don't match their crimes.

The problem with the first statement is that criminal "laws" and "liberal" lack definitions. Does the speaker mean all criminal laws or just a few like those on burglary, rape, or murder? What is meant by "liberal"? The way judges sentence criminals? Loopholes in the law that help criminals avoid prosecution? Or that sentences don't match the crimes? The second statement defines the speaker's specific intent, using precise terms.

Formulate the Specific Purpose in a Single Concise Statement A long and unwieldy statement of purpose may hinder the preparation process and confuse the audience. State your goal in a clean, crisp sentence.

Confusing: To persuade the audience that term limits for elected representatives would lead to better representation because careerism would be eliminated.

Clear: To persuade my audience to support term limits for elected representatives.

The first statement is too detailed and cumbersome. The second statement is direct and to the point.

Make Sure Your Topic Can Be Covered in the Allotted Time Experienced speakers are given an allotted time to speak just as you are in your classroom speeches. So select a topic you can cover in the specified time. A topic that is too narrow may make for too short a speech and not meet the expectations of the audience. A topic that is too broad cannot be covered in the allotted time and your presentation will appear superficial.

Unrealistic: The problem of alcoholism in the United States.

Realistic: To describe to the audience the harmful effects of alcoholism on American industry.

The first statement means that the speaker is going to discuss the entire problem of alcoholism in the United States. That could take weeks or months. The second statement specifies a much more limited and reasonable goal.

A speaker's skill and experience, along with an accurate assessment of the audience's ability to understand a subject, determine if the goal can be achieved in the designated time. The number of main points will also determine length. However, the more thoughtfully the goal is phrased, the better you can determine its feasibility as well as the preparation requirements for the speech.

DISCOVERING AND PHRASING THE CENTRAL IDEA

After formulating the specific purpose, you want to begin thinking about the central idea. The central idea is the underlying premise of the speech. It expresses the most important idea you want the audience to have about the speech and acts as the unifying thread tying the message together (Figure 4-2). It is like the message the movie director wants the audience to take with them after they see the film. It is the moral of the story and your speech.

Determining the Central Idea

Lloyd George once told the young Winston Churchill, "Don't deliver an essay with so many points. No one can absorb it. Just say one thing." The central idea captures the essence of the speech in a single sentence. Ask

FIGURE 4-2
Specific purpose/central idea objectives.

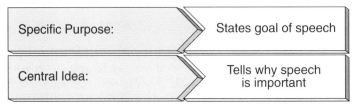

A strong central idea gives you confidence.

yourself: What do I want the audience to know, feel, or do about my presentation? Let's look at an example.

Specific purpose: To demonstrate for the audience the Heimlich maneuver for choking victims.

Central idea: The Heimlich maneuver is a simple and easy-to-learn first-aid technique.

The statement of the central idea emphasized that the Heimlich maneuver was simple and easy to learn. That was the single most important conclusion the speaker wanted the audience to reach. The speaker could have chosen a different central idea. What if he wanted to emphasize the benefits of the first-aid technique? In that case the central idea might read as below:

Specific purpose: To demonstrate for the audience the Heimlich maneuver for choking victims.

Central idea: The Heimlich maneuver saves lives and reduces serious injury.

Thus, as a speaker you have options as to what conclusion you want the audience to draw from your specific purpose. The key is to determine what you want that conclusion to be, because that will influence how the speech is developed. Richard W. Riley, Secretary of Education, in a speech about the importance of family to educational achievement, expressed the central idea of his speech this way: "To my mind, there is no more important place to begin putting our house in order than by recognizing that our children's expectations about the future are rooted in the day-to-day family activities that help children learn and develop good character. America needs to give up its get-it-now, live-for-today mentality and start looking down the road to make sure that we give all our children the America they deserve."[1] Riley went on to develop the speech around that theme.

Figure 4-3 shows a formula for discovering the central idea for your presentation. Use it to discover the central idea of your presentation.

FIGURE 4-3
Specific purpose/central idea formula.

Specific Purpose/Central Idea Formula

The following approach can help you discover the central idea for your presentation. For an informative speech write out your specific purpose and then follow it with a statement that states why the subject is important.

Specific Purpose:
to inform the audience how to perform CPR,
Goal of Speech

Because

Central Idea:
Learning CPR saves lives and reduces injury
Importance of Topic

For a persuasive speech the formula would work in a similar fashion;

Specific Purpose:
to convince the audience to practice safe sex
Goal of Speech

Because

Central Idea:
Practicing safe sex will save your life
Importance of Topic

Phrasing the Central Idea

Once you discover the central idea, phrase it clearly and concisely in a sentence. If you have difficulty phrasing the central idea, it may be that you are unclear about the purpose of your message. Give more thought to the objectives of the speech or do more research until the statement becomes clear. Discuss your speech with a friend or your professor until the central idea crystallizes in your mind. Figure 4-4 shows the relationship among the general purpose, specific purpose, and central idea.

A clearly stated central idea has many advantages. First, it gives you a strong sense of direction while you are preparing and delivering a presentation. Your selection of main points and supporting material will be guided by the response you want from the audience. For example, if your central idea is "Seat belts save lives and reduce serious injury," then you will select main points and supporting material that support that theme. Study the following example:

General purpose: To persuade.

Specific purpose: To persuade my audience to wear seat belts.

Central idea: Seat belts save lives and reduce serious injury.

Body

Main Points: I Seat belts save lives.

II Seat belts reduce serious injury.

The central idea guided the speaker in the selection of main points.

A strong central idea also increases your confidence because you are certain what your objectives are. You are leading the audience to a specific conclusion. It is easier to channel your energy and emphasize certain information during a presentation when you are seeking a specific outcome.

FIGURE 4-4
Tying the major ideas together.

General Purpose	Specific Purpose	Central Idea
To inform	To inform the audience how to skydive.	Skydiving is easy to learn and safe.
To persuade	To persuade the audience to support a ban on selling handguns.	Banning handguns will save lives.
To present an award	To praise Maria Ramos' academic achievements	Maria Ramos is an outstanding student and humanitarian

Discovering the central idea of your presentation may be challenging as you prepare your first speeches. You may be unfamiliar with the structure of a message or may have had little practice identifying and phrasing theme statements. Sometimes a clearly identifiable central idea may not emerge until after you have started the preparation process. Nevertheless, identifying and clearly phrasing the central idea is critical to effective communication.

SUMMARY

Selecting a topic for a speech involves examining your knowledge, interests, and concerns. Jobs, skills, contemporary issues, and the subjects that you talk about every day are all potential speech topics. Tailor your topic to the needs and interests of an audience.

Three general purposes for speeches are speaking to inform, speaking to persuade, and speaking for special occasions. The specific purpose states what you want the audience to know as a result of your speech. The central idea is the conclusion you want the audience to draw as a result of your speech.

PROBES

1 Briefly explain why a topic selected for a classroom speech may differ from a topic selected for outside the classroom.
2 Besides choosing a subject about which you have knowledge, what factors must you consider when you are selecting a topic for a speech?
3 Briefly explain the specific purpose of a speech. Give three examples.
4 Identify each step for formulating a speech's specific purpose.
5 Briefly explain the central idea of a speech. How does it relate to the specific purpose?
6 Briefly explain how you can link your topic with the needs and interests of the audience.
7 Briefly describe three general purposes of public speaking. How are they linked together?

APPLICATIONS

1 Take inventory of your interests, knowledge, and experiences using Figure 4-1 as a model. If some areas overlap, that's fine. Discover the wide range of topics that you could speak about. Do not exclude any possibilities.
2 Prepare specific purposes for the following topics: (a) Recycle. (b) Child abuse. (c) High school dropouts. (d) Voter apathy. (e) The national debt.
3 Write central ideas for each specific purpose in item 2 using the specific purpose/central idea formula.

4 Apply the guidelines for formulating a specific purpose to each of the following phrases and sentences. Where necessary, rewrite the phrase or sentence to reflect appropriate goals: (a) Legalize marijuana. (b) Power in government. (c) To demonstrate how to adjust ski bindings. (d) Schools need reform. (e) Backpacking.

5 Write down in a single sentence the central idea—the underlying premise—of the two most recent movies you've seen.

6 Prepare a two-minute speech about a personal experience from which you learned a lesson—a story with a moral, if you will. Conclude the presentation with a statement of the lesson (the moral). This speaking experience helps you learn how a central idea and specific purpose are related. The goal is to inform about the experience, and the moral is the central idea.

NOTES

1 Richard Riley, "Strong Families, Strong Schools," *Vital Speeches,* Vol. 60, October 1, 1994, p. 746.

GATHERING INFORMATION

Einstein said, "Intelligence is not the ability to store information, but to know where to find it." Finding information for your speech does not have to be frustrating and time-consuming. In fact, research can be simple and easy if you have a plan and know where to look.

Let's put research in perspective. Typically, experienced presenters are asked to speak on subjects about which they are knowledgeable. Research would be supplementary—used to update, revise, verify, or add to their existing knowledge. A school board president asked to speak on budget objectives for the coming year already has knowledge about the subject. The president's research would probably consist of collecting the latest revenue and expense figures, both current and projected, to support that knowledge.

Thus, the purpose of research is to complement existing knowledge rather than to develop the entire contents of a message. That is why you should speak on subjects about which you already have some knowledge. Suppose you have worked as a tutor at your college and the subject of your speech is learning disabilities. You might supplement your experience by interviewing college counselors about their experiences working with students with learning problems. The counselor might recommend additional sources such as a periodical that deals specifically with learning disabilities or the title of the definitive work on the topic. You would use this information to supplement your knowledge about the subject.

DETERMINE YOUR RESEARCH GOALS

Before beginning your research, you can determine the amount and type of information you will need by assessing your objectives, assessing your knowledge of the subject, and reviewing your audience analysis.

Assess Your Objectives

A clear and precise objective can help you determine investigative goals. If your objective is to persuade, you will be looking for facts and testimonials that support your argument. That will lead you to different sources of information than if your objective is to inform, in which case you will need descriptive or explanatory data to clarify and amplify your idea. Suppose that your objective is "to persuade the audience to donate blood," and at the end of your speech you will give them specific information on how to do that. You then have a specific research objective: to gather the names, addresses, phone numbers, and operating hours of blood banks.

Assess Your Knowledge

Reflect on your knowledge about your topic and sketch it briefly on paper. Suppose your objective is "to inform the audience on how to administer first aid to an accident victim." You have taken a course in first aid and recall some of the training. A book or manual about first aid could assist you in preparing visual aids or demonstrations for the audience. You could obtain the book from the library or a first-aid instructor to refresh your memory or to use it as a source for visual aids. You could interview a first-aid instructor to validate your approach.

Use Your Audience Analysis

Your audience analysis can help you determine research needs. If your audience is indifferent about your point of view, you need to gather facts and testimonials from credible sources to show its validity. Suppose your objective is to persuade the audience to spay or neuter their pets and the audience is indifferent about the issue. To overcome their indifference, you would gather evidence showing how they are adversely affected by fertile animals. Thus, you have a research goal: finding studies that show how humans are harmed when pets are not spayed or neutered.

PLAN THE INVESTIGATION

After assessing your informational needs, plan your research as systematically as possible. It will save you time and help avoid repetition. The following guidelines can be helpful.

Explore Preliminary Sources

Don't rush into research. If you are uncertain about where to find specific information, or you are inexperienced at locating information, examine some general sources or interview credible persons who can lead you to relevant sources.

Go to a good encyclopedia like the *Encyclopaedia Britannica* or *Academic American Encyclopedia* for background information. Even a one-volume encyclopedia like *The New Columbia Encyclopedia* or the *Random House Encyclopedia* can give you basic information on a subject. Talk to people who can help. Your professor can recommend people to talk to on campus. Discuss your topic with the reference librarian. His or her sole function is to help you with your research needs. These general sources will lead you to specific references: a book, magazine article, person, speech, newspaper article, scholarly paper, microfilm, or phamphlet. From here you can move to the next step in planning the research.

Organize Your Investigation

Develop a plan for obtaining the needed information. Your goal is to save time and use the sources of information efficiently. Establish a priority for obtaining information. For example, interviewing credible sources may be the first order of business before doing library research. The interviewee may be able to recommend specific reference material that will reduce research time in the library.

Developing a research planner may be helpful in organizing your investigation. List the sources of information, both preliminary and specific. Prioritize them and set dates for completion (Figure 5-1).

SOURCES OF INFORMATION

The sources of information available to you are almost unlimited. A brief example of a source list might look like this:

Direct sources

Oneself: the primary source

Personal interviews

FIGURE 5-1
Research planner.

RESEARCH PLANNER

Speech Topic: Animal rights   **Speech Date:** Oct. 4

General Purpose: To persuade

Specific Purpose: To persuade audience to help   **Audience:** Class

stop unnecessary testing on animals.

No.	Information Needs	Source	Seq.	Date	Hours	Comp. Date
1.	General information on animal cruelty	Interview Duf Fisher	1	9/15	1:00 PM	
		Get book The Animal Rights Crusade				9/15
2.	Types of animal testing	Newspapers Index and Magazine Index	2			9/17
3.	Examples of cruelty	Write to RESO animal rights groups	5			9/19
4.	Protest groups	Encyclopedia of Associations	4			9/18
5.	Reputable authorities on subject	Review Time and U.S News articles	3			9/18
6.	Organizations testing on animals	Visit University research center	6	9/20	11:00 AM	

Printed sources
  Newspapers
  Magazines and professional journals
  Books
  Encyclopedias
  Pamphlets
Electronic Sources
  Databases, such as periodical indexes
  Internet
  Compuserve
Nonprint sources
  Television
  Radio
  Film
  Audiotapes
  Videotapes
  Computers
  Microfilm
Organizations
  Government agencies: local, state, federal
  Private companies
  Community organizations: Chamber of Commerce, health clinics, others
Special interest groups
  Planned Parenthood
  NAACP
  National Rifle Association

These are a few of the sources available to you. Let's explore some specific ways of getting information.

Personal Interviews

Personal interviews are valuable sources of information. You can choose as interviewees people who are on the firing line and can give you unique insights into issues and events. They can give you new information about a topic or put into perspective information you have already gathered. To observe experienced interviewers at work, you might watch the hosts of PBS' *News Hour,* interview newsmakers and experts who put important events into perspective.

Interviews should be a part of your research efforts. Contrary to what you may think, people enjoy being interviewed. It boosts their egos to know they have been consulted on a subject of value to others. Interviewees are usually extremely helpful. This is especially true of your professors, who enjoy discussing their disciplines. Remember, too, that as an investigator you have influence because you are an individual looking for information.

Prepare for the Interview   Being prepared will help get you the information you need and make the interview an enjoyable learning experience. Here are some guidelines to help you prepare for an informational interview.

Define Your Informational Goals   To define your informational goals you must determine what information you want to impart to your audience. Let's assume that your objective is "to persuade the audience to get involved with the prevention of child abuse." You would need to inform your audience of the legal definition of "child abuse" and any possible ramifications of reporting it.

You decide to interview the district attorney in charge of child abuse cases. Knowing the information you want to bring to your audience, you would ask the D.A., "How would you define child abuse? What is the liability or legal exposure for the individual who reports it if the suspect is not arrested or indicted?"

In this scenario you examined your needs, and then were able to clearly identify your informational goals.

Prepare Your Questions   Prepare your questions carefully. Begin with the goal in mind. That is, prepare your questions so the interviewee responds with the information you want. For example, suppose you wanted to know the socioeconomic status of the average child abuser. You might phrase your question this way:

Question: What is the profile of the typical child abuser?

This question should result in a detailed description of a child abuser. Here are some guidelines for phrasing effective questions:

1 Define the informational objective for each question before phrasing it. List the information you need and then formulate the question to obtain the answer. This is what reporters do when they prepare questions. Suppose you wanted to know if the abuser was abused as a child. You might ask:

Question: Are the people accused of child abuse themselves victims of child abuse?

2 Use clear and specific language for questions. Concrete language pinpoints meaning and makes it easier for interviewees to respond because they immediately know what information you want. An example of a poorly worded question occurred recently in a widely publicized survey about the Holocaust. Based on the survey one in five Americans doubted the Holocaust happened, a finding that shocked many people and became headline news. The conclusion was based on a question that was so poorly written it confused the respondents and lead to the erroneous result. The question read: "Does it seem possible or does it seem impossible to you that the Nazi extermination of the Jews never occurred?"[1] That is a confusing question. Some people may have been answering no when they meant yes and yes when they meant no. In a follow-up poll with a clearly worded question only 1 percent believed the holocaust never happened.[2]

The following questions are phrased clearly and directly:

Question:	Does a person reporting child abuse expose herself to a lawsuit?
Question:	What is the typical punishment for a parent found guilty of child abuse?
Question:	Do you recommend citizens coming forward with allegations of child abuse?

3 Avoid the appearance of asking loaded or trap questions. "When is the last time you beat your child?" assumes the interviewee has committed the heinous act. The interviewers on *60 Minutes* sometimes build a circumstantial case against a person, invite the person on camera, and then conduct a highly confrontational interview. This is not the kind of interview you will be doing as you research your speeches. If you see that a question could be misconstrued, preface the question so the interviewee understands your intent. Suppose the conviction rate for abusers is very low. The implication could be that the district attorney's staff is not doing the job. Phrase the question so that your intention is clear. You might say:

Question:	The conviction rate for abusers is very low. That does not imply it is not a priority for you and your staff or that you are not doing your best to prosecute the abuser. Can you tell me the reasons for such a low conviction rate?

Two important types of questions are open-ended questions and closed-ended questions. Open-ended questions are designed to encourage the interviewee to elaborate at length on a topic. The interviewee does the talking, not you. Some examples of open-ended questions are:

Open-ended:	Please explain, in layperson's terms, the legal definition of child abuse.
Open-ended:	If a person observes child abuse, how should it be reported to the authorities?

In each instance the questions seek extended answers from the interviewee.

Closed-ended questions, on the other hand, seek yes/no responses or short factual answers. They place the burden of talking on you, the interviewer. Closed-ended questions often establish the basis for follow-up questions. Here are some examples of closed-ended questions:

Closed-ended: How many child abuse cases have you prosecuted?

Closed-ended: Is the number of reported child abuse cases increasing?

With the first question the interviewer seeks a numerical answer and in the second one, a yes/no answer.

You should phrase your questions carefully. They should be clear, specific, and concise. Larry King, one of the most successful interviewers on television, attracts hard-to-get personalities because he asks specific, nonthreatening questions that relax his guests and encourage them to speak openly and freely. When Tommy Lasorda, the Los Angeles Dodgers' manager, was a guest, the first question King asked was "Why Blue?" in reference to the name "Dodger Blue," a label frequently given to the team. King is a good interviewer to watch to learn how to phrase very specific questions.

Examine these examples:

Ambiguous question: What is your experience prosecuting child abuse cases?

Specific question: What is your success rate prosecuting parents accused of abusing their own children?

The ambiguous question has no focus. What does the questioner mean by "experience"? Number of cases tried? Trial strategy? Emotional feelings about victims? The specific question has a concrete objective: to find out how successful the district attorney has been in prosecuting child abusers.

One final note about preparing your questions. Arrange them in some kind of order. There may be some questions you feel are more important than others. You might want to ask these first. Some questions may logically precede others. Journalists often employ a strategy of opening an interview with easy-to-answer questions to relax the interviewee, and then proceed to more difficult questions.

Arrange the Interview Don't be bashful or defensive about asking for an interview. Professionals are open and receptive to granting them. However, be businesslike and flexible in arranging an appointment. People are busy. Explain who you are, the purpose of the interview, and the amount of time you will need. Offer to send an agenda so the interviewee has time to prepare answers and possibly recommend other resources.

Ask if they have any special requirements. If you plan to tape-record the interview, ask if that is acceptable.

Establish an Agenda Having an agenda is helpful because it states the goal of the interview and outlines your questions. It will also impress upon the interviewee that you are a person with professional instincts.

Preparing an agenda is similar to preparing a speaking outline. Arrange the parts of the interview in the order in which you will be presenting them. Figure 5-2 shows an example of an interview agenda.

Rapport: Thank you for taking the time to see me.

Speech Objective: To persuade the audience to report child abuse.

Ground Rules: 1 hour time limit. No questions about present cases.

Interviewee's Credentials: County District Attorney

Order of Questions:

1. How is child abuse legally defined?
2. What is the liability for an individual who reports child abuse?
3. What is the typical punishment for someone found guilty of child abuse?
4. Do you recommend citizens' coming forward to report cases of child abuse?
5. How does one report child abuse to the authorities?
6. How many child abuse cases have you prosecuted?

Other sources of information:

FIGURE 5-2
Sample interview agenda.

Decide on a Method of Recording the Interview You have the choice of either tape-recording or taking notes. If the interviewee objects to tape recording, then obviously note taking is your only option.

Even if the speaker allows tape recording, you still run the risk of the speaker being uncomfortable and less than candid. Also, keep in mind that transcribing information from tape can be cumbersome. Therefore, you should take extensive notes and use a tape recorder as a backup system, a way of ensuring that your notes represent an accurate interpretation of the speaker's remarks.

Conduct the Interview Follow the prepared agenda. Conduct yourself in a polite and businesslike manner. As the interview progresses, you should:

1 Ask follow-up questions and clarifying questions when appropriate. Don't fake it. If you don't understand a point, ask for clarification. Ask follow-up questions to probe deeper. Suppose you ask, "Are the instances of child abuse increasing?" If the interviewee says "Yes," then you could follow up by saying, "Why do you think it is happening more frequently?"

2 Keep the interview on track. Don't allow the interview to drift. If it does, politely tell the interviewee you have digressed and get back to your agenda.

3 Wrap it up on time. Show your appreciation by respecting the interviewee's time. If you end early, so much the better.

Review the Information Following the interview you should immediately review and complete your notes. Don't trust your memory to remember words, abbreviations, or spontaneous codes three, four, or five days later.

Convert that shorthand into sentences that express the ideas and facts relayed by the interviewee.

In fact, you should completely rewrite your notes to maintain their coherence. It will pay off later as you integrate the outline into your presentation.

Using the Library[3]

Retrieving information from the library is not a difficult task if you know what you're doing. Numerous resources are available to help you understand the operation of a library. Brochures, handouts, and videotapes explaining the procedure for locating materials are available in most libraries. Most colleges offer (and in some cases require) courses in using the library. You can ask for a personal tour from the librarian.

Important sources of information in libraries include librarians, books, periodicals, electronic databases, and other resources such as films, pamphlets, and government documents. The following is an introduction to using these important sources of information.

Working with the Reference Librarian The job of the reference librarian is to help you find information in a library. Reference librarians know how information is organized and where it is located. They have detailed knowledge of what sources to turn to for particular types of assignments. They can be of great help to you in finding the data you need for your speeches. Explain to the librarian as clearly and specifically as you can what information you are looking for.

Locating Books All books in the library are listed in a catalog according to author, title, and subject. Listings are filed alphabetically and include the following information (see Figure 5-3):

1 Call number: this number indicates where the book is located in the library

2 Author

3 Title

4 Publication information: city, publisher, date

5 Descriptive data about the book: (a) number of pages and size; (b) information about diagrams, maps, bibliography, and index

Many libraries have replaced their traditional card catalogs with automated (computer) catalogs. These catalogs provide the researcher additional ways (not just author, title, and subject) to find or access library materials. Automated catalogs may include films, videotapes, and other databases as well as books. Sometimes these catalogs include local area information, periodical indexes, and even gateways to other libraries and to the Internet.

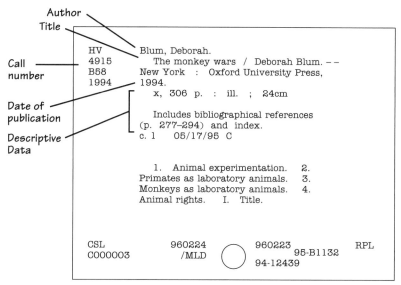

FIGURE 5-3
Library catalog card.

A typical automated catalog record includes the same information as a catalog card, but the information may be arranged differently. The computer record often adds important information such as whether the book has been checked out or not (see Figure 5-4).

Locating Relevant Periodicals If you are looking for very current information, you will want to search for recent periodical articles. Periodical indexes tell the researcher exactly which issue of a magazine includes an article on a specific topic. There are a variety of indexes for the thousands of periodicals or magazines published every year. You may already be familiar with the *Reader's Guide to Periodical Literature,* which indexes more than 240 popular or general subject magazines. The author and subject index lists articles from such popular periodicals as *Newsweek, Time,* and *U.S. News & World Report.* Every entry in the *Reader's Guide* lists the following information (see Figure 5-5):

1 Subject
2 Title of article
3 Author of article
4 Publication in which article appears
5 Volume and page number(s)
6 Date of publication

```
AUTHOR    Blum, Deborah.
TITLE     The monkey wars  /  Deborah Blum.
IMPRINT   New York  :  Oxford University Press, 1994.
DESCRIPT  x,  306  p.  :  ill.  ;  24cm
NOTE      Includes bibliographical references (p. 277–294) and index.
SUBJECT   Animal experimentation.
          Primates as laboratory animals.
          Monkeys as laboratory animals.
          Animal rights.


     LOCATION           CALL NO.                    STATUS
1 > STACKS              HV4915 .B58 1994
```

FIGURE 5-4
Automated library catalog card.

In addition, some specialized fields have their own indexes; some of the available subject-specific indexes are:

Art Index
Business Periodicals Index
Education Index
Humanities Index
Applied Science and Technology Index
Social Science Index

Computerized data bases make finding information quick and easy.

ANIMAL RIGHTS MOVEMENT
  See also
  In Defense of Animals (Organization)
  People for the Ethical Treatment of Animals
Animals, vegetables and minerals [defense of animal ex-
  perimentation] J. Szymczyk. por *Newsweek* v126 p10
  Ag 14 '95
Children and the animal rights agenda. G.S. Blankenau.
  il *Field & Stream* v100 p56-8 Ag '95

FIGURE 5-5
Reader's guide to periodical literature.

Sometimes it is necessary to consult several different indexes in your search for information.

Periodical indexes are now available in a variety of formats: print, CD-ROM, online to a database, and on microform. Electronic periodical indexes are increasingly available in libraries. These databases may correspond to printed indexes such as the *Reader's Guide to Periodical Literature* or the ERIC indexes (Resources in Education and Current Index to Journals in Education). Or, as in the case of InfoTrac databases, which we'll discuss in a moment, they may have no print counterpart (see Figure 5-6).

Using Computer Databases   Computer databases, either online or in CD-ROM format, provide quick subject access to newspaper or journal articles in hundreds of publications. These electronic indexes often cover several years and may provide abstracts and/or full text of the articles.

One CD-ROM disc can hold as much information as 272,000 printed pages or over 2,000 floppy diskettes! Compared to printed media, it is easier to find information on CD-ROMs. It is not necessary to flip through pages in a book or search through a dozen volumes before you find the information you need. Software included with the disc allows you to search through all this data within seconds.

FIGURE 5-6
Computerized periodical index.

---

6   The prospects for consensus and convergence in the animal
   rights debate. Gary E. Varner. The Hastings Center Report,
   Jan–Feb 1994 v24 n1 p 24(6). Elec. Coll. : A14954250.
   – – Abstract and Text Available – –
7   Animals and science benefit from "replace, reduce, refine
   effort. (Medical News & Perspectives) Paul Cotton. JAMA, The
   Journal of the American Medical Association, Dec 22, 1993 v270
   n24 p2905(3). Elec. Coll.: A14658322.

Like the automated library catalog, electronic indexes and databases provide several access points or methods of searching, such as author, key word, subject, browse, and the ability to combine words using Boolean logic for retrieving information. The indexes may also include cross references—that is, guides to other sources of information.

If your library does not have the periodical you need, ask a librarian if interlibrary loan services are provided. Many libraries are willing to locate the article you need and request that a photocopy be sent to you.

Selecting Quality Information Increasingly, students often find too much information! New research skills are becoming necessary as we speed ahead into the Information Age. Quality research necessitates learning new ways to evaluate what is sometimes an overwhelming amount of information. What do you do, for example, when your periodical search turns up 250 citations to journal articles? Consider analyzing the results of your large search in one or more of the following ways:

1 Select the articles that are in the more scholarly periodicals—or in the periodicals that seem best for your topic. How do you decide which are the best or most appropriate articles to read? Become familiar with the various types of magazines and journals that are published and learn to identify their content, bias, and style (see Figure 5-7).[4]

2 Look for articles in reputable periodicals or for articles whose authors you have heard of.

3 Select the most recent articles.

4 Redo your search using more specific terms or key words to trim the selections.

5 Redo your search as a subject search—this means you need to enter in a "correct/exact" Subject Heading. (Ask a librarian for help on this one!)

6 Look in *Magazines for Libraries* (a reference book by Bill Katz, R.R. Bowker) to find a description of the strength, bias, or political slant of a particular periodical.

7 Print the citations for several articles and then confer with the librarian or your instructor for suggestions.

Locating Other Printed and Electronic Sources of Information Many other sources of information can be located through your library.

1 *Government publications.* Government publications may be located through the *Monthly Catalogue of Government Publications,* which organizes data according to agency and also includes a subject index.

2 *Newspapers.* There are indexes to many of the larger newspapers. *The New York Times* compiles semi-monthly and annual indexes of its daily issues. Bell and Howard Supply printed or electronic subject and author indexes for some

Type	Sensational Publication	Popular Magazine	Professional Substantive News	Scholarly
Purpose	Arouse curiosity and interest by stretching and twisting the truth: outrageous startling headlines are used to pique interest	Summarizes important recent news stories. Designed to entertain and advertise	Provide industry specific information for professionals usually educated readers groups. Greater depth of news coverage	To inform report or make available original research for the rest of the scholarly and professional world
Sources	Rarely cite sources and sources cited are difficult to verify	Rarely cite sources; original sources may be obscure	Occasionally cite sources; this is the exception rather than the rule.	Sources are cited in footnotes and bibliographies. Articles signed and credentials given
Format	Cheap newspaper format	Slick and glossy, brief articles	Attractive glossy pages	Plain and serious
Language	Simple language often with an inflammatory, sensational style	Simple language for a general audience	Language for educated audience	Uses the terminology and jargon of the discipline: reader assumed to have similar background
Graphics	Startling photographs	Many photographs, illustrations to enhance articles	Photographs, illustrations and sophisticated graphics	Many graphs and charts; drawings, few photographs
Examples	National Enquirer Star Sun Globe	Newsweek People Sports Illustrated Ebony Time	Scientific American Science News Business Week Economist New Republic	New England Journal of Medicine Harvard Business Rev. Journal of Nutrition Education Journal of American Medical Assoc.

FIGURE 5-7
What's the difference? Journals and Magazines.

papers with large circulations, including *The Los Angeles Times, The Washington Post,* and the *Chicago Tribune.* The *National Newspaper Index,* another database on InfoTrac, indexes five national newspapers: *The Christian Science Monitor, The New York Times,* the *Wall Street Journal, The Los Angeles Times,* and *The Washington Post* (see Figure 5-8).

3 *Statistical data. Statistical Abstracts of the United States, World Almanac, Survey of Current Business,* and *Monthly Labor Review* provide easily accessible statistical data.

FIGURE 5-8
Computerized newspaper index.

```
 InfoTrac  EF    |        Academic ASAP          Brief Citations
 _____|_____
|  Subject:  animal rights                                             |
|                                                                      |
|                           1 of 42                                    |
 ──────────────────────────────────────────────────────────────────────

   1      Futility hasn't dulled lawyer's ardor for animal rights.
          (Gary L. Francione takes extreme position on animal rights;
          Rutger University's Animal Rights Law Center) (National Pages)
          .Neil MacFarquhar.  The New York Times, Nov 15, 1995 v145
          pC19 (N)  col 1 (29 col in).
               Press Enter for extended citation.
```

4 *Encyclopedias.* Both printed and electronic encyclopedias are excellent first sources because they provide a concise overview of subjects and give important background information and useful bibliographies. You can find what you need to know very quickly. Some popular general encyclopedias are the *Encyclopedia Americana,* the *Encyclopaedia Britannica, World Book Encyclopedia,* and *Academic American Encyclopedia.* There are also specialized subject encyclopedias such as the *Encyclopedia of Psychology, Encyclopedia of Religion,* and *The McGraw-Hill Encyclopedia of Science and Technology.*

5 *Pamphlets.* Many libraries have a pamphlet file (or collection). Ask the librarian.

6 *Biographies.* See *Biography Index, Notable American Women, Who's Who,* and *Current Biography.*

7 *The Internet.* The Internet, often confusing and seemingly unorganized compared to traditional resources, holds the promise of a great deal of information for researchers. Through the Internet it is possible to connect to and search the catalogs of other libraries, search the electronic text of many books and periodicals, and connect directly to resources at universities and government agencies. You can communicate with other people through e-mail or join a Listserv of your interest. Files of data can be sent from one computer to another.

Almost every source of information in the library—be it printed, electronic, or multimedia—is listed in an index or catalog.

Contacting Local Agencies and Special Interest Groups

Other important sources of information are local agencies and companies. A phone book lists all local, county, state, and U.S. government agencies, in addition to most businesses in your area. If you want statistics on the local high school dropout rate, consult the school district's office. If you need information on AIDS prevention, contact the local health services agency. The local Chamber of Commerce can provide you a list of every business, large or small, in your vicinity. The local offices of your elected representatives can also be excellent resources.

Audiovisual Sources

Suppose your specific purpose is to demonstrate how to swing a golf club. You could review a tape of the swing made by a golf professional and use those tips to supplement your demonstration. You might also decide to use an excerpt from the video during your presentation.

Most colleges have audio/video or media centers that contain videos, films, slides, filmstrips, audiotapes, and records. These resources are listed in the computer database or catalogs located in the library and/or the media center.

The *Educational Film and Video Locater* lists the title and the distributor's address for every educational video or film made in the United States. The *Video Source Book* lists the title, company, and address of every commercial and documentary video made in the United States. Both are in computer databases.

Sending for Information

The *Encyclopedia of Associations* lists the addresses of thousands of organizations in the United States and abroad such as Greenpeace, The International Brotherhood of Teamsters (the Teamsters' union), and Planned Parenthood. These groups usually respond quickly and do not charge for information. Keep in mind that these organizations are biased and only promote the interests of their group.

If you need an address, there is a directory that lists it. For example, if you want to write to the president or CEO of a major corporation, you can get the address of the corporation through *Standard and Poor's Register of Corporations.*

You might even try calling some of these organizations. Many have toll-free numbers so there is no cost to you.

You should follow certain guidelines when sending for information. Clearly specify your goal and the types of information you are seeking. Set a deadline for receiving the information. While companies and special interest groups are usually prompt, you should have backup sources just in case your request is lost or delayed.

RECORDING INFORMATION

Recording the information you find accurately is as important as doing the research itself. Taking poor notes or trusting your memory can make hours of valuable research meaningless, forcing you to retrace your steps to find forgotten information or clarify illegible notes. Taking thorough notes and compiling a bibliography will make your research efforts fruitful.

Taking Notes

Record information accurately the first time. Here are some suggestions for taking good notes.

1 Record the information on 3 × 5 index cards; 3 × 5 cards are big enough to hold plenty of data and small enough to organize easily. If you have a computer, you can transfer this information to files, such as Hypercard, that will index them automatically. Avoid the temptation to use the backs of folders, the leaves of books, or paper napkins. This information will get itself lost.

2 Use one card for each source. If you put two sources of information on one card, they may be unrelated, making it difficult to organize the cards in a simple way. It may also make it difficult to find the data. Using a computer file will simplify this process.

3 List all the pertinent information about the source. Write down the subject heading, title, author, publisher, source (call number also), date, and page number (see Figure 5-9). If you should need to reexamine material or are asked for the source of your facts, this information is invaluable. You might create a template or standard form on a PC that labels and lists all the information you need to record. You can store this information on your computer as well.

4 Take concise notes. Focus on the key ideas and summarize them. Jot down any facts you find significant or compelling. If you quote a source, make sure the quote is complete and in context. Avoid copying large sections of text. Remember, you want the key ideas (Figure 5-10).

5 Leave space for your comments. If a source is of unusual value, make a note of it. If one source ties in with another, make a note of that connection. These kinds of comments will come in handy as you put your speech together. This can be done easily on a computer.

Preparing Bibliography Cards

A bibliography is a list of the sources—periodicals, books, interviews—you consulted for your presentation. The sources are listed in alphabetical order by author. Each listing is similar to the way you recorded the source of your notes in step 3 above. In a bibliography you list:

FIGURE 5-9
Sample note card (periodical).

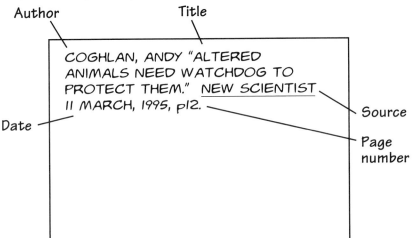

FISCHER, DUF. ANIMAL PROTECTION
INSTITUTE OF AMERICA. PERSONAL
INTERVIEW. 30 SEPT 1995

Reforms are coming but not
fast enough. Millions of
animals are being slaughtered
daily.

[interview]

FIGURE 5-10
Sample note card (Interview).

1 Author's name (last name first)
2 Title of the publication
3 Publisher
4 Place of publication
5 Date of publication

Figures 5-11 and 5-12 show two sample bibliography entries. Create a template on your computer for your bibliographic data and file it using file-maker software.

FIGURE 5-11
Bibliography card (periodical).

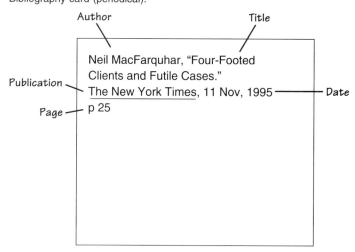

Author   Title

Neil MacFarquhar, "Four-Footed
Clients and Futile Cases."

Publication

The New York Times, 11 Nov, 1995 ——— Date

Page — p 25

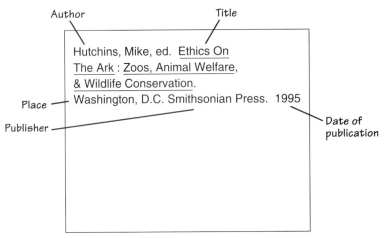

FIGURE 5-12
Bibliography card (book).

SUMMARY

Research requires planning. Such planning includes determining your research goals and planning the investigation. Major sources of information are personal interviews, the library, local agencies and special interest groups, personal correspondence, audiotapes, and videotapes. Understanding how to prepare and conduct an interview and learning how to take advantage of all the sources of information available through a library are important for conducting research. Taking accurate notes makes research successful and saves time.

PROBES

1 What sources would you consult for information about the following subjects? (a) History of your city or town. (b) A controversy in your town/city. (c) A campus issue. (d) A U.S. senator. (e) Drug trade in Colombia.
2 You need the most current information on a pressing issue such as teenage births or AIDS. How would you go about finding it?

APPLICATIONS

1 Select a local or campus issue that interests you. Select a person to interview. Prepare interview questions and an agenda. Then proceed with the interview. What was the result? Did you get the information that you wanted? What was the interviewee's attitude toward you? To the questions? How well did you conduct yourself? What was your reaction to the assignment?

2 Select a subject of interest to you, and using InfoTrac or a current edition of the *Reader's Guide to Periodical Literature,* review how many sources of information are available to you.

3 As an investigator, you have influence. Let's test that influence. Prepare a letter to the president, the Pentagon, your congressperson, or some other government official or agency, seeking information about their position or past statements on a particular issue. Suppose, for example, that the Secretary of Defense had made a major policy speech and you would like to have a copy of that message, or that you want to seek information about a person or group through the Freedom of Information Act. Whatever your choice, be specific about the information you want and your reasons for wanting it. How long did it take to get a response? Was the information, when you received it, relevant to your question?

4 Prepare a research planner as a guide for your investigation.

NOTES

1 John Kifner, "Pollster Finds Error on Holocaust Doubts," *New York Times,* May 20, 1994, p. A6.

2 "Consulting the Oracle," *U.S. News and World Report,* December 4, 1995, p. 55.

3 I am grateful to Betty Bortz, and the library staff at Diablo Valley College, for their assistance in planning the section on using the library.

4 Idea adapted from Purdue University Library handout.

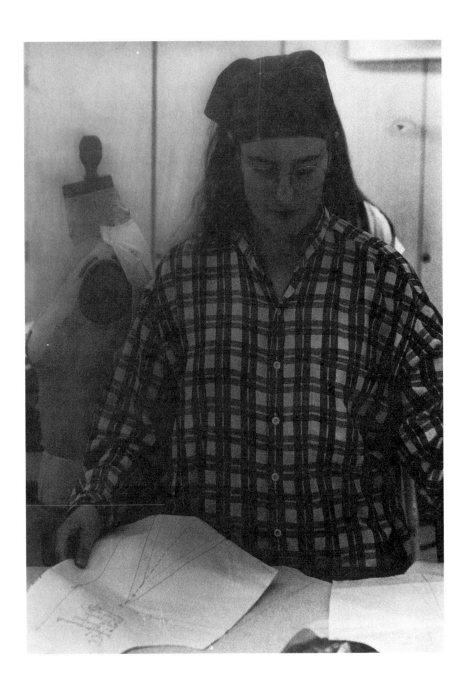

6

ARRANGING THE BODY OF THE SPEECH

CHAPTER OUTLINE

Would you plan a trip across the country without preparing a route or the means of traveling to your destination? Would you plan a surprise birthday party without notifying people of the time and place and making arrangements for refreshments and activities? Of course you wouldn't—because these activities require organization to achieve the desired result. The same is true of preparing a speech for delivery.

Speech organization is the process of arranging information to achieve a specific goal. It is your blueprint or strategy for achieving your specific purpose. You first carefully select, arrange, and phrase the main points for the body of the presentation. Your objective here is to organize information so the audience can easily understand and follow the speech. Next, you prepare the opening and closing of the presentation so you capture the attention of the audience at the beginning and conclude with a strong reinforcement of your ideas.

The importance of organization to the success of your speeches cannot be overestimated. The clear and logical arrangement of information helps the audience follow the presentation and improves their comprehension and retention of information.[1] Good organization helps the audience apply the information in your speech to their lives.[2] If your goal is to explain a first-aid technique, the audience's ability to apply the process is greatly enhanced if your speech is well organized.

Good organization improves your credibility and persuasiveness. This should not be surprising. Organization reflects your thought process. When information is clearly and logically arranged, audiences view the speaker as knowledgeable about the topic.[3] Poor organization gives the opposite impression.[4] At the same time, audiences are swayed to accept a speaker's proposal when arguments are clearly and logically presented.[5] Sound organization also improves your delivery because you're focused. You have a blueprint or plan for presenting your remarks.

THE MAIN POINTS

Umberto Eco said, "Construct the framework and the words will follow." After you have formulated the specific purpose and phrased the central idea, your next step is to select and organize the main points in the body of the speech. The main points are the key ideas from which you develop your presentation. They may be the steps of a process you want the audience to remember. They may be the reasons you select to convince an audience to accept your proposal. In the following example, the main points describe the steps of how to hot-wax skis:

Specific purpose: To inform the audience how to hot-wax skis.

Central idea: Hot-waxing of skis is accomplished by filling the grooves, smoothing the bottom, filing the edges, and applying wax.

Main points: I Fill the bottom grooves.

II Smooth the bottoms of the skis.

III File the edges of the skis.

IV Wax the bottoms of the skis.

In the next example, the main points are the reasons a speaker presents to convince an audience that nuclear power is unsafe:

Specific purpose: To persuade the audience that nuclear power is unsafe.

Central idea: The use of nuclear power has serious consequences.

Main points: I It has grave potential for disaster. (Reason)

II It entails the danger of exposure to radiation. (Reason)

III Nuclear waste cannot easily be disposed of. (Reason)

In each of the above instances, a speaker selected main points on which to then build the presentation.

Well-designed main points enhance your chances of success and save you time. Ask yourself: Do the main points give the audience a clear picture of the topic? Are the main points logically related to the specific purpose? Are my reasons the most persuasive for this audience? If you ask yourself these questions first, you can save yourself long hours spent preparing the message only to discover that your main points were weak and must be changed.

DISCOVERING MAIN POINTS

Where do main points come from? How do you find main points for the body of your speech? One way is to ask questions about your specific purpose. For example, suppose your subject is "how to prepare for a job interview." You could discover the main points for that speech by asking "What steps does a person take to prepare for a job interview?" The steps might be: (1) learn about the company, (2) select proper apparel, and (3) rehearse answering anticipated questions. These steps would then be converted into main points as follows:

Specific purpose:	To explain to the audience how to prepare for a job interview.
Central idea:	Preparing for a job interview is a simple and easy process.
Main points:	I Learn about the company.
	II Select the proper attire.
	III Practice answering anticipated questions.

If your topic is persuasive, you can discover main points by asking the question "Why?" For instance, if your goal is "to convince the audience that TV is harmful to children," asking "Why?" can generate many reasons. Look at the reasons in the following example:

Specific purpose:	TV watching is harmful to children. (Why?)
Central idea:	Watching TV has damaging effects.
Main points:	I It presents a false picture of reality.
	II It is filled with violence.
	III It psychologically manipulates children.
	IV It suggests damaging behavior patterns.
	V It creates unnecessary needs.

Asking "Why?" generated five reasons. Research might uncover even more.

Research

Research is another way of discovering main points. Encyclopedias, pamphlets, books, periodicals, and other source material can help you find important major ideas for your presentation. An encyclopedia will divide a subject into major topical areas that suggest main points. A defense lawyer will examine the evidence and draw conclusions that will become the main points of her strategy. *Opposing Viewpoints* is a book series giving pro-and-con arguments on complex and sensitive issues such as death and dying, censorship, AIDS, and racism. Another reference, *Taking Sides: Clashing Views on Controversial Issues,* discusses such topics as "Moral Issues" and "Business Ethics and Society." These books can give you a perspective on controversial issues and help you discover main points for your topic. If your topic is to "ban alcohol advertising," research might reveal the important issues to be that advertising encourages young people to drink and all alcohol users to increase consumption:

Specific purpose:	Alcohol advertising should be banned.
Central idea:	Alcohol advertising is harmful.

Main points: I Advertising encourages young people to drink. (Reason)

                  II Advertising encourages people to drink more. (Reason)

Audience Analysis

Analyzing your audience is another way to discover main points. Audiences have needs, wants, concerns, and problems that can become the source of main points. Politicians use public opinion polls and focus groups to discover what concerns their constituents and then build their major appeals around those issues. President Clinton uses pollsters extensively to discover persuasive appeals for his speeches.[6] A business presenter in analyzing her customers learns that their important decision-making criteria when buying her product are price, morale, and productivity. These issues then become the main points of the presentation:

Specific purpose: To persuade my audience to buy the XYZ laptop computer.

Central idea: XYZ laptop computers have many benefits.

Main points: I XYZ laptop computers are cost-effective.

                  II XYZ laptop computers increase morale.

                  III XYZ laptop computers increase productivity.

The main points sprang from the needs of the audience.

Sometimes discovering main points is challenging. If you have problems, talk with your classmates and instructor.

ARRANGING MAIN POINTS

After you select the main points, you arrange them in a strategic order; what order you choose depends on your plan—your strategy—for achieving the specific purpose. A teacher preparing a lesson plan might arrange the information going from the simple to complex so his students learn the basics before tackling more advanced concepts. A lawyer in preparing her client's case might arrange her arguments from strongest to weakest in hope of convincing the jury of the merits of her case at the beginning of the trial. It is no accident, for instance, that newspapers organize information by topics—sports, entertainment, national news, local news, editorials—so their readers can easily find the information of most interest to them.

There are many ways to organize main points. Five of the most common ways are (1) by time—temporal sequence; (2) by aspects of the topic—topical sequence; (3) by space—spatial sequence; (4) by problem/solution; and (5) by cause/effect. Let's look at when each method might be used.

Temporal Sequence

If a speaker's specific purpose is to teach the audience a process, the most effective form of organization would be a temporal sequence. In a temporal sequence, events or steps are described in the order in which they occur or should occur. For example, a shipping supervisor might use a temporal sequence to teach new employees how to deal with shipments ("First, check the packing slip to make sure that everything is included; second, check the invoice against the original order. . . .") or to explain the history of a project in progress that he is turning over to a subordinate. The temporal sequence is used in an "education" situation in which each progressive step is dependent upon the completion of the step before it.

A speaker whose specific purpose is to describe a historical event might also choose to use the temporal sequence format. That speaker would describe the event by establishing the sequence of events that led up to it. Observe how the temporal sequence is used in the following examples:

Specific purpose: To demonstrate how to take photographs indoors.

Central idea: To take indoor photographs, position the camera, focus, adjust the flash, and release the shutter.

Body

Main points: I Position the camera.

II Focus the subject.

III Adjust the automatic flash.

IV Release the shutter.

Specific purpose: To explain the history of women's rights in America.

Central idea: Women have made slow but steady progress in their quest for equal rights.

Body

Main points: I Women's struggle from 1774 to 1900.

II Women's struggle from 1900 to 1965.

III Women's struggle from 1965 to present.

Topical Sequence

Topical sequences are used when main points do not fall into or follow a specific order. In these instances, the speaker arranges the main points based on their common relationship to the specific purpose. For example, if you were telling your social club about the charter trip you were proposing they take, you might talk about the transportation arrangements, the hotel accommodations, the sightseeing they could do, the activities they could participate in, and so on. These main points could be arranged in any order. A personnel officer of a corporation, explaining the benefits package to new employees, might talk about vacation, insurance, pension plans, and investment options. In the body of either speech, the main points could be arranged in any sequence that was convenient. Study the following examples:

Specific purpose: To explain the three units of measure in the metric system.

Central idea: The units of measure in the metric system are meter, liter, and gram.

Body

Main points: I The meter is used for measuring length.

II The liter is used for measuring volume.

III The gram is used for measuring mass.

Specific purpose: To explain how to create a characterization in a play.

Central idea: Appearance, voice, and motivation combine to create a character.

Body

Main points: I Appearance of the character

II Voice of the character

III Motivation of the character

In each of the above examples, the main points together form a complete sequence, although the sequence of points could be rearranged.

Spatial Sequence

Spatial sequences are most commonly used when the specific purpose is related to establishing an idea based on a physical location. Spatial sequence organizes information in a directional pattern such as east to west, left to right, front to back, inside to outside, or top to bottom. A speaker discussing a backpacking trek through Yosemite National Park would speak in terms of up and down, and of east, west, north, and south, and would arrange her remarks in that order. A director choreographing movements for actors on stage would speak in terms of foreground, background, stage right and stage left, thus organizing his remarks in a spatial order. Study the following examples:

Specific purpose:	To describe the levels of the earth's atmosphere.
Central idea:	Three levels of the atmosphere are ionosphere, stratosphere, and troposphere.

Body

Main points:	I The outer level is the ionosphere. **TOP**
	II The middle level is the stratosphere.
	III The inner level is the troposphere. **BOTTOM**

Specific purpose:	To describe the two halves of the brain.
Central idea:	The brain functions intuitively and analytically.

Body

Left to Right

Main points:	I The left side of the brain is intuitive.
	II The right side is analytical.

In each of the above examples the main points are based on location.

Problem/Solution Sequence

If it is the specific purpose of a speech to address the problems inherent in a situation and at the same time present possible positive alternatives, the organizational format that would be appropriate is a problem/solution sequence. As the name suggests, in this sequence the speaker arranges information by presenting first the problem and then the solution. A good example of this type of speech is stump speeches of politicians. The candidates point out what the problems are that the voters face, and then they outline the actions they would take as officials to effect solutions to these problems. Most television commercials establish a problem and then offer a product as the be-all and end-all solution to that problem. The problem/solution sequence is one of the most effective organizational formats for persuasive speaking.

| Specific purpose: | To persuade the audience that parents should be allowed to send their children to the public school of their choice. |
| Central idea: | Choice enhances the quality of education. |

Body

Main points:	I Lack of competition reduces the quality of education. (Problem)
	II Parents should be allowed to send their children to the public school of their choice. (Solution)
Specific purpose:	To persuade the audience that drunk drivers should receive mandatory jail terms.
Central idea:	Drunk driving is criminal behavior.
Main points:	I Present laws against drunk driving are too lenient. (Problem)
	II Mandatory jail terms will reduce the number of drunk drivers. (Solution)

The first main point states the problem, and the second main point states the solution.

Cause/Effect Sequence

Another very effective organizational style is cause/effect. The cause is stated in the specific purpose and the effects are the main points. A business speaker may want to show that rising costs are due to mismanagement. She would then state that there is a problem with the management style at the start; she would follow with examples of situations where poor management had cost the company money, time, and productivity. A shop instructor might explain that there is a relationship between the use of safety equipment and a decrease in classroom accidents.

Specific purpose:	To persuade the audience not to use cocaine. (Cause)
Central idea:	Cocaine is a dangerous drug.
Main points:	I Cocaine is addictive. (Effect)
	II Cocaine damages the heart. (Effect)
	III Cocaine use can be fatal. (Effect)

This process may be reversed. You may choose to state the effect in your specific purpose, and then give the causes. For example:

Specific purpose:	To explain to the audience why some people become child abusers. (Effect)
Central idea:	Child abuse has a number of causes.
Main points:	I The abuser was abused as a child. (Cause)
	II Parents have unrealistic expectations. (Cause)
	III Either or both parents are under excessive stress. (Cause)

REFINING MAIN POINTS

After selecting and arranging your main points, the next step is to edit them for clarity and logic. This is similar to the process of formulating the specific purpose discussed in Chapter 4. You have several objectives here. You want

Focus on the main points in your speech.

to phrase the main points so they are clear and distinct. This helps the audience grasp the main ideas and easily follow the flow of information. Well-designed main points divide the body of the speech into small units of information, and people learn best when they receive information in small increments. Finally, by refining your main points you can test the logic of your outline.

Phrase the Main Points Clearly, Concisely, and Consistently

Sharply phrased main points stand out and maintain the integrity of the sequential pattern. This helps the audience identify the main ideas and the flow of information. In the following example the main points are phrased inconsistently and confuse the audience:

Specific purpose:	To explain how to select a still-life camera.
Central idea:	Three criteria to use when buying a camera are cost, operation, and versatility.
Main points:	I One of the greatest differences in camera systems is the cost of those systems.
	II Basic ease of operation.
	III Versatility.

Here, the topical sequence is appropriate, but the main points are not similarly phrased. Observe how phrasing the main points consistently increases clarity and understanding:

Specific purpose:	To explain how to select a still-life camera.
Central idea:	Three criteria to use when buying a camera are cost, operation, and versatility.
Main points:	I Determine a target price for the camera.
	II Determine the ease of operation of the camera.
	III Determine the versatility of the camera.

In the next example the main points are out of sequence. Note how that breaks the flow of information and makes the speech seem illogical.

Specific purpose:	To explain to the audience how to discipline problem employees.
Central idea:	Disciplining problem employees should be done fairly and legally.
Main points:	I Give a written warning.
	II Discuss problem with employee and document problem.

III Terminate the employee.

IV Suspend the employee.

Divide Information Equally among the Main Points

The main points should divide the body into small, distinct units of approx-imately equal size. This establishes a well-balanced flow of information and makes it easier for the audience to understand ideas. If one main point con-tains 50 to 60 percent of the information in a four-point outline, you should reexamine the sequence because you may have selected inappropriate ideas or a faulty sequence. No pattern will be perfectly balanced, but your pattern should fall within these guidelines:

30–40%   I Main point.

30–40%   II Main point.

30–40%   III Main point.

Limit Your Main Points

Regardless of the organizational sequence you use, the number of main points should be limited to a maximum of four, ideally three. Selecting more main points makes your speech too complex and dilutes the importance of your main ideas. Study the following example:

Specific purpose: To demonstrate how to make a clay pot.

Central idea: Making a clay pot is easy if you follow the steps.

Main points: I Gather the equipment.

II Buy the clay.

III Prepare the clay.

IV Center the clay pot on the wheel.

V Shape the pot.

VI Trim the pot.

VII Fire and glaze the pot.

VIII Clean up.

Eight main points are too many. The audience will be unable to follow all the steps. Reorganize the main points to condense them into four or fewer points. Many professional speakers limit their presentations to three main points, and many speech consultants recommend three. If you cannot con-vince an audience with three main points, a fourth one will not help either. Look how much easier it would be for an audience to understand the above outline if the main points were reduced to four:

Main points: I Prepare the clay.

II Center the clay on the wheel.

III Shape and trim the pot.

IV Fire and glaze the pot.

If you have more than four main points, edit your list by eliminating or combining some points. Remember, your objective is simplicity and clarity. If necessary, change your specific purpose to a more modest objective.

Test for Logic

The main points should logically follow from the specific purpose and central idea. If you say that Martina Navratilova is the greatest women's tennis player who ever lived, then your main points should logically develop that statement by establishing criteria of greatness: tournament wins, grand slam titles, longevity. If a main point does not support that goal, then you are being illogical and you may confuse the audience. In the following example, one of the main points doesn't flow logically. Note how it limits the impact of the message:

Specific purpose: To persuade the audience that TV is detrimental to children.

Central idea: TV has many harmful effects.

Main points: I TV retards the learning capacity of children.

II There are some benefits to watching TV.

III TV exposes children to violence.

The second main point doesn't follow logically. The theme of the speech is the harmful effects of TV on children and the second main point refers to benefits.

One way of testing the logic of your main points is to state your specific purpose and then ask "How?" and "Why?" Now, see if the main points directly answer those questions. If you are satisfied they do, then your main points are probably logical. Another method is to read your main points and then, beginning with the word "therefore," see if you can conclude your specific purpose and central idea. If you can, then the main points are probably logical.

FOCUSING ON THE MAIN POINTS IN THE SPEECH

The main points are your major ideas and they provide the road map for your presentation. You want to bring them center stage during the presentation so they stand out in the minds of the audience. You also want to break up the information into small units for easy comprehension and smooth flow during the presentation. You can achieve these objectives by previewing the main points after the introduction, using transitions among them, and summarizing after each main point. Let's discuss each one of these.

Preview the Main Points: The Big Picture

Introduction of the main points—often called the preview—reveals the major divisions in the body of the speech after the introduction. It is like the marquee of a movie theater displaying the names of the feature attractions. Audiences like a preview because it tells them what to expect. Carmen Policy, President of the San Francisco 49ers, used the following preview when he spoke before an audience in San Francisco:

> I'd like to give you a view into the NFL today and discuss what we're facing, what we're doing, how successful we really are, what our problems are, what we have to do to stay on top, and how we have to be smart in handling the outside world and our inside problems.[7]

Previews are normally presented after the specific purpose and central idea and before the first main point in the outline, as the following example demonstrates:

Specific purpose:	To inform the audience about the judiciary proceedings following arrest.
Central idea:	There are four steps in the judiciary proceedings.

[Preview: There are four steps in the judiciary proceedings following arrest of a suspect: (1) arraignment of the accused, (2) preliminary hearing for the accused, (3) trial of the accused, and (4) sentencing (if convicted).]

Main points:	I The suspect is arraigned.
	II A preliminary hearing is set.
	III A trial is held.
	IV The convicted is sentenced.

List the main points on a chart, using bold lines and colors. Your chart gives the speech a context and increases clarity and comprehension. Experienced speakers frequently use this technique to preview main ideas and you should as well. Refer to the main points as the speech progresses so you are reinforcing them for the audience.

Transitions: Connecting the Parts of the Speech

Audiences need to be reminded of where they are, where they have been, and where they are going. Transitions are sentences, phrases, or words that highlight the main points and tie the speech together. They are like stoplights directing traffic. They may be used: (1) to signal movement from one main idea to the next and (2) to connect passages within the body of the message.

Moving from One Main Point to the Next Transitions highlight and link the main points. Transitions are used at the end of a main point and just before the beginning of the next one. The following are some examples of transitions among main points:

Now that the first major step has been completed, let's move to the second major step, putting the parts together.

Where do we go from here? The second step revealed the process; now let's apply it.

Up to this point we have discussed some of the causes of the problem. Now let's turn our attention to some of the harmful effects.

You can use the same approach to move from the introduction into the body of the speech and from the body into the conclusion.

Transitional Words and Phrases Certain words and phrases are helpful in linking statements and thoughts within the body of the message. They improve comprehension by emphasizing important ideas. Here are some common transitional phrases:

To summarize material: in other words, in conclusion, to sum up, to repeat
Example: "Before moving on let me repeat, tofu contains all the daily nutrients your body needs."

To add material: furthermore, similarly, moreover, nevertheless
Example: "Let me add one more feature; you will lose weight too."

To contrast material: however, on the other hand, on the contrary
Example: "On the other hand, you must be careful to observe protocol."

To reach conclusions: therefore, accordingly, consequently, as a result, hence
Example: "As a result you will kill two birds with one stone."

To illustrate a point: for example, for instance
Example: "For example, don't lose sight of your objectives."

Transitions are valuable devices for tying major points and passages together. As you outline a speech, it is important to include transitions because they emphasize or reinforce major ideas and use the audience as the copilot.

INTRODUCTION A. Attention material
                         B. Orientation material
                         C. Specific purpose
                         D. Central idea

BODY **(PREVIEW)**
      I. Main point
         A. _____
            1. _____
               a. _____
               b. _____
            (TRANSITIONAL WORDS & PHRASES)
            2. _____
               a. _____
               b. _____
          (SUMMARY)
          (TRANSITION)
         B. _____
            1. _____
               a. _____
               b. _____
            (TRANSITIONAL WORDS & PHRASES)
            2. _____
                a. _____
               b. _____
          (SUMMARY)
          (TRANSITION TO MAIN POINT)
      II. Main point
         A. _____
            1. _____
               a. _____
               b. _____
            (TRANSITIONAL WORDS & PHRASES)
            2. _____
                a. _____
               b. _____
          (SUMMARY)
          (TRANSITION)
         B. _____
            1. _____
               a. _____
               b. _____
            (TRANSITIONAL WORDS & PHRASES)
            2. _____
                a. _____
               b. _____

CONCLUSION A. _____

FIGURE 6-1
Preview, transitions, and summaries in an outline.

Summaries: Reinforcing Main Points

Summaries are often used at the end of major points or after complex passages. They reinforce the important ideas and signal the beginning of a new passage. The following are examples of summaries:

To sum up the first major point: Compulsory prayer in public schools may serve only to alienate and confuse many children.

Before I move to the next point, keep in mind there is a strong correlation between certain personality traits and cancer.

Before I close, let me say that the Heimlich maneuver saves thousands of lives every year. Remember these steps: First position yourself behind the choking victim. Second, wrap your arms around the victim at the waist below the sternum, make a fist with either hand, and grip it with the other. Third, execute four quick upward thrusts to force air from the lungs. Repeat if necessary.

Because listeners cannot go back and review what has been said, brief summaries within a speech help them keep relevant information in mind and make the speech easier to understand.

Figure 6-1 shows where previews, transitions, and summaries may be used in the body of the speech.

SUMMARY

Speech organization means arranging information to achieve a specific goal. The body of the speech is composed of the specific purpose, the central idea, and the main points. The main points divide the body of the speech into equal parts and along sequential lines. Five important ways of arranging the main points are in terms of time, topic, space, problem/solution, and cause/effect. Focus on the main points in the speech by using a preview, transitions, and summaries.

PROBES

1 What are main points?
2 What are the advantages of using main points effectively?
3 In the beginning of the chapter, organizing informative speech was compared to planning a trip. Explain the relationship.
4 Describe three methods for discovering main points for your speech.
5 Describe five ways of arranging information for a speech.
6 How does refining the main points improve clarity?
7 How can you make the main points stand out in the speech?

APPLICATIONS

1 Recall and write down five instances where you organized an activity or event. Possible examples could be planning a backpacking trip, preparing a recipe, or transplanting a plant. Select three of these activities and state what you organized and how you did it. The following examples will serve as models:

What:	Organized a clothing drive for the needy.
How:	1 Got volunteers.
	2 Advertised.
	3 Scheduled pickup.
	4 Distributed clothes.
What:	Directed a short scene from a play.
How:	1 Selected a scene.
	2 Assigned roles.
	3 Scheduled rehearsal.
What:	Planned a bicycle trip.
How:	1 Determined destination.
	2 Planned route.
	3 Tuned up bike.
	4 Prepared food and gear.

Bring your outlines to class and discuss whether the sequences are temporal, spatial, or topical. You should discover through this assignment that organization is not new to you; that, in fact, you have been creating temporal, spatial, and topical patterns long before you knew you were.

2 Following the guidelines in the section on phrasing main points, revise the following examples:

Specific purpose:	To explain how to impeach the president of the United States.
Central idea:	Impeaching a president is a four-step process.

Body

Main points:	I Impeachable offenses
	II Proceedings begin with the House of Representatives
	III Senate
	IV Conviction
Specific purpose:	To explain how to develop an appreciation of wine.
Central idea:	Appreciating wine requires knowledge of its history, manufacture, and selection.

Body

Main points: I A few basic facts about wine and its history are important to know.

II Second, a basic knowledge of winemaking is helpful.

III The third and final aspect in wine appreciation is selection.

3 Devise transitions for the above two examples.

4 Consider the kinds of organizational patterns you might use with each of the following topics: (a) Illiteracy. (b) Term limits. (c) Payment for housework. (d) Synthetic fuels. (e) Junk food.

NOTES

1 C. Spicer and R. E. Basset, "The Effect of Organization on Learning from an Informative Message," *Southern Speech Communication Journal,* Vol. 41 (1976), p. 298; Tom D. Daniels and Richard F. Whitman, "The Effects of Message Organization, Message Structure, and Verbal Organizing Ability upon Learning of Message Information," *Human Communication Research,* Vol. 7 (1981), pp. 147–160.

2 Richard F. Whitman and John H. Timmis, "The Influence of Verbal Organizational Structure and Verbal Organizing Skills on Select Measures of Learning," *Human Communication Research,* Vol. 1 (1975), pp. 293–301.

3 James C. McCroskey and R. Samuel Mehrley, "The Effects of Disorganization and Nonfluency in Attitude Change and Source Credibility," *Speech Monographs,* Vol. 36 (1969), pp. 13–21.

4 Eldon E. Baker, "The Immediate Effects of Perceived Speaker Disorganization on Speaker Credibility and Audience Attitude Change in Persuasive Speaking," *Western Speech,* Vol. 29 (1965), pp. 148–161.

5 Raymond G. Smith, "An Experimental Study of the Effects of Speech Organization upon Attitudes of College Students," *Speech Monographs,* Vol. 18 (1951), pp. 292–301.

6 Elizabeth Drew, *On the Edge: The Clinton Presidency* (Simon & Schuster: New York, 1994), pp. 124–125.

7 Carmen Policy, "A View of Professional Sports through NFL Binoculars," *The Commonwealth,* Vol. 89, September 11, 1995, p. 11.

7

SUPPORTING THE MAIN POINTS: TELLING AND DOING

In the movie *Stand and Deliver,* the main character is Jaime Escalante, a high school math teacher. Escalante, whose character is based on a real-life math teacher, faces a serious challenge: how to teach an honors calculus course to a class of inner-city Latino students. The school's administration and many of Escalante's colleagues are skeptical that the students can learn the complex concepts and pass a standardized test administered by the school district. They believe the students will fail and the failure will reinforce their negative self-image. To the surprise of many, all the students pass.

How did that happen? Much of the students' success is attributed to the creative and entertaining way Escalante communicated the difficult concepts and processes of calculus to the students. He used drawing, rhymes, slogans, definitions, analogies, stories, demonstration, and pictures. He had the students play roles, do skits, and play games. In short, he used supporting material in a compelling manner to foster understanding in the minds of his students.

TYPES OF SUPPORTING MATERIAL

There is an old saying, "Tell me, I'll forget. Show me, I may remember. Involve me, I'll understand." Supporting material is the lifeblood of your presentation. It develops your major ideas using language, audience activities, and visual aids. Used effectively, supporting material illuminates your main points and makes your presentation interesting, memorable, and convincing.

The three ways of presenting supporting material are telling, showing, and doing. *Telling* uses different types of language devices to amplify main points; these include definitions, descriptions, analogies, illustrations, statistics, and testimony.

Showing combines telling with visual aids and/or demonstration. Common kinds of visual aids include charts, graphics, slides or video, and exhibits.

Doing combines telling and perhaps showing with physical participation by the audience in some aspect of the message. The audience might complete a survey, duplicate a process, or emulate a demonstration.

USE EACH TYPE OF SUPPORTING MATERIAL IN YOUR SPEECHES

Using each type of supporting material improves comprehension, holds the attention of the audience, and makes your speech more believable (Figure 7-1). Audiences understand information more easily and retain it longer when they are able to hear it, see it, and experience it. A volleyball coach, showing the team how to serve a volleyball, will achieve far better results if, after explaining and showing, he has the players execute the maneuver. A prosecutor strengthens her case against a defendant when she uses a multisensory approach to present evidence to a jury. She presents verbal and eyewitness testimony, shows physical evidence—gun, fingerprints, bloodstains—reenacts the crime, and has the jury touch or hold the exhibits. This

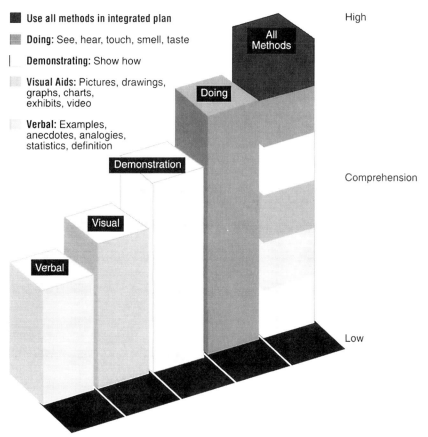

FIGURE 7-1
Learning effectiveness: use all the channels of communication.

approach makes the case more real and thus makes her arguments more per-suasive.

Audiences have short attention spans and become restless and bored when a speaker uses language alone to communicate the message. A multi-media approach increases and maintains attention during a speech because it draws an audience deeper into a presentation. Language uses the auditory senses; pictorials, the visual senses; and doing, the tactile senses and possi-bly motor skills. That is why professional and very experienced speakers use a variety of media—colorful slides, video, overhead transparencies, partici-patory activities—in their presentations. They flood the senses. The more channels you use, the greater the involvement of the audience.

In this chapter we will discuss how to use language and physical activities to support main points. In the next chapter we will discuss how to use visual aids to develop and support ideas.

TELLING: VERBAL CHANNELS OF INFORMATION

Language is a rich resource for making your ideas clear, interesting, and convincing. Even very complex processes and concepts can be converted to easily understandable statements using language. Bill Walsh, the famous football coach who won three Super Bowls, has the ability to communicate complex strategy and tactics using clear language his players can easily understand. An engineer, when discussing complex technology with a group of nontechnical managers, uses analogies that link the audience's experience with her subject to help them understand the presentation.

The following are among the many types of verbal devices available to you: (1) definition, (2) example, (3) stories and anecdotes, (4) comparison and contrast, (5) description, (6) statistics, and (7) testimony.

Definitions

Definition clarifies unfamiliar or abstract words that may be barriers to understanding or cause misunderstanding. Take the word "homeless," for example. It is a popular label used to classify a group of people in social difficulty. Does "homeless" refer to a family temporarily without shelter because their home was destroyed by fire? Or does it refer to mentally disabled people unable to fend for themselves? Or does it refer to the people whose life is disrupted by substance abuse? Or does it refer to drifters and transients who move from place to place? A specific definition of "homeless" would pinpoint your meaning and avoid confusion.

New or unfamiliar terms also require definition. For example, a tax accountant telling a group of new business owners how to set up their books may need to define such terms as "credit" and "debit." A computer field representative showing a client how to operate a microcomputer may need to define such terms as "DOS" and the special meaning of "exit" and "access." Supreme Court justice Stephen G. Breyer used definition to define the law to a group of nonlawyers:

> Isn't law, after all, simply a body of rules, standards and practices, developed by, and applied to, groups of human beings, as part of their inevitable effort to live together peacefully and productively, justly and with freedom.[1]

The definition gave the audience a common basis for understanding his remarks. Four types of definitions are etymology, classification, use of a synonym, and operational definition.

Etymology Etymology defines by giving the root or origin of the word. These definitions are short, very informative and usually very interesting because they tell how a word was originally used. This helps audiences grasp meaning quickly. "Democracy," for instance, derived from the Greek *demos,* "people," and *kratta,* "rule." So democracy originally meant "people rule." "Govern" originated from the Greek word *kubernan* meaning to "steer a ship." "Jail" derived from Latin meaning "little cage." Warren Bennis, well-known authority on leadership, defined the word "retirement" in a speech using the etymology of the word:

> The ultimate source of the word is the old French word *retirer,* made up of the prefix "re" meaning "back" and the verb *tirer* to "draw together," meaning to withdraw, to take back. The first English use recorded in 1553 refers to a military force that withdraws and retreats.[2]

→ grouping into categories

Classification Classification is the kind of definition found in dictionaries. It provides a handy point of reference for unfamiliar and abstract words. Suppose you are going to use the word "sophist" in your speech and you need a quick and clear definition for the audience. Consult a standard dictionary such as Webster's *Ninth New Collegiate Dictionary* or *The American Heritage Dictionary* and quote it verbatim: "sophist . . . a person skilled in devious argumentation."

There are a number of specialized dictionaries that contain definitions for a particular industry or subject. The *Dorsey Dictionary of American Politics* gives concise definitions for any person, institution, or subject associated with American politics. *The Dictionary of Business and Management* defines words and concepts related to business. Here is its definition of the frequently used Latin phrase *caveat emptor:*

> Caveat emptor, let the buyer beware (Latin). When merchandise is sold without a warranty by the vendor, the buyer takes the risk of loss due to defects. If you buy a used car without a warranty and the engine blows up driving it home, then you must pay the cost because you assumed the risk.

The library also has dictionaries focusing on art, music, fine arts, economics, social science, and many other fields.

Synonym A synonym is a word that has the same or nearly the same meaning as another word. Synonyms define by associating a word or phrase known to the listener with one that is unknown to that person. For example, you might define the term "parity" by stating that it is synonymous with "equality." A lawyer might use "before" rather than "heretofore" when talking to a client. If a dentist were speaking to a group of laypeople about dental care and used the word "caries," he would almost certainly follow up by telling them that he was talking about tooth decay. A thesaurus is a dictionary of synonyms. It is a valuable reference for finding synonyms easily understood by the audience.

Operational Definition   An operational definition defines by describing what someone or something does. In some instances, a classification definition may be inadequate to convey meaning. For example, the classification definition of a manager as "someone who supervises others" is inadequate because it does not explain the actual responsibilities of a manager: coaching, motivating, planning, decision making, hiring, and so on. In the following example, Ted Koppel, host of ABC's *Nightline,* uses an operational definition in his famous speech, "The Vannatizing of America," to describe the magic of television. His central idea may be stated this way:

Central Idea: The viewer, not television, supplies the meaning for its programs.

> It seems unlikely, but lest there be among you someone who has not thrilled to the graceful ease with which Ms. White (Vanna) glides across our television screens, permit me to tell you what she does: She turns blocks, on which blank sides are displayed, to another side of the block, on which a letter is displayed. She does this very well; very fluidly, and with what appears to be genuine enjoyment. She also does it mutely. Vanna says nothing. She is often seen smiling at and talking with winners at the end of the program; but we can only imagine what they are saying to each other. We don't hear Vanna. She speaks only body language; and she seems to like everything she sees. No, "like" is too tepid. Vanna rejoices, adores everything she sees and therein lies her magic.
>
> We have no idea what, or even if, Vanna thinks. Is she a feminist, or every male chauvinist's dream? She is whatever you want her to be. Sister, lover, daughter, friend; never cross, nonthreatening, and nonjudgmental—to a fault. The viewer can, and apparently does, project a thousand different personalities onto that charmingly neutral television image, and she accommodates them all.[3]

Examples

Examples are specific representative instances used to define a statement or idea. If a person said that "honesty" was a characteristic she admired most in others, then she would need to give a concrete example of how an "honest" person behaves before her meaning was clear.

Examples may be short, crisp statements or longer illustrations that nail down concepts or prove points. In the following illustration, the speaker uses a short example to clarify an idea:

Idea: Many types of cancer are preventable.

Example: Lung, breast, colon, and prostate cancer have all been directly linked to diet and fat intake. Groups with high incidences of these cancers tended to have fatty diets low in fiber.

In the next instance, the speaker uses a more detailed example to support an assertion:

Idea: Today, we are exposed to great quantities of information.

Example: If you were to read the entire Sunday edition of *The New York Times,* you would absorb—or at least be exposed to—more information in that one reading than was absorbed in a lifetime by the average American living in Jefferson's day.

The more concrete your example, the greater the impact it will have on an audience. In the following example, the speaker uses vivid examples to describe the dangers posed by the availability of assault weapons:

Idea: Police are unable to protect civilians from criminals with assault weapons.

Example: Recently, a man was able to kill twenty-one hostages over the course of an hour. S.W.A.T. teams were unable to move in and take control because the assailant was firing a Uzi assault weapon.

Stories/Anecdotes

Stories and anecdotes have special qualities as supporting material. (An anecdote is a particular kind of story: a short narrative, sometimes funny, often describing an incident that personally happened to the teller.) Stories and anecdotes bring ideas or persuasive appeals to life. They have beginnings, middles, and ends and strong central themes. They may be funny, sad, dramatic, or satirical.

Audiences love stories! Audiences may forget many of the details of a presentation, but they remember the stories a speaker tells and repeat them to others. Circuit speakers, well-known people who travel from city to city giving speeches for money, tell many stories in their presentations because they understand the entertainment and informational value of stories. Motivational speakers fill their presentations with stories.

In the following example, the speaker uses a story about people falling into the water to dramatize the problems facing an overwhelmed criminal justice system:

Two men are walking along a river when they hear cries for help. They see a man thrashing about in the water, jump into the river, and pull him to shore. But just as they reach the bank, they hear more cries for help. They look up and see not just one, but a whole line of bodies coming downstream, each one in trouble. The rescuers jump into the river, time and again, to save as many people as they can. But they can't save everyone. Finally, one of the rescuers says to the other: "Hey, you stay here and do what you can. I'm going upstream to see if I can keep people from falling into the river in the first place."

Our criminal justice system, like our heroes, is overwhelmed. Each of the three parts of that system—police, courts, and corrections—cannot handle the increasing number of people falling in the river of crime.[4]

Stories may be factual, describing something that actually happened, or they may be fables or parables. In the following example, from a speech by Christopher Matthews, a Washington correspondent, the speaker uses a factual illustration to describe how former President Ronald Reagan prepared for press conferences. Matthew's idea could be stated this way:

Idea: Former President Reagan prepared for news conferences the same way he rehearsed for performances.

Here is his factual account:

When Ronald Reagan prepared for a press conference, he treated it as a performance. For two hours each week he rehearsed in the family movie theater with the faces of the reporters on each chair and a seating chart in front of him. He had flash cards with individual pictures of the press corps, and memorized the nicknames of everyone.

Before he came out to meet the press, he watched a reverse camera facing the audience. He panned the room and got a fix on everyone's face. He is up to date on who everyone is, and he can go out there and perform. He knows that he is really selling his own debonair style, his "regular guy status." He is not a snob, he is one of the boys. That makes us like him.[5]

Comparison and Contrast

Comparison and contrast can be a powerful tool for creating understanding. You use information—facts, experiences, knowledge—known to the audience to explain what is unknown to them. This is one of the quickest and most efficient means of clarifying new or complex information for an audience. In the following example, Peggy Noonan, journalist and author, compares today's television programming with her generation:

When I was a kid there were kids who went home to empty houses, and they did what kids do, put on the TV. There were game shows, cartoons, some boring nature show, an old movie, "The Ann Sothern Show," Spanish lessons on educational TV, a soap opera.

Thin fare, boring stuff; kids daydreamed to it. But it was better to have this being pumped into everyone's living room than, say the Geto Boys on channel

25, rapping about killing women, having sex with their dead bodies and cutting off their breasts.

Really, you have to be a moral retard not to know that this is harmful, that it damages the young, the unsteady, the unfinished. You have to not care about anyone to sing these words and to put this song on TV for money.[6]

Analogies may make a single, brief comparison, or they may be extensive and detailed.

In the following example, the speaker uses a brief metaphor (we'll discuss metaphors in Chapter 11), followed by a series of vivid comparisons, to describe the size of a microchip:

Idea:	The microchip is a tiny electronic brain.
Use of comparison:	The microchip, the brain of all computers, is one-tenth the size of a postage stamp and about as thick as the cover of a paperback book. If dropped on the ground, it could be dragged off by a large insect.

The sharper and more vivid you can make the comparison, the greater the impact will be on the listener.

One way to support an argument is by drawing sharp contrasts. In the following example, the speaker uses this technique to show the hypocrisy of laws regulating weapons.

Idea:	Laws regarding weapons are illogical.
Use of contrast:	In California, if you are caught carrying mace or a billy club without a license, you are guilty of a felony and could be sent to state prison. However, if you are caught carrying a Uzi assault weapon, don't be concerned; that is perfectly legal.

In the next example, the speaker contrasts Amish society with modern society:

Amish society violates every modern rule. Relative to the industrial economy, they use true horsepower rather than tractors in the fields. They rely on horse-and-buggy for transport, rather than auto and truck. They make their own clothes, furniture, and candles. They avoid credit. They resist most uses of electricity and electronic devices. And they build and sell products using hand labor, dedicated to craftsmanship.

Relative to the state, the Amish are, at their request, exempt from Social Security and Medicare. They refuse welfare, relying instead on help from their neighbors and relatives in time of crisis. They keep their children out of state schools, operating their own schools through the eighth grade, after which children learn trades from their parents and neighbors.[7]

Description

When using description as supporting material, you are looking to create a mental picture or scenario that allows the audience to put your idea or concept into a context they can understand. The more vivid a description you can create and the more senses you draw on to describe a topic, the closer you can bring the audience to what you want them to understand.

Suppose a sales manager is giving a presentation to bolster her salespeople's output. She might have permission to offer a trip to Hawaii to the most successful salesperson of the year. She begins to describe the soft warm breezes, the faint smell of coconut, the warmth of the white sand underfoot, the festive atmosphere of the luau, and the clear water of the ocean with its myriad of colorful fish. The next thing she knows, the salespeople are fleeing the room to make sales calls. It's because her description has produced a clear mental picture of what they can achieve.

In the following example, the speaker's one-sentence idea is: "Young gangsters are sophisticated and wealthy." In the description, the speaker paints a vivid picture of how urban gangs control communities.

> Public-housing tenants are under siege by young gangsters. Increasing numbers of young dope dealers, twelve, thirteen, fourteen, and fifteen years old, roam these areas with sophisticated beepers, weapons, and bodyguards. Gangs have formed better distribution networks than Amway or Avon. A new fad for the dope dealers is to recruit young girls for prostitution, sexual gratification, and information.
>
> Many of these children carry large wads of $100 bills and have become a major economic force in the community. Young drug dealers drive Mercedeses and Ferraris and live at five-star motels. They are living straight out of "Miami Vice." Why should they get a job at McDonald's for $4 an hour when they can make hundreds or even thousands of dollars for an afternoon's work.[8]

When you are speaking to persuade, description can be a very effective method for appealing to the emotions. In the following example, the speaker describes the plight of children living in the inner city. The idea is: "For many Americans, life is hopeless."

> Our cities have given birth to sprawling ghettos populated mostly by minorities. In the ghetto, families of eight, ten, and twelve share two-room apartments with rats so large they endanger infants. These same rats carry rabies and TB and typhoid, and gnaw infants' fingers while they sleep. In the ghetto 1 in 3 mothers is unwed and a teenager. These girls do not go to school because they have to work to feed their babies—that is, if they can find work. In these ghettos, 1 out of every 7 young men will die before the age of 25 from a wound inflicted by another young male. In the ghetto, the chokehold of crack cocaine has become so tight that the police are afraid to confront those responsible for its production and sale, and will not enter those houses where its users dwell.[9]

Statistics

Statistics are facts presented numerically. Everywhere we look there are statistics: Michael Jordan's scoring average, the number of Big Macs consumed, prison immates, and SAT scores. We are inundated with statistical data to clarify ideas and prove assertions.

Statistics are a popular type of supporting information, and, used effectively, they add clarity, impact, and believability to your presentation. Statistics are frequently used in business presentations to show such things as increases or decreases in sales, a company's market share, or how many people liked a product that was being tested in the market.

Statistics may be used to make generalized statements or to make comparisons between or among things. The following example contains some generalized statistical statements:

Idea: Drug and alcohol use are commonplace in American life.

Statistics: Today an estimated 50 million Americans have smoked marijuana; 35 million Americans, most under the age of 21, are smoking it regularly.

Five thousand people a day try cocaine for the first time, and an estimated 5 to 7 million are addicted.

Tell, show, do to create understanding.

Today 15 million Americans, most of whom are women, are addicted to Valium.

Today over 25,000 tons of aspirin are consumed annually.

Today 75 percent of Americans drink alcohol.

Statistics are most effective when they are used to make comparisons. We attempt to measure the effectiveness of education by comparing how today's students scored on SAT scores versus ten years ago. A sales executive measures the performance of his staff by comparing sales on a quarterly and yearly basis. In the following example, the speaker makes a simple comparison between the incidence of breast cancer in women:

The incidence of breast cancer has been escalating in the last several years. In the 1950s, the rates were 1 in 20 women in her lifetime. Today, breast cancer will affect 1 in 8 women over her lifetime.[10]

In the next example, the speaker uses a series of statistical comparisons to describe the social changes in New York City between 1944 and 1994. The speaker's idea might be summarized as follows: "New York City has changed dramatically since 1944." Here's how the speaker uses statistics to support that assertion.

In 1944, New York City had 150,000 more inhabitants than it does in 1994. Yet 97 percent of all children born in 1944 were members of two-parent families. In 1994, only 50 percent go home to households headed by a mother and a father. In 1944, a total of forty people died of gunshot wounds. In 1994, forty people are shot and killed every ten days. In 1944, one hundred babies were sent to orphanages. In 1994, thousands of babies are abandoned, some merely deposited in trash cans and restrooms. What happened to New York between 1944 and 1994?[11]

Communicating Statistics   Used skillfully, statistics clarify ideas and help support arguments. Used poorly, they confuse, bore, and mislead an audience. Here are some guidelines for presenting statistics when speaking:

1   Simplify the Statistics   Present statistics so they are easily understood. One way is to use round figures whenever possible without sacrificing accuracy. Rounded numbers are easier to remember and have greater impact.

Complex:	The population of the United States is 228,783,930.
Rounded:	The United States has over 228 million people.
Complex:	There are 9,863,412 unemployed people in the United States.
Rounded:	There are almost 10 million unemployed people in the U.S.

Another method for communicating statistics is to use simple and distinct comparisons along with repetition to reinforce the point you are making. Read the following example:

> Among the 500,000 sixth- and twelfth-graders tested, the twelfth-graders who watched zero to one hour of television (29.8 percent of the total) per day averaged more than 72 percent correct on mathematics tests. The score declined for each hour watched, with those who watched six hours or more daily (5.5 percent of the total) averaging 58 percent correct.

The statement is confusing and you probably had to read it more than once to understand its meaning. A simplified version might read:

> In a study of 500,000 students in grades six through twelve, performance on math tests showed a relationship between the number of hours of TV watched and math scores. Students who watched less than one hour of television scored 14 points higher in math than students who watched many hours of TV. The more TV students watched, the more their scores declined.

In the second example, a distinct comparison was made between math performance and watching television and the main idea was repeated at the end.

2 Limit the Use of Statistics   Avoid reciting long lists of statistics. Audiences are unable to absorb large amounts of numerical data. If many statistics are necessary, employ other means to aid comprehension, such as visual means. A simple chart or graph can simplify statistics. A common practice in business presentations is to prepare handouts with complex data and distribute them following the presentation. Remember, a confused audience is an unhappy audience.

3 Make Your Statistics Meaningful to the Audience   Avoid general and abstract statistics. Show how the statistics impact the audience. In the following example, the speaker relates the statistics to his audience of upper-middle-class parents:

> Only 3 percent of the U.S. high school graduates are able to write a good letter or essay. Only 5 percent of those graduating can do problems in simple, elementary algebra or read a newspaper like *The New York Times* or *Washington Post,* which is written at the eighth-grade level. I am not talking about those children to whom life has dealt a bad hand. I am talking about the most privileged youngsters who have ever walked the face of the earth, youngsters who haven't suffered from discrimination, lack of health care, books, or opportunities to travel. I am talking about your kids.[12]

In the next example, the speaker states a statistic about the amount of time a family spends watching television per week:

Example: According to the Nielsen report on television, the average family watches 49 hours of television per week.

This statement does not reveal the significance of the statistic. The speaker could expand this figure by comparing television watching to other activities to dramatize its influence:

Example: According to the Nielsen report, the average American family watches television over seven hours a day and that television ranks third, behind work and sleep, as a consumer of time. Almost a third of the average person's life is spent watching television.

4 Make Your Statistics Memorable Comparing your statistics to something bizarre or unusual helps the audience remember them easily. Read the following examples:

The amount of information an individual uses in a lifetime is equivalent to 20 billion bits of data. That amount of data can be sent around the world in seven seconds. In other words, everything you ever think and say in your entire lifetime can be sent around the globe in seven seconds.

How safe is air travel? If an airline traveler flew in a commercial airplane every day to random destinations within the United States, it would take an average of 26,000 years before he was killed in a crash.

Of all the people who have lived to age 65 in the history of the world, more than half are alive today.

Your Statistics Must Be Credible Your statistics must not only be clear, they must also be truthful. Unfortunately, the misuse of statistics has become a major problem, aggravated by the popular media that sensationalize information rather than report it accurately. According to Steven A. Holmes of *The New York Times,* "With so many causes and problems clamoring for attention and government money, boosting figures becomes a way of moving to the head of the priority queue."[13] Holmes goes on to say:

If America is the land of the free, it is also the home of the telling statistic, numbers proffered by politicians, interest groups or businesses to cajole, comfort or frighten the public into accepting their particular view of the world. Increasingly . . . the statistics are confusing, contradictory or just plain wrong.[14]

Using statistics dishonestly may have short-term gain but will fail in the long run because people will discover the deceit and you will lose your believability. As a presenter you want your statistics to be accurate, current, and reliable. Here are some guidelines for demonstrating the credibility of your statistics:

*1 **Your Statistics Should Be Used Accurately*** Statistics can be easily distorted. Take the word "average," for instance. It is defined as a measure of central tendency, but in statistics there are several kinds of average, such as median, mode, and mean. *Median* is a point above and below that all items of measurement fall. *Mode* is the number that appears most frequently. *Mean* is the figure that results when all numbers are added up and divided by the total. Each of those figures could show a very different result. So define what you mean by "average," as the speaker does in the following example.

Example: The average hit in baseball is a single. By average, I mean that more players hit singles than doubles or triples. It is the mode.

Another method of using statistics to mislead is using a faulty base from which to measure events. A speaker who stated that the educational system in this country was not working for the entire Latino community claimed that only 50 percent of all Hispanics graduate from high school. Strictly speaking, this figure is accurate. But when you analyze the population from which the figure is taken, you see that the figure is misleading. Second-generation Hispanics have been lumped together with immigrants from Mexico. When the groups are analyzed separately, figures show that 80 percent of second-generation Hispanics graduate from high school and only 25 percent of the immigrants from Mexico graduate from high school.

*2 **Your Statistics Should Be Current*** Use the most up-to-date statistics. This shows you have done your homework and are using the most current information to support your ideas. Also, situations change quickly, and statistics two, three, or four years old may be an inaccurate representation of today's realities.

*3 **Your Statistics Should Come from Reliable Sources*** Draw your statistics from sources that will be judged objective and credible by the audience. To advocate the right to bear arms, quoting figures from the National Rifle Association to support your case is self-serving and weakens your appeal, not to speak of your credibility. Some objective sources of information include the *Statistical Abstract of the U.S.,* which compiles statistics from many government sources such as the Centers for Disease Control, the *World Almanac,* and *Congressional Research Reports.*

In the following example, the speaker quotes from a credible source to prove an important point:

According to a study by the *American Journal of Public Health,* 90 percent of the scientists surveyed believe that smoking causes most deaths from lung cancer. Even scientists who do research for the tobacco industry believe that smoking causes a wide range of diseases and is addictive, despite repeated denials from industry leaders.

Testimony

Testimony is opinions and conclusions stated by others that you use to clarify ideas and prove arguments. Testimony adds depth to your presentation and increases your credibility. Testimony includes excerpts from interviews, speeches, and printed sources such as books, magazines, and newspapers. A quote may be used to dramatically enhance a point or to inspire or motivate the audience.

In the following example, the speaker uses a quotation to support his assertion that education has strayed from its traditional goal of enlightening people:

Idea: Today students are taught to be afraid.

Example: In a recent speech, Dr. Edward Teller, the eminent nuclear scientist, expressed his concern about the direction of public education. He said and I quote, "Thirty years ago, students were taught that progress is wonderful. Today they are indoctrinated not to enlighten, but to be afraid."

Expert opinion is a type of testimony used to prove an argument. Expert opinion supplements facts and statistics to enhance believability. The opinion of an individual with broad evidence, extensive knowledge, and established reputation serves as evidence for the speaker's argument. For example, Henry Kissinger—Harvard professor, diplomat, former Secretary of State, and presidential advisor—is often called upon to give his expert opinion on international events. In the following example, the speaker uses expert opinion to support his argument that smoking causes cancer:

Argument: Smoking causes cancer.

Example: Dr. Robert Schweitzer, surgeon and former president of the American Cancer Society, says smoking is a primary cause of cancer: "We have known about the hazards of smoking for over twenty years. Smoking contributes to 30 percent of all cancer deaths."

Communicating Testimony Communicate testimony in such a way that your point is clear and meaningful to the audience. Here are some guidelines for presenting testimony to the audience:

1 Be Concise Quoting verbatim is appropriate when the citation is short and the language gives unusual clarity and impact to your ideas. However, reciting long passages may be cumbersome and result in confusion and boredom. If the citation is long, paraphrase or summarize the passage, or combine paraphrasing with a direct quote. In the following quote, the speaker summarized the results of a study by the American Heart Association:

Idea: Heart disease is the number one killer of Americans.

Quote: According to the American Heart Association, nearly half of all the deaths in the U.S. are caused by arteriosclerosis. It is not only a prime cause of heart attacks, but also of stroke, chronic kidney ailments, and vascular disease. More people die of heart disease annually, than of any other disease including cancer.

2 Be Accurate   Respect the intended meaning of the person you are quoting. It may be tempting to distort or misrepresent testimony, especially if you feel strongly about the topic. Politicians often distort opponents' statements to win a debate. Unprofessional journalists take statements out of context to create controversy or to support questionable conclusions. Tabloids like *The National Enquirer* and *The Washington Star* rely heavily on gross distortions to sell newspapers. The following story shows how comments can be taken out of context:

An English diplomat was interviewed by reporters on his arrival in Washington, D.C. Before leaving London he was warned that American journalists frequently take comments out of context, and he should therefore be careful how he responded to questions. "Are you going to visit any nightclubs during your stay in Washington?" was the first question asked. "Are there any nightclubs in Washington?" was the diplomat's reply. The next day he opened the morning newspaper and read an account of his interview. According to the news story, the first question he had asked was, "Are there any nightclubs in Washington?"[15]

Making the Testimony Credible to the Audience   Select testimony that gives credibility to your message. Here are some guidelines for building the credibility of your testimony:

1 Use Testimony from Credible Sources   Draw testimony from sources that are respected for their knowledge and admired by the audience. Oprah Winfrey, Phil Donahue, and Geraldo Rivera might be well-known television personalities but they are entertainers, not experts, and to quote them as authorities would damage your credibility. Planned Parenthood and right-to-life groups may be sincere organizations dedicated to their causes, but they are highly biased special interest groups and cannot be relied on to give objective opinions.

You might quote Tom Peters or Peter Drucker in a business presentation because they are world-renowned management consultants. Quoting Jacques-Yves Cousteau, explorer and environmentalist, about water pollution would be persuasive testimony because he is admired and has expertise. If your source is reputable but unknown to the audience, give a brief description establishing the person's qualifications.

You might use testimony from unknown but credible sources such as people who have unusual insights into or experience with your subject. Suppose you are advocating that adopted children have the right to privacy when a birth parent tries to locate the child. You might interview a person who has adopted a child and use that testimony in your speech.

2 *Document Your Sources*   Tell your audience the source of the testimony. This establishes your integrity and strengthens your argument. Give the name of the person who made the statement and the source from which it was taken. If the source is a magazine that doesn't give bylines, cite the publication. If you quote a person, give the name of the person you are quoting and identify the document that contained the statement. Here are some examples of how to cite a source:

Syndicated columnist Molly Irvins revealed that . . .

Conservative columnist George Will, writing in *Newsweek,* says that . . .

In a recent editorial, *The Los Angeles Times* expressed opposition to . . .

ABC news anchor Peter Jennings, in a recent speech, expressed concern about freedom of the press.

DOING: STRUCTURED EXPERIENCES

Doing uses participatory experiences to support a main point. Doing is a valuable aid to comprehension because the listener can actually "experience" the idea or process as well as hear and see it. For some members of the audience, seeing and hearing about a process will have less impact than being able to perform it. For these types of listeners, direct experience leads to greater understanding.

Some topics require activities if they are to be understood by the audience. Would you be able to apply a tourniquet to a wound efficiently if you were only told how to do it and did not practice the procedure? Probably not. Would you be able to communicate effectively in a job interview if you were only told how to do it and did not rehearse? Probably not. So doing is a helpful form of support in a presentation.

Moreover, audiences like structured experiences, especially when a presentation is long. Activities give them the opportunity to stand, move around, and become physically involved with the topic, speaker, and other members of the audience. Structured experiences help maintain attention.

Keep the audience together as you lead them through activities.

Planning Activities

Structured activities can be used in many ways to support main points or to reinforce telling and visual aids. They can be role-playing exercises done by the audience in their seats that simulate real-life situations, or simple physical movement such as modeling good posture or practicing relaxation techniques. You might even ask for volunteers to perform a process.

In a presentation on aerobic exercise, the presenter had the audience locate pressure points in their necks and wrists and count the number of heartbeats in 30 seconds. In a speech about the importance of proper posture, the presenter had the audience practice the technique. In a presentation on management communications, the speaker had members of the audience pair off and practice active listening techniques.

A rule of thumb is to use structured activities when they will enhance comprehension. In instances where an audience is expected to duplicate a process or action, doing may be necessary. In a speech describing the Japanese art of origami (paper folding), the speaker had the audience make a simple figure. In a speech explaining sign language, the speaker taught the audience to say hello in sign language.

Finding activities to support main points is challenging, especially when the subject is conceptual. Nevertheless, you should look for ways to use them in your presentations.

Leading Groups through Structured Experiences

Structured experiences require careful planning. Your goal is to give the audience hands-on experience to clarify or reinforce a point that you are trying to make. In most instances, you will be leading the whole group through a series of steps. You also have a limited amount of time in which to execute the activity. So you want to prepare the activity carefully and lead the audience smoothly through the process. Planning the activity includes:

1 Determine the objective of the activity. What point or idea in the presentation are you seeking to clarify, reinforce, or preview for the audience?

2 Determine whether conditions exist for the activity to be performed smoothly and efficiently in the allotted time and setting.

3 Determine how the audience will be organized for the activity. Will you divide them into pairs, triads, small groups? Or will you lead the whole group?

Next, prepare and rehearse your instructions. If you were going to lead the whole audience through the same activity, you might use the following sequence:

1 Explain your objective—what the experience is intended to accomplish.

2 Preview the steps of the experience—tell and show the group what they are going to do.

3 Present the steps in an organized sequence.

4 Use concise, clear, and simple language.

5 Keep the audience together.

The following example communicates a set of instructions using the five steps.

> *(Objective)* Before we proceed to the next step I want to make sure each of you knows how to grip a choking victim using the Heimlich maneuver. *(Preview)* In a moment, everyone will pick a partner. Decide who will be the victim and who will administer the technique. I will check each of you to make sure your grip and placement are correct. Then you will switch roles. I will again check to make sure the hold is correct.
>
> *(Instruction)* Now pick your partner. Good. Place your arms around the victim. Make a fist with one hand and place it against the sternum, thumb side in. Place your other hand over the fist and gently pull in with four quick thrusts. Under normal conditions, you would squeeze with greater force.

The presenter stated the objective of the activity, previewed the steps, and presented the steps in sequence. Clear, specific language was used, and the instructions were phrased so as to keep the group moving through the steps together.

SUMMARY

Telling, showing, and doing are three important types of supporting information and should be used in every speech. Verbal channels include definitions, examples, stories and anecdotes, comparison and contrast, description, statistics, and testimony. Doing includes planning activities and leading groups through structured experiences.

PROBES

1 Why should a speaker use all channels to convey information?
2 Briefly describe three types of definitions.
3 Why should stories be used in a speech?
4 Briefly describe four ways of communicating statistics.
5 Briefly describe three ways of making your statistics credible.
6 How can you make testimony credible to the audience?

APPLICATIONS

1 How would you use telling, showing, and doing to explain each of the following? (a) Self-defense techniques. (b) Bullet train. (c) Shooting a free throw. (d) The concept of honesty.
2 You want the audience to try some stretching exercises you will be discussing in your speech. How would you prepare for their participation?
3 Select a speech in *Vital Speeches* that contains statistics and analyze how effectively the speaker used them. Review the discussion about statistics in the text, and use it in your analysis. Were the statistics clear? Simple? Limited? Meaningful?

NOTES

1 *The New York Times,* "The Nominee, In His Own Words: a 'Mandate of Equal Justice Under Law,' " May 15, 1994, p. 16.
2 Warren Bennis, "Reflections on Retirement," *Vital Speeches,* Vol. 61, October 1, 1995, p. 752.
3 Ted Koppel, "The Vannatizing of America," delivered at Duke University Commencement, May 10, 1987, from a manuscript sent by the speaker.
4 Robert D. Raven, "A Criminal Justice System Overwhelmed," *The Commonwealth,* Vol. 33, June 30, 1989, p. 348.
5 Christopher Matthews, "Hardball: How Politics Is Played," *The Commonwealth,* Vol. 45, November 7, 1988, p. 479.
6 Quoted in Newton Minow's speech, "The Communications Act," *Vital Speeches,* Vol. 61, April 15, 1995, p. 390.
7 Allan Carlson, "The Family and the Welfare State," *Vital Speeches,* Vol. 61, July 15, 1995, p. 600.

8 Daniel H. Weinstein, "Our Children's Future," *The Commonwealth,* Vol. 40, October 5, 1987, p. 433.

9 Joseph D. McNamara, "The Los Angeles Riots and the Crisis in American Policing," *The Commonwealth,* Vol. 27, June 12, 1992, p. 389.

10 Susan Blumenthal, M.D., "Making Sense of Women's Health," *The Commonwealth,* Vol. 89, September 4, 1995, p. 2.

11 Gary L. Bauer, "Who Counts the Most Important Things of All?" *Imprimis,* Vol. 23, July 1994, pp. 2–3.

12 Albert Shanker, "What Schools Should—and Shouldn't—Learn from Markets," *The Commonwealth,* Vol. 47, November 25, 1991, p. 766.

13 Steven A. Holmes, "Even If the Numbers Don't Add Up," *New York Times,* August 14, 1994, p. E5.

14 Ibid. See also, Cynthia Crossen, *Tainted Truth: The Manipulation of Fact in America* (Simon & Schuster: New York, 1994); Paul Weaver, *News and the Culture of Lying* (Simon & Schuster: New York, 1994); Nicholas Eberstadt, *The Tyranny of Numbers* (Washington D.C.: American Enterprise Institute, 1995); and Robert Aberson, *Statistics As Principled Argument* (Hillsdale, NJ: Lawrence Erlbaum Associates, 1995).

15 Adapted from *The Executive Speechwriter Newsletter* Sample Issue, 1987, p. 2.

8

SUPPORTING THE MAIN POINTS: VISUAL AIDS

CHAPTER OUTLINE

PRESENTING VISUAL AIDS
    Maximize the Audience's View of the Visual Aids
    Introduce and Describe Visual Aids to the Audience
    Maintain Eye Contact with the Audience
    Conceal Visual Aids until You Use Them and Put Them Away after Use

The power of visual media to persuade was dramatically demonstrated a few years ago when a citizen videotaped the beating of Rodney King by members of the Los Angeles Police Department. The police stood over the prostrate and defenseless man and continuously struck him with batons and stung him with electrical prods. The shocking video caused nationwide revulsion and a riot when the police were acquitted of criminal behavior.

Aristotle said, "The soul never thinks without a picture." Visuals used skillfully increase comprehension and retention of information as well as enhance your credibility and the persuasiveness of your ideas.[1] Visuals add color, images, and motion to your spoken words. Instead of telling an audience about an exotic place, you can describe and show it using pictures, slides, or videotape. If you were arguing that Social Security entitlements are completely disproportionate in the federal budget, the most effective tool you could use to sway your audience would be to show a pie graph of the federal budget. The entitlements would be completely dominant.

In this chapter we will discuss the uses of visual aids, when to use them, the types of visual aids, selecting the appropriate medium, preparing visuals, and finally how to present them.

TYPES OF VISUAL AIDS

There are many types of visual aids you can prepare to support your main ideas. Among them are you, charts, graphs, other pictorial exhibits, video, and exhibits (objects).

You

You are an important source of visual information because you can gesture, demonstrate, and show material. You can contrast the size of two objects with your hands. You can execute an athletic movement such as a jump shot, and you can model clothing, uniforms, or sporting equipment.

Charts

Charts are popular forms of visuals and are usually designed to illustrate or reinforce in a simple and straightforward way important ideas, processes,

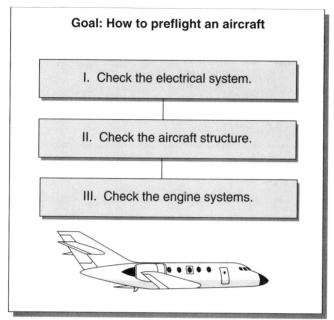

FIGURE 8-1
Main point outline.

and terminology. A common type of chart used in professional presentations is a main point outline. The audience sees the major ideas to be covered and gets a road map of the presentation (Figure 8-1). You should preview the main points on a chart.

An organizational chart shows the structure of an organization or the relationship between interconnected parts (Figure 8-2). A flowchart shows how steps of a process work together. You may use words, symbols, or pictures to illustrate the point (Figure 8-3).

FIGURE 8-2
Organizational chart for the delegation process.

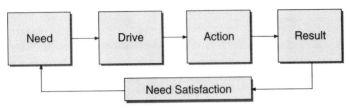

FIGURE 8-3
Flow chart for the need-satisfaction process.

A chart may be used to show statistics in a creative way. In Figure 8-4 the speaker uses a chart to present statistics about violence in comic books. Charts can be used to show statistics in a straightforward manner. In Figure 8-5 the speaker shows the number of AIDS deaths and the number of AIDS cases in the U.S. through 1994.

FIGURE 8-4
Violence in comic books. Average number of violent acts per issue.

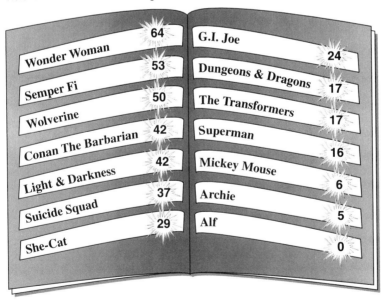

FACTS ABOUT AIDS

U.S. AIDS Deaths	Through 1994
Adults/Adolescents	267,465
Pediatric (under age 15)	3,405
Total	**270,870**

U.S. AIDS Cases	Through 1994
Adults/Adolescents	
Male	376,889 (86%)
Female	58,428 (13%)
Subtotal	435,319
Pediatric (under age 15)	6,209
Total	**441,528**

Source: Centers for Disease Control and Prevention

FIGURE 8-5
Sample chart.

Graphs

Graphs are especially useful for showing statistical data. Line graphs are effective for showing trends (change over time), such as sales trends and changes in market share (Figure 8-6). Line graphs can be presented creatively with drawings (Figure 8-7). Bar graphs are effective for showing trends and for comparing statistics. For example, you could show the causes of death of young people between the ages of 18 and 24 on a bar graph (Figure 8-8). You can also be creative in designing bar graphs (Figure 8-9). Bar graphs can also be presented horizontally (Figure 8-10). A pie graph—a circle divided into wedge-shaped segments of various sizes—dramatically shows relative proportions. For example, if you wanted to show how men and women contract AIDS, you could use pie graphs to show the relationships (Figure 8-11).

Other Pictorial Exhibits

Sketches, maps, cartoons, diagrams (Figure 8-12), pictures, photographs, and slides are all valuable visual devices. They are also very entertaining. Pictorial exhibits can be enlarged easily and at little cost. Photographs can be blown up at a photo shop or in the campus photo lab. Many copy centers

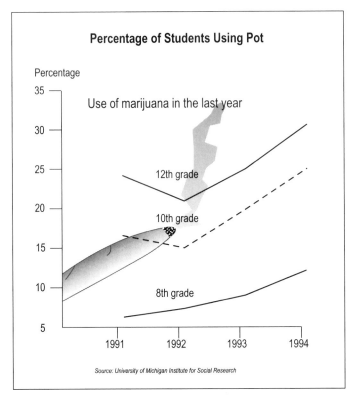

FIGURE 8-6
Line graph showing increase in pot use among students.

have Poster Makers that enlarge 8½ × 11 sketches, diagrams, and maps into 24 × 36 posters at low cost. One student had a Gary Larson "Far Side" cartoon blown up because it captured an idea he was explaining in his presentation.

The campus media center may have slides relevant to your topic that you can borrow. Some campus photo labs will convert your personal photographs into slides.

Video

Video has high impact because it combines sound, image, and motion. You can show excerpts from actual events, demonstrations along with commentary from experts, or snippets from television and movies to clarify, dramatize, or prove points. For example, you might describe and show how to

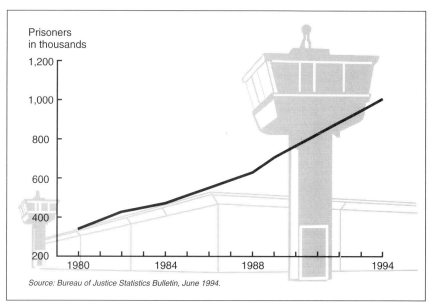

FIGURE 8-7
Line graph: number of prisoners.

serve a tennis ball and then show a short video excerpt of a professional performing the maneuver.

Obtaining videotapes is easy. Most colleges have large video libraries and many video stores have large inventories of instructional videos at low cost. Some students make their own videos to use in speeches. One student who worked at a marine park made a short video of a trainer teaching baby whales to jump through a hoop and showed it in her presentation.

Exhibits (Objects)

Exhibits are valuable because an audience can actually see the objects or the model. A laptop computer, a mountain bike, a piece of volcanic rock, or a wetsuit—all add a vivid and realistic dimension to a presentation that words cannot provide.

Melvin Belli, a well-known personal injury attorney, uses exhibits extensively in his presentations to a jury. In one trial, he carried a long cylindrical object wrapped in brown paper into the courtroom every day and laid it on the table in front of the jury. The mystery object aroused everyone's curiosity and there was wild speculation about the contents of the package. It soon became the focal point of the trial. Finally, during his summation at

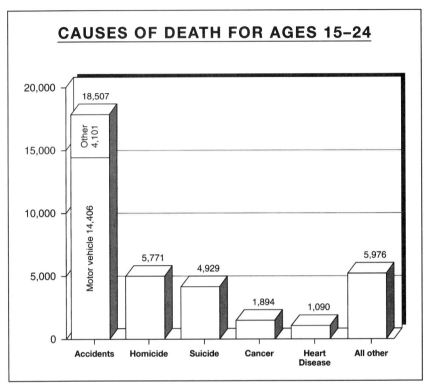

FIGURE 8-8
Bar graph.

the end of the trial, Belli picked up the package and slowly and deliberately began to unwrap it. He held up an artificial leg and asked the jury how much it was worth. His client had lost a leg in an accident and was seeking damages.

SELECTING THE APPROPRIATE MEDIUM

After selecting the type or types of visual aids you will use, you want to determine the most effective way of presenting them to the audience. In some circumstances the method will be obvious. If you have an object, it will be a matter of holding it up so the audience can see it easily. If you are going to demonstrate, it is a matter of practicing the steps and then going through them when you give the speech.

However, if you want to use a chart or graph, what is the most effective way to present it? On a poster, slide, or flip chart? Professional presenters

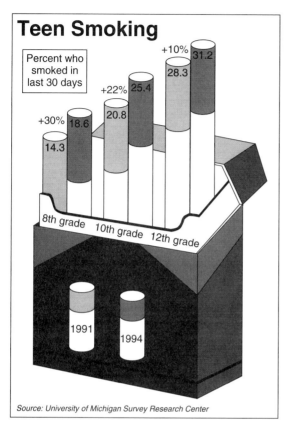

FIGURE 8-9
Bar graph.

wrestle with these questions, too, because they want to present their visuals with the maximum impact for a specific audience. Part of the answer lies in the type of visual you want to present and the resources that are available.

Experienced presenters have a broad variety of technology from which to choose a medium. As a student you may not have these resources at your disposal. Let's discuss some of the ways of presenting your visual in a classroom setting along with their advantages and disadvantages.

Posters

Graphs, charts, diagrams, and drawings can be easily prepared on posters and are popular with students because they are cheap and allow for creativity.

Use exhibits to inform.

Posterboard is typically 24 × 36 inches, an ample size for a classroom audience. Campus bookstores carry large supplies of posterboard in many colors. Remember, too, that smaller charts and graphs can be enlarged using a Poster Maker. Ringed artist pads, 24 × 36 inches, also work nicely as posters and can be displayed on a table or easel.

Determine the resources available to you for displaying your visuals. Are there clips, easels, or poster stands available? If not, you may have to bring tape or tacks to hang your posters. Whatever method you use, be certain they can be displayed easily for audience viewing. Then rehearse, using the visuals as you will use them in the speech.

Video

You need a TV monitor, a VCR, and a stand. The monitor should be easily seen by all; ideally it should be positioned just above eye level so the audience can see it comfortably. Professional presenters speaking before large audiences use projection equipment to transfer the video image onto a movie screen. When using a monitor and a VCR, it is a good idea to use a remote control device so you can easily operate the equipment.

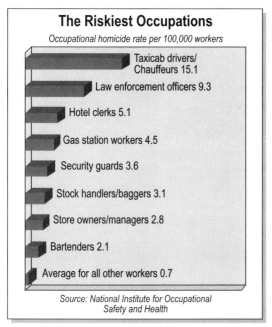

FIGURE 8-10
Horizontal bar graph.

Rehearse carefully, using the video. Familiarize yourself with the equipment so you can operate it easily and effortlessly when you make the presentation. Pre-set the videotape so it starts precisely at the point you want. Do not rewind and fast forward the tape during the presentation. Maintain eye contact with the audience as you use the video. Video can be cumbersome, and if not handled carefully can be distracting and defeat your purpose in using it.

Tell the audience what you want them to focus on before showing the video. Videos have movement and images that may detract from the example you want observed.

Remember that the goal of using video is to support, not dominate or overshadow, your ideas. The video excerpts should be short and directly support the main point.

Overhead Transparencies

Overhead transparencies are a popular medium for showing charts and graphs in business and professional presentations. They provide the impact of projection and can be prepared in rich colors and three-dimensional designs that impress the eye.

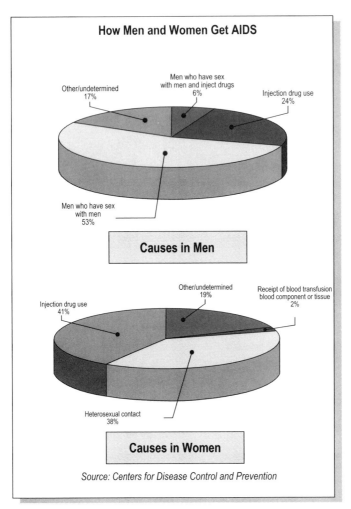

FIGURE 8-11
Pie graph.

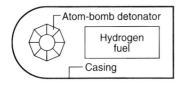

FIGURE 8-12
Hydrogen bomb diagram.

You should consider using transparencies in your presentations. They are easy to make. You can design a transparency on a computer. You can also design a chart or graph on paper and then transfer the image onto a transparency using a transparency copier, a piece of equipment that most campus media centers now have. Copy stores will make transparencies for a small fee, usually less than a dollar.

Transparencies are easily enhanced: you can highlight them with colored markers. You can also write on them during the presentation to emphasize important data or add information.

Practice with the overhead projector and transparencies so they integrate smoothly into the presentation. Turn off the projector after you have described the transparency. The glare of the light or the continuous display of a graph after you have explained it is distracting to the audience. If the screen is low, be sure to stand to the side so your body doesn't block the audience's view. If the screen is above your head, then you may stand next to the projector.

LCD Projection Panel

An LCD (liquid crystal display) panel projects images from a computer or video onto a screen using an overhead projector. The LCD panel is placed on the stage of the overhead projector, plugs into a computer or video, and then projects the images onto the screen for audience viewing. The LCD panels are small and lightweight and fit easily into a briefcase and are quite popular for business presentations. For example, a businesswoman may create visuals for her presentation using a laptop computer, attach it to her LCD panel, and use it to present the visuals during the speech. This is a very simple and efficient means of using visuals.

Flip Charts

Flip charts are a very popular medium for business and professional presentations. Flip-chart paper comes in standard 24×36 pads and attaches to easels. Flip charts are very effective for presenting charts, diagrams, and sketches and are usually used for audiences of 25 people or fewer. They are best used for informal presentations such as briefings and reports.

Preparing flip charts is relatively easy. Lightly outline in pencil the words or diagram you are going to show and then draw over the lines with many contrasting colored markers to create vivid and striking lists and drawings. Use double sheets of paper to prevent the marker from bleeding through to the next sheet.

You can write notes in pencil lightly in the margin. Your audience can't see these notes and you can use them to cue yourself for additional comments or to make a transition to the next page.

Stand to the side of the easel as you present the visuals. Face the audience as you discuss the visuals, and only occasionally glance at the chart. Be sure to point to the flip chart with the arm closer to the visual. When you are finished with the visual, cover it with the next blank sheet and then you are ready to present the next one.

Slides

You may take pictures of a subject that support an important point in your speech and have them made into slides. Or you may have existing negatives that can be made into slides. The media center on campus may have slides on the subject of your presentation. The campus photo lab may have slide libraries as well. Ask a student who is majoring in photography. Check these sources before you make your own.

Using slides requires good planning. Rehearse with the projector. Make sure the slides are placed in the tray correctly and that you know how to retrieve and replace a jammed slide. Use a remote control device. Designate a member of the audience to turn the lights on and off. Determine where you will stand when using the projector.

Demonstration

Demonstration shows the audience how a process works. You may want to show the audience how to karate kick, to perform a ballet step, or to handcuff a criminal suspect, or you may want to model a process such as applying pressure to a wound to stop bleeding.

If you are going to demonstrate, you should follow certain steps. First, describe the steps and then give a preview. Second, demonstrate each step precisely and correctly. Third, repeat the process to ensure that the audience understands the movements.

Chalkboards

The best policy is to prepare your visuals before the speech and avoid the chalkboard. If you must use a chalkboard, write only brief information such as a name or a new word, or draw simple diagrams. Extensive writing and drawing will divert your attention and break your contact with the audience. Audiences are turned off when your back is turned to them. Chalkboards are dull, and drawings and graphs have less impact because they lack color and contrast.

Handouts

Handouts supplement your oral presentation. They may contain complex information or supporting data that you cannot include in your speech because of time constraints. Distribute handouts at the end of the presentation. If you pass them out before or during the speech, some members of the audience will be reading them as you are talking. Tell the audience at the appropriate point in the speech that you have handouts for them and that you will be passing them out at the end of your presentation.

PREPARING VISUAL AIDS

After you have selected your visual aids and the medium for presenting them, you want to design them to maximize their impact. Let's discuss how to design visual aids and some of the features of presentation software, used for making visuals on a personal computer.

Principles of Design

The purpose of visual aids is to clarify and support ideas as well as to make your speech interesting. They also impact your credibility. What conclusion would you draw about a speaker whose visuals were cluttered and unreadable or sloppily prepared with irregular lines, smudges, messy lettering, or misspelled words? Undoubtedly it would be a negative impression. Let's discuss some guidelines for preparing your visuals.

Present One Idea Per Visual   Ideally the audience should understand the idea presented by the visual in a single glance. Trying to explain two or three or more ideas on one visual may confuse the audience and diminish the impact of the point you are trying to make.

Keep the Visuals Simple   Visual aids should stand by themselves. They should be simple, clear, and quickly understood. Remember, visuals support your presentation of ideas; they are not the whole presentation. If they are too complex or cluttered, they confuse the audience. Laypeople often complain that technical speakers such as engineers make their transparencies and slides too complex by using schematics and blueprints.

As suggested earlier, present one idea. Condense paragraphs into concise sentences, sentences into phrases, phrases into words. Many charts are presented in what is called "bullet" form: three or four well-spaced lines with two or four words per line preceded by a large dot (Figure 8-13). (The dots are called bullets because of their resemblance to bullet holes.)

When presenting statistics, clearly show the trend and the time frame, the two most important pieces of information.

DEADLY TALLY: AIDS BY RACE

- White   58%
- Black   26%
- Hispanic   15%
- Asian   1%

FIGURE 8-13
Chart with a bullet list.

When using charts, position the information on the upper part of the chart because audiences can see it better.

Drawings should be simple and you should avoid excessive labeling. Maybe six items or fewer should be listed in bold lettering and bright colors (Figure 8-14).

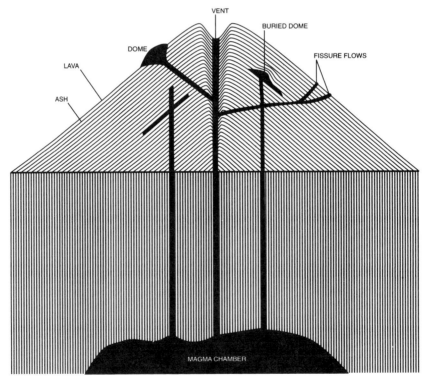

FIGURE 8-14
Interior of a volcano.

Follow a Consistent Format Each visual should follow a similar format. If you use a particular type of lettering for one chart, you should use the same lettering for subsequent charts.

Make Visuals Large Visual aids should be large enough to be seen easily by all members of the audience. In a typical classroom a 24 × 36 poster-board may be the minimum size for a graphic. You should also consider some of the media we have discussed above, such as transparencies, slides, or flip charts. Small pictures, photographs, or drawings have no impact; have them enlarged at a photo shop or copy shop.

One way to determine if your unprojected visuals are adequate in size is to stand ten feet away from them. If you can easily see and read them, then their size is okay. If you cannot, make them larger.

Use Bold Colors and Lines Use bold colors and broad lines that are vivid and contrasting. Blue, green, black, purple, and red give impact to words and drawings. Use bold type or felt markers with flat tips so the lines are broad and striking. Do not use pastel colors or yellow markers. They cannot be seen. Use white or very light-colored backgrounds for your graphics and charts. A dark background diminishes the impact of your colors.

Use Pictures with Words If you are listing words or short sentences on a chart, draw pictures that correspond to the ideas. For example, if you have a dynamite idea, draw a stick of dynamite. The visual association will improve memory and impact.

Must Be Easy to Handle You should be able to smoothly introduce and withdraw the visual. Heavy or bulky objects or flimsy poster paper that is noisy or difficult to hold flat can be distracting and interfere with the flow of information. Look for alternative solutions if your visuals are cumbersome. One student, whose topic was how to windsurf, used a miniature windsurfing model to describe the process of getting up and sailing the board because bringing a windsurfer and sail was impractical.

If you are using presentation equipment such as a VCR or slide projector, rehearse extensively so that the equipment operates flawlessly during your speech.

Limit the Use of Visuals

There is no formula for the number of visuals to be used in a speech. They are strategic and designed to highlight ideas and prove points. Too many visuals lose their impact and the main ideas are lost or diluted. The best approach to take is to ask yourself: How can I use visuals to clarify my ideas and reduce complex information to a simpler form? Keep in mind that your purpose is to communicate ideas and that visuals are one tool to help you achieve that goal.

Presentation Software

Presentation software allows you to prepare graphs, charts, and diagrams on a computer. You can make slides, overhead transparencies, handouts, outlines, and posters that can be blown up. There is a variety of templates—standard patterns for graphs and charts—from which you can choose. You can work in black and white or color. Your campus computer center should have presentation software you can use, and probably offers a short course on how to use it.

Presentation software can be as sophisticated as you want it to be. There are full-blown programs made by a number of software companies. You can also create effective visuals with a word processor and a basic drawing program available on standard computers. These are easy to use and you can create entertaining charts, graphs, and drawings using them.

PRESENTING VISUAL AIDS

Present your visuals so they can achieve the objective of clarifying ideas and proving points as well as enhancing your credibility. Here are some guidelines for presenting your visuals effectively.

Maximize the Audience's View of the Visual Aids

Before your speech, plan where you will place your visuals and then view that spot from different places in the room to determine if they can be seen easily. Adjust the position to maximize the view.

When presenting the visuals, position yourself so you do not obstruct the audience's view. Bring tacks, tape, easel, or whatever supplies you need to display charts and posters. If you are going to display a poster, you might attach tape to the back before the speech and just press it against the wall or board before you show it.

Introduce and Describe Visual Aids to the Audience

Introduce the visual, describe it, and explain its relationship to your idea. Don't assume the audience will understand the visual without your commentary. For example, a speaker describing a bar graph showing the types and percentages of crimes committed by teenagers under 17 might say:

This graph shows the types of crimes committed by teenagers under 17. The left side, or vertical axis (point to it), of the graph shows the percentage and the horizontal axis (point to it) shows the type of crime. As you can see the highest percentage of crime is the theft of property.

Maintain Eye Contact with the Audience

Don't talk to your visual aid; talk to the audience. Look at how your audience is responding to the visual so you can adapt your remarks if necessary. Turning to the side or turning your back to the audience breaks contact.

Stand to the side of the visual, facing the audience. Keep your feet pointed to the audience—that will keep you from turning. Glance quickly at the visual and point to the item you want the audience to focus on with the arm closest to the visual. This way you have your body directing the attention of the audience to the visual and at the same time you are looking at the audience.

Conceal Visual Aids until You Use Them and Put Them Away after Use

Do not show your visual until you get to the section of the speech in which you will use it. After you discuss it, put it away. If you leave a poster hanging up and then introduce another one, the first one will compete for the audience's attention.

The exception is if there is continuity among the posters—for example, if the posters show the steps of a process. Then hanging up more than one is necessary because you are showing the relationship among steps. Sometimes a speaker will display a list of the objectives for a speech and refer to them as they are met in the presentation. But as a rule of thumb, put your visuals away after you have used them.

SUMMARY

Visual aids help clarify ideas, prove arguments, create interest, and increase your credibility. The different types of visual aids include you, charts, graphs, other pictorial exhibits, video, and objects that you exhibit to the audience. Methods of presenting visuals include posters, video, overhead transparencies, flip charts, slides, demonstrations, use of the chalkboard, and handouts. Visuals should be easily seen, made with bright colors and broad lines, simple, and easy to manage, and you should limit their use. Presentation software allows you to make your own visuals on the computer. When presenting visual aids, maximize the audience's view of them, describe them, maintain eye contact with the audience, and put away after use.

PROBES

1 Briefly describe the different types of visual aids.
2 Briefly describe the different ways of presenting visuals.
3 What principles should you follow in designing visuals?
4 What is the best way to present visuals?
5 Briefly describe three types of graphs.
6 Briefly describe how to present information on a flip chart, on overhead transparencies, and on slides.

APPLICATIONS

1 You have a series of statistics about the number and causes of traffic accidents in your state. What kinds of visual aids would you construct for the message? What guidelines would you follow in the preparation and use of them in the speech?
2 What kinds of visuals could you use with the following subjects? (a) Space shuttle. (b) Child abuse. (c) The drug trade. (d) Unemployment. (e) The federal deficit.
3 You want to show a series of drawings related to the Egyptian pyramids. How would you prepare and display them?

NOTE

1 William J. Seiler, "The Conjunctive Influence of Source's Credibility and the Use of Visual Materials on Communication Effectiveness," *Southern Speech Communication Journal,* Vol. 37 (1971a), pp. 174–185; Donna Baron, "Graphics Presentations at Your Fingertips," *Office,* Vol. 112, July 1990, pp. 32–34; "Persuasion and the Role of Visual Presentation Support," Research paper, Management Information Systems Research Center, School of Management, University of Minnesota, Minneapolis, June 1986; "Graphics Help People See What to Do," *Meeting Management News,* Vol. 4, No. 3, September 1992, pp. 3–4; Virginia Johnson, "Picture-Perfect Presentations," *Training and Development Journal,* Vol. 43, No. 5, May 1989, pp. 45–47; "Brilliant Meetings: The Art of Effective Visual Presentations," The 3M Company, 1993.

9

OPENING AND CLOSING
THE SPEECH

In a speech about effective problem solving the speaker opened her presentation by remarking how wonderful it would be if, by magic, we could make our problems disappear. As she was uttering these words she held up a bright red silk handkerchief in her right hand and made a closed fist with her left hand. She began to stuff the red handkerchief into her closed fist until it disappeared. Then, she dramatically opened her hands to show the audience that the red silk handkerchief had disappeared.

At the end of her presentation she repeated her theme that our problems won't disappear by magic. In that instant she reached into her breast pocket and pulled out a bright red handkerchief just like the one she had made disappear in the introduction to her speech.

The opening and closing are the book ends of the presentation. In the introduction you must get the audience's attention focused on you and then your topic. You want to establish a positive personal and professional relationship and demonstrate the relevance of your topic. You may even have to establish your credentials. In the conclusion you want to strongly reinforce the major ideas of your presentation and their value to the audience.

PREPARING AN EFFECTIVE INTRODUCTION

You should prepare the introduction as carefully as you prepare the body of your presentation. Your opening remarks must get the attention of the audience and pave the way for the message. You want to consider certain strategic questions: What is the best way to open my presentation to get the attention of the audience? How can I show the relevance of my topic so the audience will immediately see the benefit? How do I establish a positive relationship and demonstrate my qualifications for speaking on the topic, so the audience will like me and respect my knowledge about the topic?

Figure 9-1, the "introduction matrix," shows five steps for building an effective introduction, the goal of each step, and the desired audience response.

FIGURE 9-1
Introduction matrix.

Step	Goal	Audience Response
Attention	To get attention	"I want to listen."
Rapport	To establish positive relationship	"I like the speaker."
Relevance	To show value of the topic	"I will benefit."
Credibility	To show qualifications	"The speaker is knowledgeable."
Agenda	To prepare audience for body of speech	"I understand the objectives of the speech."

Capture the Attention of the Audience

Picture yourself at the movies. You're sitting comfortably in your seat, a jumbo box of popcorn in one hand and a diet soda in the other. The lights dim and all of a sudden the screen explodes with action and your senses become riveted to the screen. The opening has captured your attention and drawn you into the movie.

Your opening remarks should grab the interest of the audience and draw their attention to the speech. Numerous factors, internal and external, are competing for the audience's attention. A group of managers may be thinking about important appointments or unfinished projects. A student audience might be focused on midterm exams or daydreaming about upcoming weekend activities. The room might be hot and stuffy. Students may be milling about just outside the classroom door talking in loud voices. Your first step is to get control of the audience's attention and draw the audience into your speech.

There are a number of popular ways of getting the attention of the audience. Whatever method you use should be thematic and appropriate to your personality and audience. Below are some common methods of getting the attention of the audience.

Provocative or Stimulating Statement A provocative or stimulating statement is designed to excite the audience emotionally or intellectually. The goal is to get the audience's attention by making a penetrating observation that challenges perceptions. In the following example the speaker makes a statement designed to challenge a cherished assumption:

Specific purpose:	To convince the audience to support scientific research.
Central idea:	Scientific development is the key to success and advancement.
Provocative statement:	We like to think of ourselves as a scientifically advanced people. We are not. The astounding technical achievements of our age were not made by the masses, but by a tiny fraction of 1 percent of the population against the apathy, inertia, and sometimes bitter opposition of the remaining 99 percent.

An Amusing Statement, Incident, or Joke Humor is a popular opening method. Audiences like humor and it quickly establishes rapport. The entertaining opening may be a statement, a humorous anecdote, or a joke. You might open with a quote from a famous person—for example, Yogi

Berra, famous for statements like "Ninety percent of the game is half mental" and "You can observe a lot just by watching."

Humorous anecdotes are entertaining and establish rapport with the audience.

Specific purpose:	To persuade the audience to turn adversity to opportunity.
Central idea:	Negative experiences help us grow.
Personal story:	The first time I ever spoke in public was when I was three years old. My sister and I recited *Little Robin Red Breast* for a church audience. I felt that since I was mature enough to recite the poem, I was mature enough to dress myself for the occasion. I put on my pretty little red dress but I blew it with my underwear. I somehow ended up with my oldest sister's pair. When I stood up on stage and started reciting, my underwear fell right down to the floor. Needless to say, I was a hit.

Humor is an effective tool for defusing hostility and creating rapport. When Barbara Bush was announced as the commencement speaker at Wellesley College, the news was not favorably received by some of the students. Many felt she was unqualified, that she had been asked to speak because of her husband's position, not her own accomplishments. However, she won the audience over with statements like this one: "Somewhere out in this audience may even be someone who will one day follow in my footsteps and preside over the White House as the president's spouse. I wish *him* well."

If you choose humor to open your speech, practice the joke or story several times, so you can deliver it with confidence and hit the punch line hard. (See Chapter 15.)

If you need sources for humor, look in *The Return of the Portable Curmudgeon* (John Winokus; Plume), a book of jokes and humorous stories designed for public speakers. *Oxford Dictionary of Humorous Quotations* (Ned Sherrin; Oxford University Press) also contains many humorous anecdotes. Many speeches published in *Vital Speeches* have humorous openings.

A Startling Statement   A startling statement is designed to jolt the audience to attention. The statement may be a shocking statistic or fact unknown to the audience. Suppose you said "Many children die every year from starvation." Not much impact. But what if you said "Forty million children die of starvation each year." That is an astonishing statistic and, for many in the audience, a revelation. If you use this approach, use good taste and be thematic.

Specific purpose:	To inform the audience about the problem of child abuse.
Central idea:	Child abuse is a serious problem.
Startling statement:	The headline read, "Child Tortured to Death." A four-year-old girl was burned with cigarette butts, beaten, tied up, and left on a kitchen shelf seven feet above the floor. She eventually fell from the shelf and broke her arm. If you think this story is journalistic sensationalism, you are wrong. Hundreds of thousands of children are physically and mentally abused every year.

A Quotation   An interesting or thought-provoking quotation can capture the attention of the audience and help them focus on the topic. The quote should be fairly short and focused. In the following example the quote works naturally into the topic:

Specific purpose:	To persuade the audience to get involved in education.
Central idea:	The quality of education has disintegrated.
Introduction begins:	Every 8 seconds of the school day, a student drops out; 700,000 a year. Every 67 seconds, a teenager has a baby. Every 7 minutes a child is arrested for drugs. Every year 700,000 students graduate who cannot read their diplomas. *A Nation at Risk,* the landmark report on the status of education in America, concluded,
Quotation:	"If an unfriendly foreign power had attempted to impose on America the mediocre education performance that exists today, we might well have viewed it as an act of war."

A Story   Telling a story is an effective way of opening a presentation. Audiences like stories and opening with an entertaining or dramatic anecdote sets a positive tone for the speech. Useful types of stories include dramatic accounts, personal experiences, and short anecdotes. A dramatic account stirs the imagination or emotions of the audience and draws them into the presentation.

Specific purpose:	To persuade the audience that security should be provided for students on campuses at night.
Central idea:	Students are endangered at night.

Story: It was a cold and foggy November evening. I had finished studying in the library and was walking to my car. I usually walk with my friends, but that night they were busy. Besides, I felt safe. As I walked through campus, the fog became very thick, and I could barely make my way. As I walked along I began to feel that someone was watching me. Suddenly, someone grabbed my arm and threw me to the ground. Fortunately, my screams scared the intruder away. Many women on campus have had similar experiences, some with much worse consequences.

In the following example the speaker opens with an entertaining story that focuses on his theme:

Specific purpose: To persuade the audience to get the facts before making a decision.

Central idea: Look before you leap.

Short anecdote: One night while at sea, the ship's captain saw what looked like the lights of another ship heading toward him. He ordered his signal man to flash the other ship: "Change your course ten degrees south." The reply came back: "Change your course ten degrees north." The ship's captain answered: "I am a captain. Change your course south." To which the reply was: "Well, I am a seaman first class. Change your course north." This infuriated the captain, so he signaled back: "Dammit, I say change your course south. This is a battleship!" To which the reply came back: "And I say change your course north. This is a lighthouse!"

Rhetorical Question   A rhetorical question is a skillfully phrased question designed to stimulate thought. Rhetorical questions demand that the audience mentally participate in your speech, forcing them to assess both their own position and the one that you offer. In the following example, the speaker poses a question that forces the audience to query themselves about the cultural values of our society:

Specific purpose: To persuade the audience to support the National Endowment for the Humanities.

Central idea: The National Endowment for the Humanities preserves lasting values.

Rhetorical question: Imagine a nation that can make room on its airwaves for "Beavis and Butthead," but not for Ken Burns's documentaries on the Civil War and Baseball, or that can make room on its bookshelves for Howard Stern's *Private Parts,* but not for the writings of Abraham Lincoln, Frederick Douglas, or Mark Twain; that can make room in its public places for video games but not for exhibits about Thomas Jefferson. Is that the country of our dreams?[1]

Other Opening Approaches   There are many other ways of opening your speeches besides the ones discussed above. Here are some ideas:

One speaker approached the podium pushing a shopping cart; he wore a sign on his chest stating "I will work for food." The speech was about homelessness.

A speaker opened with a video showing a head-on collision as the introduction to a speech about wearing seatbelts.

The speaker had the audience close their eyes and played relaxing and soothing music as a prelude to a speech about relaxation techniques.

A speaker showed sections of a rock video advocating violence against women to introduce a speech discussing how women are depicted in pop culture.

The speaker played a recording of a pilot's last communication with the tower before his plane crashed. The speaker's topic was air traffic control.

The speaker took out a menu from McDonald's and began waving it in the air and asking the audience: "How many calories? Fat? Carbohydrates? Cholesterol? are contained in one Big Mac? What I am going to tell you will amaze and scare the heck out of you."

One speaker asked the audience to take out a pencil and paper and answer the following questions:

1 Why are manhole covers round?

2 How many pizza restaurants are there in the U.S.?

3 If you were to put artificial turf on all the Major League ballparks, how many square yards would you need?

4 Why do vending machines and jukeboxes have both letters and numbers?

5 If you were a product, how would you position yourself?

He then explained that these were examples of job interview questions asked by employers. The purpose was to test an applicant's analytical skills. The speaker's topic was "how to answer job interview questions."

A provocative statement, humor, quotations, stories, rhetorical questions, and creative behavior are effective ways of getting the attention of the audience. Now let's talk about establishing rapport, another important goal of the introduction.

Build Rapport

Audiences respond favorably to speakers they like and respect, and therefore it is very important to establish a positive personal and professional relationship as you deliver your introduction. Building rapport for a speech is similar to meeting someone for the first time at a dinner party and creating a positive first impression. As you learn more about each other—such as discovering common interests and experiences—you develop a positive relationship.

Building rapport begins even before you speak. A smile, eye contact with members of the audience, natural gestures and movement, a relaxed posture—all show openness and accessibility. You are reaching out to the audience and communicating that you are happy to be there speaking to them.

Build rapport with audience.

Experienced speakers use a variety of verbal approaches to build rapport with their audiences. A simple "thank you" and expression of appreciation to the audience for the opportunity to speak to them is a standard example of rapport building. If you were speaking to a service organization such as the Kiwanis or the Rotary Club, you might acknowledge their community service and cite one or two of their latest projects. You may refer to members of the audience by name.

Here is an example of how Maggie Kuhn, a spokesperson for the elderly, established rapport with her audience at a conference on aging:

> There are three things that I like about being old. First, I can speak my mind, and I do, and I'm always surprised at what I can get away with. I can be outrageous, and I can ask you to rate me today—have I been outrageous? And I hope you'll give me a brownie point for that. The second thing that I like about being old is that I have outlived much of my opposition. The people who said to me, "Maggie, that will never work; it's just a crazy idea," they're gone. But the third thing in my life in my old age is the honor and the privilege and the sheer joy of reaching out to people like you and being a part of your future. What a blessing and a privilege—and fun.[2]

As you prepare your classroom speeches, think of ways to build rapport with your audience. You might acknowledge one or more previous speeches that were beneficial. You might make a personal reference to one or two members of the class who have received special recognition. One speaker referred to the pressures students feel at midterm time and another referred to the difficulty of selecting a major or the right career. In the following example, the speaker establishes rapport with an audience of classmates:

> A real problem for me and I'm sure for many of you is registration for classes. There are the required classes you have to take. You are limited to certain hours because you work part-time. You put together a schedule that meets these needs and you go to registration—and what do you find? The courses you want are closed, and you have to improvise quickly to get what's left. Most of the time you don't.

Whatever approach you use to build rapport should be a genuine expression of respect. Do not patronize or pander to an audience. Audiences can instantly detect insincerity and will respond less than favorably. Rapport does not imply you are subordinate to or even equal to an audience. Audiences want to view speakers with respect, as a source of information and leadership.

Establish Common Ground

This technique is used when a speaker's topic is controversial, or likely to be unpopular. Presenters using this technique attempt to mitigate some of the differences by showing that many areas of similarity exist between themselves and the audience. They might cite membership in common organizations, or shared social, political, or religious views. The goal is to expose enough similarities to get a fair hearing. In the following example, former FBI Director William Sessions attempts to establish common ground with an audience of lawyers:

> Its members (a profession) must be proficient in their discipline—but they must do more than simply perform for money. They must work for the social good, within the discipline of the profession.
>
> What qualities must lawyers and judges have if we are to preserve our legal traditions? Dedication to scholarship, broad vision, and equanimity—balance—an evenness and fairness of mind, a strong ethical underpinning and, of course, integrity and honesty.[3]

In your classroom speeches, you may speak on controversial subjects. One classroom speaker advocating a pro-life position on abortion attempted to create common ground this way:

> I know many of you believe and have a sincere conviction that abortion on demand is every woman's right. And I applaud and respect your sincerity. I feel differently and base my beliefs on experience and sincere convictions as well. In the next few minutes I would like to explain my position and ask that you listen with an open mind and heart.

Demonstrate the Relevance of Your Topic

Audiences have expectations about speeches, listening with keen awareness when a speech addresses their needs and interests, and possibly sleeping through a speech that does not. Demonstrating relevance means showing the audience how your speech will help them achieve important objectives, such as saving money, improving performance, gaining new insights, or solving important problems. Even experienced speakers who have captive audiences are careful to show the benefits of their speech to the audience.

Here is an example of how a student speaker linked her topic to the needs and interests of the audience:

Topic:	To describe to the audience a process for studying more effectively.
Relevancy statement:	As students one of our biggest problems is managing time effectively. We work part-time, take a full load of courses, and do homework. What I want to talk to you about today is how to reduce your homework time by 25 percent.

The speaker showed the audience how learning about the topic would help them achieve an important objective: relieving the pressures of a full schedule.

In the next example the speaker, Julie Packard, demonstrates the relevance of her topic, the ecology of the oceans, to the audience:

> Ask any person what image they associate with the sea, and you'll get one word—mystery. The oceans are the last frontier on Earth. They're the only place yet to be explored. With more than 5 billion humans on the planet, there are very few places that people have not been.
>
> And of course, there's the beauty. Few things can match the grace of a shimmering school of sardines ambling in perfect unison through a swaying tower of kelp forest plants. But today I'd like to talk about why we need to focus on the oceans—how our very fate as a human race is entwined and dependent on them.[4]

In the next example the speaker anticipates that some members of the audience are indifferent to the problem of alcohol addiction and must be convinced of the importance of the issue and how it affects them directly:

Topic:	Alcoholism is a serious problem.
Relevancy statement:	Many of you are probably saying to yourself, "I have heard about the problem of alcoholism so often I don't need to hear any more." That may be true, but it doesn't diminish the problem. In fact, it probably compounds the problem.
	Alcoholism is a crisis. If I asked how many of you know someone who has a drinking problem, every one of you would raise your hand. We all know not one but many people who have drinking problems. Five of you sitting in the audience will wrestle with alcohol addiction in your lifetime. Some of you may already have a drinking problem.

Establish Your Qualifications to Speak on the Topic

Another objective of the introduction is to establish your credentials. Audiences listen with greater attention and respect when they perceive the speaker as an expert. Professional speakers weave their credentials into the introduction in a number of ways. They may have the master of ceremonies cite their relevant training, education, and experience. In the introduction a speaker may subtly refer to her background and allude to success stories that highlight or reinforce her qualifications. In the following example, the speaker built his credibility by telling the audience that his organization did important work that drew national attention:

> I am delighted to be here to talk about important subjects—education and international competitiveness. As you may know, the organization I represent, the Business-Higher Education Forum, first called national attention to the competitiveness crisis about a decade ago. Our report, which was front page news from New York to Los Angeles, focused extensively on the need to improve our schools and workplace programs.[5]

Although you are not a professional speaker, you have had experiences that make you uniquely qualified to speak on your subjects. Refer to these qualifications in the introduction in a way that shows the audience you know what you are talking about. Here are two examples of how students demonstrated their qualifications to speak:

> John's speech was about ski safety. He is a licensed member of the ski patrol. He has been skiing for fourteen years, and every winter he heads up a ski rescue team on weekends and holidays. In the introduction of his speech he referred to his skiing experience in a matter-of-fact way: "I've been skiing since I was six. I earned my ski patrol certification six years ago and on weekends lead a ski rescue team." He obviously knew what he was talking about, and the audience was very impressed.

> Joan learned sign language in high school when she worked with deaf children. In her speech describing sign language, she mentioned this experience: "I learned sign language in high school and work with deaf children at the Mauzy Institute." The combination of her experience and her knowledge of sign language established her credentials.

Prepare the Audience for the Body of the Speech

Another goal of the introduction is to prepare the audience for the subject matter of the speech. You may need to define key words or technical terms, reduce the topic's complexity, or establish a perspective for the message. The method and extent of this orientation depends on the subject. However, the introduction is a good place to nail down the perimeters and set the context for the presentation. The following methods are frequently used to orient an audience:

Narrow the Topic   Sometimes a topic appears to be very broad and you need to define its limits. If your topic is to "reform education" you may need to define what you mean by "education." Kindergarten through high school? College? Preschool? What do you mean by "reform"? Eliminate tenure? Use more computer-based education? Extend school hours? These terms need to be defined so the audience understands the scope of your message. In the following example, Bill Gates, CEO of Microsoft, defines the "information age" in the introduction of his speech so the audience understands what he means by that term:

> When we say that its the "information age," what we mean is that people should have easy access to information of any type, for use in business, information, entertainment, or education. Anywhere they go, they should find that easy to do.[6]

In a speech whose topic was "the comic genius of the Three Stooges," the speaker narrowed down the subject this way:

> If one were to discuss the full breadth and width of the careers of those men known as the Three Stooges it would consume days; granted they would be days well spent, for who can ever hear enough of these funny men and their antics. For the sake of time I will limit myself to a discussion of those films starring Larry Fine, Moe Howard, and Curly Howard, leaving their illustrious stage career and the films in which Shemp Howard replaced Curly for another day.

Define Technical or Unfamiliar Language   Your speech may contain new or unfamiliar language that needs definition. In the following example the speaker defines "vegetarian":

Specific purpose:	To describe a vegetarian diet.
Central idea:	Vegetarian diets can be flexible.
Definition:	Before I continue, I want to define for you what I mean by vegetarian. A strict vegetarian is someone who eats no animal products. There are varying degrees of strictness: some vegetarians eat dairy products, some eat eggs, some even eat fish. Each person adheres to the degree of vegetarianism that fits his or her own life or beliefs. I am going to discuss the diet of a strict vegetarian.

Provide a Background   With some topics a brief history may be necessary to put the subject in perspective. If you are going to propose a solution to a problem, you might briefly give some background on the issue, such as causes of a problem and other proposed solutions that failed. The goal is to give a context for the speech so your presentation will be easier to understand.

Specific purpose:	To outline a plan for developing democratic governments and a free market economy in the former Soviet Union.
Central idea:	There must be a change in the historical mindset of the Soviet people.

Historic context: One of the most common mistakes made when viewing the confusion that now reigns in the former Soviet republics is that these people are trying to reform concepts of government that have only existed since the Revolution of 1917.

    Prior to the Soviet Communists the tsars were all-powerful. As far back as history can record the Russian people have been told exactly what to do. The Russian people must now throw off a subservient mentality that has existed for a thousand years and recognize their self-sufficiency and self-determination. This is not an easy task.

SAMPLE INTRODUCTION

The following introduction was delivered in a speech persuading the audience to donate time to a youth camp for disadvantaged children:

Introduction

(Rapport) Thank you for the opportunity to speak to you this morning. *(Attention)* I'd like to show you the picture of two young children, Robert and Sonya. Robert is your typical nine-year-old. He loves to play in the dirt and fill his pockets with all sorts of treasures like rocks, string, yo-yos, and lizards. He's different from the other boys though. He watched his father shoot to death his mother in their home.

Sonya is seven and as you can see very pretty. She has long dark curly hair and loves to cuddle. In fact she craves affection. Sonya has four siblings and lives with her mother. She doesn't know who her father is, in fact none of the children do. Each child has a different father. Sonya's mother is a prostitute.

Robert and Sonya are the kinds of children we encounter every summer at Opportunity Camp. *(Rapport)* I know that each one of you gives time to charitable causes and that the summer is a time to kick back from school and make some badly needed money.

(Relevancy) But, Opportunity Camp is a real opportunity for you to spend one week of your time helping a child to learn to read, build self-esteem, and give them guidance. Your example can make a difference in shaping a child's future.

(Credibility) I have worked at Opportunity Camp for the past five summers and I can tell you wonderful success stories about the children who have attended. It has been one of the most rewarding experiences of my life.

(Orientation) Opportunity Camp was established by the county ten years ago to aid abused children, foster children, and disadvantaged children. They are referred by the Department of Social Services. My goal this morning is to encourage you to donate one week of your summer to Opportunity Camp. . . . *(Used with the permission of Victoria Hamilton)*

Getting the attention of the audience, building rapport, establishing the relevance of your topic, building your credibility, and preparing the audience for the body of the speech are important objectives of the introduction. Now, let's turn our attention to the conclusion.

PREPARING AN EFFECTIVE CONCLUSION

Your concluding remarks should be carefully planned. They should solidify the goal and reinforce the major ideas. This is your last opportunity to focus on your major ideas and leave a lasting impression on the audience. Paul Erdman, author and well-known circuit speaker, believes strong conclusions are essential for a successful speech. On one occasion as he was waiting to be introduced he realized his ending was not appropriate for this particular audience. He rewrote it on the spot and completed it just as he was being introduced by the master of ceremonies.[7] In an informative speech where you want the audience to remember important ideas or to use a process, you may want to summarize the main points to assure retention. In a persuasive speech you may want to conclude with a call to action, exhorting the audience one last time to follow the course you propose.

Figure 9-2 shows the goals and the desired audience responses for different types of conclusions. You may use one type or a combination depending on the specific purpose of your presentation.

FIGURE 9-2
Conclusion matrix.

Step	Goal	Audience Response
Summary	Long-term retention	"The major ideas were clear to me."
Show concrete results	Give the audience sense of satisfaction	"I learned helpful information"
Call for action	Have audience respond in certain way	"I will do it!"
Unify the speech	To give speech sense of completion	"Speech was unified"

Reinforce the Major Ideas

Restating the central idea and the main points is a common way of concluding a speech, especially an informative presentation. It reinforces the key
points in the minds of the audience and helps them retain the information.
There are a number of ways you can conclude a speech that focus attention
on the major ideas and the theme.

Summarize the Main Points   Reviewing the main points and supporting them with a visual aid is a very effective method of concluding a speech.
Summaries are often used in informational presentations when the speaker
wants the audience to remember or be able to execute a process following a
presentation.

Specific purpose:	To instruct the audience in the proper application of a tourniquet.
Central idea:	You may never need to know how to use a tourniquet, but if you do you may save a limb and maybe a life.
Closing summary:	In closing I would like to review the steps of applying a tourniquet. First, determine if the wound is bad enough to justify the use of a tourniquet. Second, locate a strap of some length, such as a belt or tie, and secure it into a loop. Third, slide the loop over the wounded extremity and slip a stick through the loop. Fourth, using the stick twist the loop until it closes the wounded extremity. Continue to tighten the loop, or tourniquet, until blood stops flowing from the wound entirely. Loosen the tourniquet every five minutes so that the limb is not damaged by lack of blood flow. Maintain the tourniquet until instructed otherwise by a doctor or medic.
	Remember, the proper use of a tourniquet can save a life, and a limb. Its misuse may save a life, but might cause severe complications.

End with a Quotation   A quote capturing the central idea is a common
way of ending a speech. In the following example, the speaker quotes Martin Luther King, Jr., to conclude a speech about capital punishment:

Specific purpose:	To persuade the audience that capital punishment should be abolished.

Central idea: Capital punishment will not reduce the causes of crime.

Closing quote: Thank you for taking the time to listen to me today. Before I take my seat I would like to leave you with one last thought about capital punishment. We must change how we view people and the criminal justice system. Martin Luther King gave us a hint when he said: "Man must evolve for all human conflict a method which rejects revenge, aggression and retaliation. The foundation of such a method is love."

Combining a quote with a summary is more effective than a summary alone because important ideas are connected to a memorable statement.

Tell a Story   Concluding with a story helps an audience remember key concepts. Audiences like stories and recall them long after hearing a speech. In the following example, Newton Minow concludes his speech with a story told by President John Kennedy. Minow's theme is that the nation urgently needs to define the public interest of children in the electronic age.

President Kennedy told a story a week before he was killed, a story I have never forgotten. The story was about French Marshal Lyautey, who walked one morning through his garden with his gardener. He stopped at a certain point and asked the gardener to plant a tree there the next morning. The gardener said, "But the tree will not bloom for one hundred years." The Marshal looked at the gardener and replied, "In that case, you had better plant it this afternoon."[8]

Inspire or Challenge   These methods are often used to conclude persuasive presentations. A motivational speaker, for example, may wish to conclude by exhorting the audience to take the high ground by striving for the moral, ideal, or noble path. These types of endings often use uplifting quotes. In the following example, former President Ronald Reagan closed his address to the 1992 Republican Convention with the following words of inspiration:

My fondest hope for each one of you—and especially for the young people here—is that you will love your country, not for her power or wealth, but for her selflessness and her idealism. May each of you have the heart to conceive, the understanding to direct, and the hand to execute works that will make the world a little better for your having been here.

May all of you as Americans never forget your heroic origins, never fail to seek divine guidance, and never lose your natural, God-given optimism.

And finally, my fellow Americans, may every dawn be a great new beginning for America and every evening bring us closer to that shining city upon a hill.[9]

In some presentations a speaker's solution or answer to a problem may require great effort, patience, and perseverance. AIDS, child abuse, and civil rights are great challenges that will not be solved overnight. A speaker may call upon an audience to meet these great challenges. In the following example, Marian Wright Edelman uses a story to inspire and challenge the audience:

My role model, Sojourner Truth, an illiterate slave woman, hated slavery and second-class treatment of women and never lost an opportunity to speak out for justice. One day when she was speaking out against slavery she got heckled by a man who said, "Old slave woman, I don't care any more for your old anti-slavery talk than for an old flea bite." She snapped back: "That's alright, Lord willing, I'm going to keep you scratching." Don't try to be a big dog to bring about big changes, although the Lord knows we need them right now. Just decide to be a flea against injustice, against racism, against poverty, against dishonesty and corruption in your own life, in your home, corporation, law firm, or medical practice.[10]

Demonstrate Concrete Results

An effective way of closing a speech is to show an audience how your presentation helps them achieve personal objectives. As discussed under "Demonstrate the Relevance of Your Speech," audiences have expectations when they attend speeches. They attended your speech to obtain useful information. In your conclusion, show the audience how your speech helps them. If your topic was speed reading, for example, show the audience they can now read 800 words a minute instead of 500, a 300-word-per-minute increase. A manager briefing her staff on a new time-management program concludes by showing how the program increases their productivity by 15 percent. In the following example, the speaker tells the audience how the self-defense techniques they have learned in the speech will help them:

It is sad but true, we must learn to protect ourselves against violent assault and worse. The techniques I outlined for you today can increase your chances of escape, reduce your chances of serious injury, and maybe even save your life. The next time you have to study late, walk to your car unescorted at night, or walk to your dorm, you have two self-defense techniques that can help you in an emergency.

Demonstrating concrete results gives the audience a sense of satisfaction. They leave the speech motivated. They have received information that is helpful to them. This approach boosts your credibility because you have helped the audience achieve important objectives. It also gives unity to your presentation because you have linked the opening and closing of the speech.

Give the audience a sense of satisfaction in the conclusion.

Make a Request for Action

In a persuasive speech your objective is often to move the audience to action. You want them to vote, reduce fat intake, exercise on a regular basis, or take some other action as a result of your presentation. An important part of this approach is to show the audience how they can accomplish these objectives in a practical and efficient manner. Do not expect the audience to take the action without a plan or some direction from you. Give them the resources and the means to accomplish the action. Here is how one speaker gave the audience specific and easy action steps:

> So if you want to help build housing for the homeless, call 800-HABITAT, or if you want to teach adults or kids to read, call the literacy hotline, 800-228-8813. If you can help in some other way, call the National Volunteer Center at 703-276-0542 or one of their 380 affiliates nearest you.

Suppose your goal is to persuade the audience members to vote. Hand out voter registration forms and have them fill them out on the spot. Give the audience telephone numbers, addresses, and directions to the voting stations. Arrange transportation if necessary. Remove the barriers standing between the audience and the action. When an audience has been persuaded to act, help them take the action.

Tie the Speech Together

The conclusion should give your message a sense of completeness. In business there is a phrase, "closing the loop." What it means is tying all the loose ends together. The same is true of a speech.

Many of the methods of concluding a speech discussed above can help tie a speech together, such as a memorable quote focusing on the central idea. Another technique is to close by alluding to information discussed in the introduction. This completion is often referred to as "a wrap-up." In a speech about unnecessary surgery, the speaker opened with a story of a woman whose doctor recommended removal of her uterus. She had been diagnosed as having tumors and a cyst and was told that immediate surgery was required. In the conclusion the speaker returns to that example, as follows:

Specific purpose:	Second opinions should be mandatory before elective surgery.
Central idea:	Second opinions reduce unnecessary surgery.
Wrap-up:	At the outset of my speech, I mentioned the case of Susie Wilson, whose doctor told her she must have her uterus removed because of a cyst. Susie's union had a group-insurance policy that included a second-opinion plan. Her second opinion was worth it—that cyst turned out to be a baby!

SAMPLE CONCLUSION

In the following example, the speaker closes with a plea that includes a quotation.

Specific purpose:	To persuade the audience that wildlife must be protected.
Central idea:	Wildlife is becoming extinct.

Conclusion

Before I close, let me summarize some figures on this crisis. The California grizzly is extinct; the last sighting was in 1933. The New Mexico grizzly has been extinct since 1950. The cheetah, one of the fastest animals on earth, numbers less than 100. The California condor, which used to roam over the western United States, is confined to two small breeding areas, the size of two small towns. All the whales are endangered. I could go on but let me leave you with a quote from *The Politics of Extinction:*

> Never before in recorded history have the world's wild animals faced such a desperate crisis. We are now at the point in time when the destiny of numerous species is being determined. Our generation will decide which animals live on and which die out. The decisions we make during this period will determine not only the fate of the world's wild animals, but perhaps, ultimately our own as well.

SUMMARY

The role of the introduction is to focus the audience's attention in preparation for the body of the speech and to establish a positive professional relationship between the audience and the speaker. The goals when creating an introduction are to grab the audience's attention, establish rapport with the audience, show the relevance of your topic, establish credibility, and prepare the audience for the body of the speech. Possible ways to capture the attention of the audience are to make a startling statement, tell a joke, make a provocative statement, use an interesting quote, tell a story, or ask a rhetorical question. Your concluding remarks should solidify your goals and reinforce the major ideas of your speech. Good ideas for conclusions are summarizing the main points of an informative speech, showing concrete results of the process which you have described, calling the audience into action, or just tying any and all loose ends together.

PROBES

1 Briefly explain the objectives of the introduction.
2 Briefly describe five parts of an introduction.
3 Briefly describe five ways of getting the attention of the audience.
4 Describe three ways of preparing the audience for the body of the speech.
5 Briefly explain the objectives of the conclusion.
6 Describe four types of conclusions.
7 Briefly describe the idea of common ground.

APPLICATIONS

1 For each of the following subjects, create a method for getting the attention of the audience: (a) Preventing AIDS. (b) Date rape. (c) Applying first aid to a wound. (d) Joining the Peace Corps.
2 What kinds of conclusions could you use for each of the following topics? (a) Preventing child abuse. (b) Learning to use a computer. (c) Supporting affirmative action. (d) How to improve memory.

3 Read some issues of *Vital Speeches* and see how the speakers opened and closed their speeches. Describe three methods used.

NOTES

1 Sheldon Hackney, "Lasting Values in a Disposable World," *The Commonwealth,* Vol. 89, May 15, 1995, p. 1.

2 Maggie Kuhn, "Keynote Address at the Conference on Conscious Aging," in Victoria L. DeFrancisco and Marvin D. Jensen, *Women's Voices In Our Time,* (Prospect Heights, IL: Waveland Press, 1994), p. 233.

3 William S. Sessions, "Fundamental Changes in the Legal System: Professional Priorities," *Vital Speeches,* Vol. 58, January 15, 1992, p. 197.

4 Julie Packard, "An Airbreathers's View of the Water Planet: How Our Future Is Linked to the Sea," *The Commonwealth,* Vol. 89, May 29, 1995, p. 1.

5 Don M. Bludin, "Help Wanted, Crisis in the Work Force," *Vital Speeches,* November 9, 1991, p. 281.

6 Bill Gates, "The Business and Social Impact of the Electronic Highway," *The Commonwealth,* Vol. 45, November 8, 1993, p 634.

7 Story related by Paul Erdman in video *Persuasive Speaking,* Esquire Inc. Video, 60 minutes, 1985.

8 Newton Minow, "The Communications Act," *Vital Speeches,* Vol. 61, April 15, 1995, p. 392.

9 Speech before the Republican Convention, August 8, 1992. Transcribed from videotape recording.

10 Marian Wright Edelman, "The Measure of Our Success," *The Commonwealth,* Vol. 44, October 9, 1992, p. 656.

10

OUTLINING YOUR SPEECH

CHAPTER OUTLINE

SELECT AN OUTLINE FORM
  Key-Word and Short-Phrase Outline
  Complete-Sentence Outline

COMPLETE THE BODY OF THE SPEECH
  Select the Subpoints
  Use Standard Outline Form
  Label the Preview, Transitions, and Summaries

COMPLETE THE INTRODUCTION AND CONCLUSION
  Label Each Part of the Introduction
  Label Each Part of the Conclusion

SUPPLY THE FINISHING TOUCHES

SAMPLE OUTLINE: PUTTING IT ALL TOGETHER
  Outline Option: A Storyboard

USING SPEAKING NOTES
  Outline Variations
  Note Cards
  Post-it™ Notes
  Tips for Using Notes

Now is the time to put the parts of your speech together into a complete outline and speaking notes. All good speakers follow a plan, and you should have one as well.

The outline is a picture of your speech. An artist sketches a portrait before painting it. It helps the artist see how the images fit together and to revise if necessary. Outlining performs the same function for you. It helps you manage information for the greatest impact. Suppose you had a special quote you wanted to use in the speech. Where should you put it in the speech? The introduction? Body? Or conclusion? A carefully constructed outline could help determine where to place the quote to maximize impact.

The outline helps you revise easily because you can move information around as well as add and delete content. If you had a topical outline, what main points should go first? A trial outline could help you answer that question. Last, a good outline gives you confidence because you can see your ideas on paper and you have a solid plan to follow.

Outlining should not be seen as a laborious task. Making the "portrait" of your speech can be a fun experience. You may even get some grease on your clothes. Outlining is a four-step process: (1) selecting an outline form, (2) filling in the body of the speech, (3) completing the organization and conclusion, and (4) supplying the finishing touches. Preparing speaking notes is the final step before rehearsal.

SELECT AN OUTLINE FORM

Every speaker has her or his own style of outlining a speech, and as you gain experience your style will emerge. Charles Osgood, radio commentator, writer, and frequent public speaker, likes to use a single note card with key words so he can look at the audience as he speaks. Some speakers may use an outline made up of key words or phrases, while others may use a complete sentence outline to trigger their ideas. Let's discuss both styles.

Key-Word and Short-Phrase Outline

When you use this approach, you condense ideas into key words and phrases. In the following example, the speaker uses this approach to outline a speech about heart disease:

Specific purpose:	Take care of your heart.
Central idea:	You can live a long and healthy life if you take care of your heart.

Body

I Heart disease
  A Deaths
    1 1 million yearly
    2 46% of deaths yearly
    3 50% fatalities
  B Victims
    1 1 of 3 men
    2 1 of 10 women
    3 12-year-old children
  C Disabilities
    1 33% partial
    2 19% permanent
  D Costs
    1 36% total medical costs
    2 Highest insurance costs
  E Causes
    1 Diet
    2 Smoking
    3 Drinking
    4 Drugs

The main points and supporting information are stated as words and short phrases. Now let's discuss the complete-sentence outline.

Complete-Sentence Outline

The speaker lists the main points and subpoints in short, complete sentences as previously discussed in Chapter 6, under "Refining the Main Points." This is the recommended approach for beginning speakers because it sharpens your thinking and crystallizes your ideas. Edit the main points until the ideas are razor sharp. Here is an example of a complete-sentence outline.

Specific purpose: To persuade the audience to take care of their hearts.

Central idea: You can live a long and healthy life if you take care of your heart.

Body

I Heart disease is America's most serious illness.
  A Heart attacks kill; most fatal disease.
    1 Heart attacks kill 1 million Americans per year.
    2 Heart attacks account for 46% of all deaths.
    3 50% of all heart attacks are fatal.

B Many people suffer heart disease.
    1 One in three men have heart disease before sixty.
    2 One in ten women have heart disease before sixty.
    3 Children as young as twelve years suffer from heart disease.
C Many heart attack victims are disabled.
    1 33% of victims become functionally disabled.
    2 19% of victims suffer permanent disability.
D Heart-disease costs are staggering.
    1 36% of all medical costs caused by heart disease.
    2 Skyrocketing health costs caused by heart disease.
E Heart disease caused by variety of factors.
    1 High-cholesterol diet causes fatty deposits.
    2 Smokers have 74% incidence of heart attack.
    3 Heavy drinkers have 50% risk of heart attack.
    4 Drug abuse greatly increases risks.

Take a moment to compare the key-word and short-phrase outline with the complete-sentence outline.

After you have selected the outline form, the next step is to fill in the body of the speech.

COMPLETE THE BODY OF THE SPEECH

The body is a crucial part of your speech because it contains your main ideas and supporting information. You want them to stand out and sparkle. Three steps can help you achieve this goal: (1) select the subpoints that will support the main points, (2) use standard outline form to distinguish between main points and supporting material, and (3) label the preview, transitions, and summaries.

Select the Subpoints

Subpoints are statements that support the main points. They may be supporting material—such as examples, statistics, or testimony—that directly support the main point. Or they may divide the main points into subideas that are in turn supported by supporting material. The former approach is frequent with complex subjects. In the following example, the speaker uses statistics to directly support a main point:

Specific purpose: To persuade the audience to protect themselves from sunlight.

Central idea: Unprotected exposure is harmful.

I Skin cancer is a serious problem.
   A 600,000 cases reported each year.
   B One in six Americans get skin cancer.
   C One of every three people in this audience will get skin cancer.
   D One of three fair-skinned people get skin cancer.

When a topic is complex, main points may need to be broken down into subpoints or subideas to help the audience better understand them. In the following example, the main point is divided into subideas so it can be easily understood.

Specific purpose: To persuade the audience that stronger gun control laws are needed.

Central idea: Stricter gun laws will reduce deaths and injuries caused by guns.

I The extent of gun ownership is staggering—and dangerous.
   A Americans own a vast arsenal of weapons.
      1 Americans own 60 million handguns.
      2 Americans own 140 million rifles.
      3 Americans own 1 million assault rifles.
   B Gun ownership is lethal.
      1 Firearms are used in 13,000 murders.
      2 Firearms are used in 15,000 suicides.
      3 Firearms account for 3,500 accidental deaths.
      4 Guns are used in 175,000 assaults.

The main point, "The extent of gun ownership is staggering—and dangerous," is divided into two subpoints: **A** "Americans own a vast arsenal of weapons" and **B** "Gun ownership is lethal." They in turn are backed up by concrete supporting material to prove and clarify them. The main point will be clearer and more persuasive because the audience understands the thinking behind the assertion.

When to divide a topic into subideas is sometimes difficult to determine. The broadness of your topic is one indicator, and the statement of the main point, another. In the above example, to defend the first main point, "**I** The extent of gun ownership is staggering—and dangerous," the speaker had two points to prove, that gun ownership is widespread and that it is dangerous. If the main point suggests two ideas, then you probably need to divide it into subideas.

In an oral presentation, limit your outline to a maximum of three levels of support: main point, subpoint, and concrete supporting information. More levels make a speech difficult to understand because ideas become buried in details. If the speech has complex information that you feel is important, but would take you to a fourth level, put it on a handout and pass it out after the speech.

Use Standard Outline Form

Use a consistent pattern of Roman numerals I, II, III; capital letters A, B, C; and arabic numbers 1, 2, 3 to signify your main points and their logical divisions. This outline form has a hierarchical structure with the Roman numerals representing the highest level. Indent as you develop each level so you can visualize the relationship. Remember, an outline is a visual representation of your thinking process. The point here is not to be academic but to help you think logically. The following example shows a standard subdivision sequence:

I Main point
  A Subidea
    1 Concrete supporting material (tell, show, do)
    2 Concrete supporting material (tell, show, do)
  B Subidea
    1 Concrete supporting material (tell, show, do)
    2 Concrete supporting material (tell, show, do)
II Main point
  A Subidea
    1 Concrete supporting material (tell, show, do)
    2 Concrete supporting material (tell, show, do)
  B Subidea
    1 Concrete supporting material (tell, show, do)
    2 Concrete supporting material (tell, show, do)

Keep in mind the "2 × 2 rule." Outlines should be divided into a *minimum* of two main points with two supporting statements. This helps ensure that your ideas are developed logically and completely.

Label the Preview, Transitions, and Summaries

As we discussed in Chapter 6 under "Focus on the Main Points in the Speech," highlight the main points and major divisions of the speech using a preview, transitions, and summaries. The preview is placed between the introduction and the body of the speech. Transitions can be placed between subpoints and between main points. Summaries may be used between main points. (See Figure 6.1, Chapter 6.)

COMPLETE THE INTRODUCTION AND CONCLUSION

After you finish outlining the body of the speech, outline the opening and closing. Label each step of the introduction and conclusion so each part stands out, as well as your strategy. Let's discuss how to do these important parts of the outline.

Label Each Part of the Introduction   Label each part of the introduction you plan to use in your speech. State the content in concise sentences. If your attention step is a story, briefly summarize it in a sentence or two. If it is a humorous story, write down the punchline. Don't write out the entire content. Use the same approach for other parts of the introduction. If you have a series of steps, outline them. Write the specific purpose and central idea in complete sentences. Use capital letters to identify each part of the introduction, such as "A" for "attention" material, "B" for "rapport," "C" for "relevance," and so forth. The main points are the most important parts of your outline and the Roman numerals should be reserved for them. Here is an example of an outline for an introduction:

Introduction

A *Attention material:* Describe a person having a heart attack. This happens 2,800 times a day.

B *Relevancy statement:* Heart disease is a major cause of death. One of four people in this audience is in some stage of heart disease.

C *Orientation material:* The heart is a continuously pumping muscle. Heart disease restricts or blocks blood flowing to the heart.

D *Specific purpose:* To persuade the audience to take care of their hearts.

E *Central idea:* You will live a long and healthy life if you take care of your heart.

Label Each Part of the Conclusion

Label each part of the conclusion as you did in the introduction. If you plan to use a story, write the moral or a brief summary statement. If you summarize, list the steps in a brief outline form. Use concise sentences to capture the ideas for each part. Use capital letters A, B, C to label the parts of the outline. Here is an example of an outline for a conclusion:

Specific purpose:	To persuade the audience to take care of their hearts.
Central idea:	You will live a long and healthy life if you take care of your heart.

Conclusion

A *Summary:* Reducing the fat in your diet, not smoking, using alcohol in moderation, and not using drugs decreases your chances of having heart disease.

B *Benefits:* You will live longer, feel better, and have more energy.

C *Handout:* "How to Make Your Heart Last a Lifetime."

SUPPLY THE FINISHING TOUCHES

After outlining the body of the speech and the introduction and conclusion, apply the final details: title, statement of general purpose, bibliography, and learning objective.

Title   Supply a title if necessary. If you use one, it should be catchy and get the attention of the audience. Instead of saying "Tanning Can Be Dangerous," say "Death by Tanning." More dramatic, greater impact. Here are some other examples:

Donate Organs: Two Hearts Are Better Than One
Wilderness Areas: Rocky Mountain High
Safe Sex: Life and Death
Pollution: Trashing the Planet

General Purpose   If you need to state the general purpose, you can list it above the specific purpose in the introduction or above and to the left of the introduction.

Bibliography   If appropriate, list your sources at the end of the outline, following the conclusion. See Chapter 5, under "Preparing Bibliography Cards," for proper bibliographic form.

Learning Objective   Write out your learning objective for the speech at the end of the outline. Limit to one or two; more than two will overload you.

SAMPLE OUTLINE: PUTTING IT ALL TOGETHER

Let's put all the pieces together and see what a complete sentence outline looks like for the topic on heart disease. *(Example used with the permission of Paul Johnson.)*

Take Heart

General purpose: To persuade.

Specific purpose: To persuade the audience to take care of their hearts.

Central idea: You will live a long and healthy life if you take care of your heart.

Introduction

A *Attention material:* Describe person having heart attack. It happens 2,800 times a day.

B *Relevancy material:* Heart disease is a major cause of death. One in four members of this audience are in some stage of heart disease.

C *Orientation material:* The heart is a continuously pumping muscle. Heart disease restricts or blocks flow of blood to the heart. *(Transition)*

D *Specific purpose:* To persuade audience to take care of their hearts.

E *Central idea:* You will live a long and healthy life if you take care of your heart. *(Transition)*

Preview: **I** Problem: Heart disease is America's most serious illness.

II Solution: Take care of your heart. *(Transition)*

Body

I Heart disease is America's most serious illness.
  A Heart attacks most fatal illness.
    1 Heart attacks kill 1 million people per year.
    2 46% of all deaths nationwide from heart attacks.
    3 50% of all heart attacks fatal.
  B Many people have heart disease.
    1 One in three men has a heart attack before 60.
    2 One in ten women has a heart attack before 60.
    3 Children as young as twelve have heart attacks.
  C Many heart attack victims become disabled.
    1 33% of victims become functionally disabled.
    2 19% of victims suffer permanent disability. *(Summary) (Transition)*
  D Heart-disease costs are staggering.
    1 36% of all health care costs.
    2 Causing skyrocketing insurance costs.
  E Heart disease caused by a variety of factors.
    1 High-cholesterol diet creates fatty deposits.
    2 Smokers have 74% chance of heart attack.
    3 Heavy drinkers have 50% chance of heart attack.
    4 Drug abuse greatly increases risk. *(Summary) (Transition)*
II Take care of your heart.
  A Change your lifestyle.
    1 Limit intake of high-cholesterol food.
    2 Stop smoking/don't start.
    3 Say no to drugs.
    4 Reduce intake of alcohol. *(Summary) (Transition)*
  B Action plan to follow.
    1 Eat a well-balanced diet.
    2 Keep your cholesterol below 250.
    3 Have annual physical checkup.
    4 Exercise on a regular basis. *(Transition)*

Conclusion

A Summary:

    1 Junk food, alcohol, and drugs increase your chances of getting heart disease.

    2 If you follow my plan you will live longer, feel better, and have a more energetic life.

B Handout: "How to Make Your Heart Last a Lifetime."

Learning objective:	To improve my eye contact and present the main points so they stand out and the audience can follow them easily.

Bibliography

Jane E. Brophy, "Many People Are Learning to Lower Their Cholesterol by Changing Their Patterns of Eating and Exercise," *The New York Times,* January 3, 1996, p. B7.

Bonnie Liebman, "Heart Disease: How to Lower Your Risk," *Nutrition Action Healthletter,* Vol. 22, October, 1995, pp. 1–5.

Anonymous, "Cholesterol Reduction: How Does it Help," *Harvard Heart Letter,* Vol. 6, February 23, 1995, p. 3.

Anonymous, "Averting Coronary Death," *Consumer Reports on Health,* December, 1995, Vol. 7, p. 142.

Outline Option: A Storyboard

You have another option: to create an outline in storyboard form. When you use this method, you combine the written outline with a column on the right side of the paper on which you make drawings of the visuals you will use in support as well as delivery cues, transitions, and so forth (Figure 10-1). Movie directors use storyboards so they can visualize a movie before they begin shooting it. In the same way, a storyboard helps you visualize your speech before preparing your speaking notes. You can see how the verbal content integrates with the visuals and other parts of the speech. You get the big picture.

USING SPEAKING NOTES

Your outline can be adapted in any number of creative ways into speaking notes. You may use variations of the outline or you can transcribe the points of the outline onto note cards. Whatever method you use, you want it to be compatible with your speaking style. Speaking notes should enhance your delivery, not stifle it. If you move around while speaking, note cards may work best because they are small, easy to hold, and easy to manage. An $8\frac{1}{2} \times 11$

I. **Main point: Heart disease is America's most serious illness.**

Supporting material:	Visual material:

A. Heart attacks most fatal illness.
  1. Heart attacks kill 1 million people annually.
  2. 46% of all deaths caused by heart attack.
  3. 50% of all heart attacks fatal.
 	
B. Many people have heart disease.
  1. 1 of 3 men have heart disease.
  2. 1 of 10 women have heart disease.
  3. 12-year-old children have heart attacks.
 	
C. Many heart attack victims disabled.
  1. 33% of victims functionally disabled.
  2. 19% of victims suffer permanent disability.
	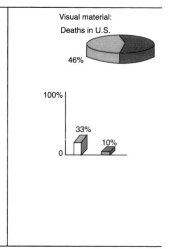

Summary: Heart disease major cause of death in America and leaves people disabled.
Transition: Now, let's look at some of the costs of heart disease.

FIGURE 10-1
Storyboard outline.

sheet of paper may flap around and be hard to manage. However, if you are standing behind a podium, an 8½ × 11 sheet of paper may work just fine. Whatever method you use, rehearse thoroughly so your delivery is relaxed and natural. Let's discuss some options for using speaking notes.

Outline Variations

Outline the speech on standard 8½ × 11 paper. If you have a PC, you can enlarge the type and darken the labels for the main points and any key words or phrases or other parts of the outline (Figure 10-2). You could use a highlighter to further reinforce the main ideas and key words. If you don't have a PC, you might type or write out or print your outline very neatly. Color-code the introduction, body, and conclusion or draw a color band on the left-hand margin for each section or draw colored lines between each section. You should color-code the transitions and summaries as well. Write the outline on the upper half of the paper so you don't have to look down so far that you lose eye contact with the audience. If you have more than one page, do not staple them together. You want to be able to shuffle one page unobtrusively under the other or place it to the side. If you are speaking outdoors, have some means of anchoring the papers so that they can't blow away.

Using notes is a popular way of delivering a speech.

FIGURE 10-2
Sample outline using a PC.

I. **HEART DISEASE IS AMERICA'S MOST SERIOUS ILLNESS.**
   A. *Heart attacks most fatal illness.*
      1. Heart attacks kill **1,000,000** people per year.
      2. **46%** of all deaths nationwide from heart attacks.
      3. 50% of all heart attacks fatal.
   B. *Many people have heart disease.*
      1. One in three men have heart attack before 60.
      2. One in ten women have heart attack before 60.
      3. Children as young as twelve have heart attacks.
   C. *Many heart attack victims become disabled.*
      1. **33%** of victims functionally disabled.
      2. **19%** of victims suffer permanent disability.
                    Summary and **Transition**

Note Cards

Note cards are very popular (Figure 10-3). Ronald Reagan used 3×5 cards extensively. They are small enough to be handled easily under most conditions and are unobtrusive. You would use one card for each major part of the speech: introduction, conclusion, and each main point with its supporting information. You can color-code each part of the speech using the traffic system: green cards for the opening, yellow cards for the body, and red cards for the ending. You can enlarge the lettering and color to highlight key ideas and facts. You can write cues for pauses, visuals, demonstrations, or other points of emphasis for content or delivery. Use a rubber band and/or paper clip to keep them in order until you speak. Number the cards in case you mix them up.

End each card with a transition and summary so the shuffling of the cards is in concert with a new point.

Post-it™ Notes

You can use Post-it™ Notes to create speaking notes. Write the main points on $2\frac{1}{2} \times 2\frac{1}{2}$ Post-it™ Notes and stick them side by side on an $8\frac{1}{2} \times 11$ sheet. Write the supporting information on separate Post-it™ Notes and place them underneath (Figure 10-4). With one quick glance you see the whole speech. You could use notes of different colors for the main points and supporting information. You could write the introduction and conclusion as well as the transitions and summaries on Post-it™ Notes. As you finish delivering each part of the speech, you can lift that Post-it™ Note off the page.

FIGURE 10-3
Sample note card.

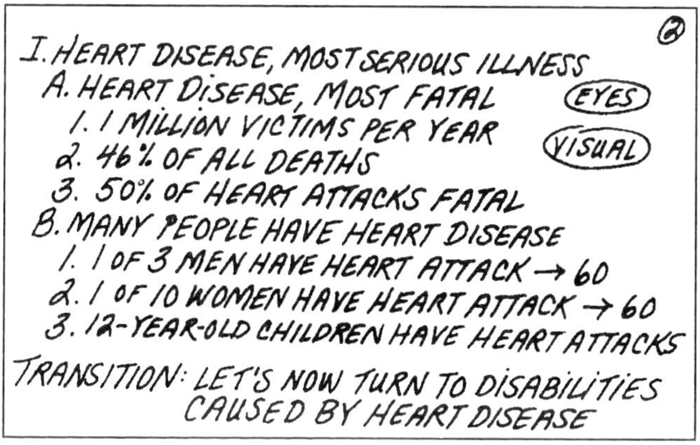

> I. Heart disease is
> America's most serious
> illness.
>
> (Eyes)

> II. Take care of your
> heart.
>
> (Eyes)

> A. Heart disease most serious
>   illness.
> 1. 1 million deaths per year.
> 2. 46% of all deaths. (Eyes)
> 3. 50% of all attacks fatal.
>
> (Visual)

> A. Change your lifestyle
>   1. Limit fat intake. (Chart)
>   2. Stop smoking/don't start.
>   3. Say no to drugs.
>   4. Reduce alcohol intake.
>
> Summary:
> Transition:

FIGURE 10-4
Post-it™ notes sample outline.

Tips for Using Notes

As you put your speaking notes together, you should follow certain guidelines. Here are some tips:

1 Maintain the logical divisions of the outline. Use the appropriate symbols: Roman numerals, capital letters, and arabic numbers. Indent. Use colors to highlight the different parts of the outline.

2 Don't clutter the outline. Keep it simple. A quick glance at the page or card should be all you need to get the ideas you need.

3 Give yourself delivery cues. If your learning objective is to improve your eye contact, write it periodically on the speaking outline. Or if you plan to use pauses, write "pause" where you want to use them.

4 Rehearse with your notes until you are comfortable and can speak naturally with them.

SUMMARY

The process of outlining your speech begins with selecting the outline form: key words and phrases or concise sentences. The next step is to complete the body of the speech by adding the subpoints, using standard subdivisions, and labeling the preview, transitions, and summaries. Complete the introduction and conclusion. Supply the finishing touches. Convert the outline to speaking notes by using a full-page outline, note cards, or Post-it™ Notes.

PROBES

1 Why is it important to outline your speech?

2 Identify two types of outline forms.

3 What are subpoints? How do they work to support main points?

4 Why do you want to avoid going beyond three levels of development for main points in a speech?

5 Why do you want to use a consistent set of symbols when outlining?

6 Describe three types of speaking notes. What are the advantages and disadvantages of using each?

7 What guidelines should you follow when preparing speaking notes?

APPLICATIONS

1 Prepare your speaking notes using one of the methods used in the book.

2 Select a speech in *Vital Speeches* and outline it. Use the outline of "Take Heart" shown in this chapter as a guide. Give special attention to how the speaker used subpoints to support the main points.

3 Identify the main point and subpoints in the following excerpt.

Drug abuse is causing serious health problems in the country. Tuberculosis is on the rise in many cities, venereal disease is increasing, and half the admissions to many city hospital emergency rooms are drug related, such as OD's and shootings. Nearly a third of all AIDS cases are the result of intravenous drug use, at a cost of billions of dollars. And how do you measure the cost of crack-addicted newborns, or the impact on society as these retarded and psychologically disturbed children enter our schools and communities?

PRESENTING THE SPEECH

11

USING LANGUAGE EFFECTIVELY IN PUBLIC SPEAKING

CHAPTER OUTLINE

THE IMPORTANCE OF LANGUAGE

IMPROVING YOUR LANGUAGE SKILLS

    Be Clear

    Be Specific

    Be Vivid

    Be Appropriate

ELIMINATE CLUTTER

USE PERSONAL LANGUAGE

A FINAL NOTE ABOUT USING LANGUAGE EFFECTIVELY

The movie *Let Him Have It* tells the story of two young gangsters confronted by the police during an attempted burglary. One of the burglars, a cunning and vicious hoodlum, pulls a revolver and threatens to shoot the police. His companion, a timid and slightly retarded teenager, surrenders and screams out "Let him have it!" The vicious young gunman opens fire, killing one police officer and wounding another.

At his trial, the fate of the timid youth rests on how the jury interprets "Let him have it." Was he telling his friend to shoot the police or to lay down his weapon before anyone got hurt? The jury believed the former. He was convicted and hanged. The moral of the story is say what you mean or pay the consequences.

THE IMPORTANCE OF LANGUAGE

Using language effectively is a key to successful communication. Like your delivery style, your language should be natural and concise. The goal of public speaking is to communicate ideas clearly and concretely to an audience. Language is the primary vehicle to achieve that goal. Fancy delivery style and glittering visuals cannot save ideas that are confusingly, vaguely, or abstractly stated. Fredrick Beuchner describes the importance of language this way:

> Words have color, depth, texture of their own, and power to evoke vastly more than they mean; words can be used to make things clear, make things vivid, make things interesting, and make things happen inside the one who reads them or hears them.[1]

Using language effectively is persuasive and gives audiences confidence. When audiences understand ideas, they are more inclined to accept them. In 1933, panicked depositors began a frantic run on American banks, a move that would destroy the banking system and further erode a depression-racked economy. President Franklin Roosevelt went on nationwide radio and announced a four-day "bank holiday" to prevent frightened depositors from withdrawing their funds. In his speech he calmly and clearly explained how the banking system worked and why it was necessary to take the radical action. He gained the public's support because they understood what he was doing and why he was doing it. Other leaders who have used language skillfully were John F. Kennedy, Martin Luther King, Jr., and Ronald Reagan.

Language also tells an audience about the inner person. Your language is your signature and reveals much about your character, values, attitudes, knowledge, and motivation (Figure 11-1). Speakers who talk around an idea may be revealing a lack of knowledge. Unnatural language may mean the speaker is attempting to inflate an image or lacks confidence in his grasp of the topic. A politician who evades a question is probably concealing her real position. A person who uses language poorly may be revealing a lack of education. Your language tells who you are. In this chapter we will discuss how to use language effectively in public speaking.

IMPROVING YOUR LANGUAGE SKILLS

Using language effectively means using words that convey your meaning—that create the correct meaning in the minds of the audience. It means selecting words that are clear and concrete and appropriate to the audience. This is

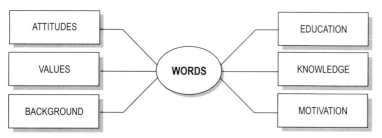

FIGURE 11-1
Your language reveals your character.

challenging because no two people have the same exact definition of a word. When you speak, people will understand what you say in the context of their own experience. They filter your words through their beliefs, knowledge, education, and motivations and then give them meaning. If you say without further clarification that you want to create a "learning organization," each member of the audience may have a different understanding of the concept. Using language effectively means creating a common understanding.

Six important language skills are (1) being clear, (2) being specific, (3) being vivid, (4) being appropriate, (5) eliminating clutter, and (6) being personal.

Be Clear

Being clear means using language the audience immediately understands. Unfamiliar words, technical words, and jargon stop communication. The audience doesn't have the knowledge or experience to understand your language. This creates frustration, and audiences tune out and may even become angry, especially if the speech is one that contains information necessary to their performance and productivity. Suppose you're trying to learn how to operate a personal computer or some new software and the instructor uses technical words unknown to you and doesn't explain or define them. You become frustrated because you are unable to understand the information.

You might think of yourself as a translator who is carefully converting meaning from one language to another. Choose your words carefully and keep them simple. Don't use "putrescence" when "decay" is clear or "proletariat" when "lower classes" will suffice. Study the following example:

Unclear: Meteorologically, the remainder of this 24-hour period should eventuate in acceptable, even above-average levels barring any unforeseen precipitation.

Clear: We should have nice weather tomorrow.

The first statement sounds like a complex mathematical formula and would take a lot of effort to understand, if you could understand it at all. The second statement is clear and direct. In the following example, the speaker strips away complexities and, using clear and simple language, describes the career criminal as:

> typically an impulsive young man who grew up in a discordant family where one or both parents had a criminal record, discipline was erratic, and human relations were cold and unpredictable. He had a low IQ and poor verbal skills. His behavior problems appeared early, often by age eight, and included dishonesty and aggressiveness. Even in kindergarten or first grade he was disruptive, defiant, and badly behaved. He had few friends and was not emotionally close to those associates with whom he began stealing and assaulting.[2]

The speaker used simple and clear language to describe the typical career criminal.

Ask yourself: "Are there any words or sentences in this speech the audience will have difficulty understanding?" This question is especially relevant if your topic is technical or involves complex processes or concepts. List them. Consult a dictionary for a clear definition. If it's a technical word, consult one of the many specialized dictionaries for a clear definition. A thesaurus can help you find a synonym that simplifies a complex term. Use comparison and contrast to clarify your meaning. Here is an example of a speaker using this technique to describe the composition of a microchip:

> The chip is made of silicon, which next to oxygen, is the earth's most abundant element. Silicon is what most of us spend a lot of time on during the summer—beach sand. Silicon is ideal for making microchips because it can be electrically charged; that is, it can carry electrical power just like a cord carries power to the lamp from the outlet. The sand is melted and molded into sausage-shaped crystals about five inches in diameter and is sliced into razor-thin wafers, like tiny slices of bread. Each wafer is then diced into hundreds of tiny squares, or chips, that become the heart of the computer operation.

The speaker used vivid comparisons and analogies—"beach sand," "lamp cord," "sausage-shaped," "razor-thin," "slices of bread"—to describe a complex process.

In the following exercise, substitute a simpler word for each of those listed:

Utilization
Optimization
Enhancement
Cognizant
Enumerate
Magnitude

Necessitate
Promulgate
Procedurally

Be Specific

Senator Howard Baker, a member of the Senate Judiciary Committee during the Watergate investigation, gained notoriety when he pinpointed the issue of President Nixon's guilt and innocence in one concise sentence: "What did he know and when did he know it?" That one statement summed up the thousands of hours of testimony and volumes of evidence that had left the nation confused and uncertain.

Words may be connotative or denotative—that is, general or specific. Connotative words are general or abstract words that have subjective meanings, such as "freedom," "homeless," "human rights," and "justice." They rely on the subjective association of the listener for meaning.

Denotative words are specific and refer directly to objects or processes—for example, "gummy bears," "apple," "laptop computer," or "bungee jumping." Proper names such as "Bill" and "Mary" and technical words such as "spectrophotometer" and "amniocentesis" fall into this category. A football coach sending in plays from the sideline uses specific language so the play is executed precisely by all eleven players. Specific words have a clear and standard meaning. This is the kind of language you should principally use in public speaking.

Specific words give your language the kind of detail that pinpoints meaning. By using them, you make sure that there will be no misunderstanding. Compare the following statements:

John performed well.
John received two A's and one B in his classes.

The first statement is abstract and doesn't tell us what John did well or what "well" means. It is left to our imagination. The second statement is precise and clear. We know what John did well.

Specific words clarify ideas and processes by answering important questions about the topic such as Who? What? When? Where? How? and Why? (Figure 11-2). The answers to these kinds of questions add depth and precision to your language by pinpointing meaning. Suppose you wanted to describe the preflight check of an airplane. You would tell *when* you do it. *What* you do. *Where* you do it. *How* you do it. *Who* does it. And, *why* it is done. Here is an example of how this process works. We begin with the simple statement "I bought some clothes."

Who?   *I* bought some clothes.
When?   *Yesterday,* I bought some clothes.

SPEAKER	LISTENER
"I bought a PC."	"What brand?"
"A MacIntosh."	"When?"
"Yesterday."	"What kind?"
"A laptop."	"For how much?"
"$1,200."	"Where?"
"ABC Discount Store."	"Why?"
"To store my files."	

Why not just say: "Yesterday I bought a MacIntosh laptop at ABC Discount Store for $1,200 to store my files."

FIGURE 11-2
Nonspecific language leads to questions.

What? Yesterday, *I bought a red V-neck cashmere sweater, a navy blue blazer, and a brown gabardine skirt.*

Where? At the *mall.*

How? *Charged it.*

Why? To *attend a special dinner.*

Being specific fills in the important information the audience needs to understand the message. Suppose you said, "Fuel conservation is beneficial." That statement lacks the specific information to give it meaning to the audience; they will understand that the speaker has a positive feeling about something, but not much more. Here is an example of how specific language makes the statement clear to the audience:

Forty-three percent *(what)* of the oil used in the U.S. *(where)* is consumed by automobiles. *(how)* If we raise the fuel efficiency of new cars by just 1.5 mpg, we can save 3.2 billion barrels of oil over a fifteen-year period *(when).* That is equivalent to all the oil estimated to be in the Arctic Refuge *(where)* drilled over a thirty-year period *(when).*

If fuel efficiency *(what)* is raised from 27.5 mpg to 40 mpg *(how)*, oil imports would be reduced by 50 percent *(how much)* and we would save 3.2 billion barrels *(how much)* of oil every two years *(when).*[3]

Naming is another way of using specific language. Use the real names of the objects and ideas you talk about. Instead of saying "that thing on the table," say "the bottle opener," or instead of saying "whatchamacallit on the door," say "my green parka is hanging on the door in the kitchen." Naming gets you in the habit of using specific language. Don't be lazy using language.

Specific language increases the efficiency of your speaking and demonstrates your expertise. Problems are pinpointed, explanations are clear, and major issues and important ideas stand out. Misunderstandings are reduced and needless discussion is avoided. You command respect because specific language shows subject knowledge.

Be Vivid

Sometimes it is necessary to be descriptive and use language that appeals to the senses—sight, hearing, taste, touch, and smell. You want to create a word picture that appeals to the emotions of the audience. You add color, action, and drama to your speech. Suppose you wanted to describe the conditions of children living in tenements. If you say, "Tenements are filthy places to live," the audience may not be moved. But if you say:

> There is excrement, piles of it, left by junkies who have turned the hallways into public toilets. Rats as big as cats move boldly through the mounds of rubbish in the hallway gnawing on trash, waste, and human flesh. In the midst of jagged glass, rancid food, bloodstained hypodermic needles, and the acrid and ever-present stench of urine and feces, little children play hide and seek.

This language puts the audience inside an urban slum—they can visualize it, smell it, feel it. Four important ways you can use descriptive language are (1) using vivid, "sensual" description; (2) using "action" language; (3) using imagery; and (4) using rhythm.

Using Vivid, "Sensual" Description   You can recreate an experience in vivid detail, as the above example demonstrated. You attempt to activate the senses, as the speaker does in the following example describing animal testing:

> The Draize Eye Irritancy Test begins by placing rabbits in stocks so only their heads protrude and to prevent them from dislodging the solution from their eyes with their paws. Then a technician holds their head and drips a caustic substance into their eyes. The pain is so intense the rabbits squeal hysterically as their bodies whip wildly back and forth. Some die from shock. Others from broken necks. Those that survive are recycled for other tests, such as the Dermal Toxicity Test where chemicals are applied to raw open sores or wounds to measure the potency of poisonous substances.

Using "Action" Language   Action scenes in a movie accelerate the tempo and draw the audience deeper into the film. "Active" language produces a similar effect. In the following example, the speaker vividly describes a skier caught in an avalanche.

Use vivid language when you speak.

He pushes off the hill, traversing the snow, looking for a little-used slope. Head bowed against the wind, he slices through the virgin snow and comes to a clearing.

He is startled. He looks behind him. The snow is moving with him. The once serene mountain has become a sea of seething and malignant fury. The snow and wind grab him like a giant wave lifting a surfer, and hurl him into the cascading snow. He helplessly tumbles forward gasping for breath and life.

Suddenly the snow stops. And like a disoriented swimmer struggling to reach the surface, he tries to dig himself out as the snow begins to strangle him with its massive weight.

Count the number of action words used in the excerpt. Here are a few: "pushes," "looking," "bowed," "slices," "startled," "fights," "gasping." Action words give life to description.

Using Imagery   Figures of speech like metaphors and similes work by putting together two things or ideas that are not obviously alike. Saying, for example, that "the federal deficit is a cancer threatening the economy" equates a serious economic problem with a fatal disease. This metaphor is effective because it is a frightening fact that the deficit, if not controlled, could destroy the economy just as cancer destroys the body. An image can convey an idea in clear and colorful language and make the idea memorable. Here are some examples of imagery used in speeches:

America is at war at home.
Words are the bugles of social change.
The schools in our country are a ticking time bomb, threatening to blow up our economy and our way of life.
Too often when people in Washington grapple with major policy issues, it is like watching a train wreck in slow motion.

Authur Miller, professor of law at Harvard Law School, used the metaphor of a boxing match to describe the conflict between the right to privacy and the right to know:

> I'd like to see both of these rights climb into the ring and go through twelve rounds of fast and furious combat. I'd like to see a series of heavy blows, maybe some low blows—that's the American way—to put rights in conflict and let them work out some social accommodation. I'll tell you what I do not want; I don't want to see either the press or privacy get knocked out, because we all lose. What I really want is for these two heavyweight rights that so affect and improve our lives to go through these twelve rounds of fisticuffs, and then I'd like the great referee in the sky to call them both to center ring and declare a draw.[4]

Using Rhythm   You can arrange language to give it a special cadence, somewhat as a songwriter arranges lyrics. The words have a melodic or poetic quality, making them entertaining, inspiring, and memorable. Famous speakers such as Roosevelt, Churchill, King, Kennedy, and Reagan used rhythm regularly in their speeches. Repetition, parallelism, and alliteration are three stylistic devices for creating rhythm in your speeches.

Parallelism   A series of words, phrases, or sentences are arranged in a similar fashion. Here are some examples of parallelism used in speeches:

"We need NEH (National Endowment for the Humanities), among other reasons, because we need more sound reasoning and fewer sound bites, more bold ideas and fewer bold headlines, more informed discussion and less uninformed pandering." *(Sheldon Hackney)*

"Voltaire once said of the Holy Roman Empire that it was neither holy, nor Roman, nor an empire. The same might be said of the Civil Justice System in the United States: that it is neither civil, nor just, nor a system." *(Stephen B. Middlebrook)*

"We were meant to be masters of destiny, not victims of fate." *(Ronald Reagan)*

"Let every nation know, whether it wishes us well or ill, that we shall pay any price, bear any burden, meet any hardship, support any friend, oppose any foe to assure the survival and the success of liberty." *(John F. Kennedy)*

Repetition The speaker repeats the same word at the beginning or end of several sentences or phrases. Here are some examples of repetition used in speeches:

"They have given us false choices, bad choices, and no choice." *(Al Gore)*

"It is now time that we listen and react with a voice so loud that our actions drown out our words.

"It is now time to circle the wagons and fight on the battlefield of excellence, self help, and economic empowerment.

"It is now time to put aside out petty differences, our negative self image, and self hatred, our crab-in-the-barrel mentality and join forces to leverage more effectively our collective resources and intellectual capital.

"It is now time to move from being the victim to being the victor." *(George C. Fraser)*

Alliteration When you use alliteration, you establish a rhythm by repeating the initial sound of adjacent or closely placed words in a sentence. Here are some examples:

"They have demeaned our democracy with the politics of distraction, denial, and despair." *(Al Gore)*

"My constituency is the desperate, the damned, the disinherited, the disrespected, and the despised." *(Jesse Jackson)*

Be Appropriate

Say what you mean, but at the same time avoid language that interferes with your message and reduces your credibility. That doesn't mean speaking in a sanitized or politically correct manner, but it does mean checking your speech to ensure that it matches the audience's expectation of the topic and your ethics. Columnist Chris Matthews was particularly critical of President Bill Clinton's reference to male workers as "them" to a Democratic audience. "This is psychologically a difficult time for them," the president uttered in reference to working males. Matthews went on to say, "Can you imagine Franklin Roosevelt or Harry Truman or Jack Kennedy referring to . . . the men who work and worry and try to provide for their families as 'them'?"[5]

The president was using condescending language and it damaged his credibility. As suggested earlier, language reveals the inner self. Slang, profanity, and pettiness all tell the audience something about you. Let's discuss ways of using language appropriately.

Avoid Profanity Profanity damages your credibility and should be avoided at all costs. If it is part of a quote or used as evidence, then it may be permissible. Most newspapers will not print offensive words, preferring instead to use the first letters followed by spaces—for example, bull - - - -."

Malcolm X gave up profanity when he realized that it took away from the power of his message. He came to that realization in prison when an inmate whom he respected told him that profanity was dishonest and covered up a lack of education. Malcolm X said of this man:

> What fascinated me with him most of all was that he was the first man I had ever seen command total respect . . . with his words. . . . That ended my vicious cursing attacks. My approach sounded so weak alongside his, and he never used a foul word.[6]

Avoid Slang, Clichés, and Worn-Out Words Slang lowers your credibility and the status of your ideas. It is like putting dirty clothes on a clean body. "Humongous," "pissed-off," "screwed up," "you guys," and "that kind of stuff" detract from your message.

Clichés are trite phrases and statements the audience has heard numerous times. Some common clichés include:

Leave no stone unturned
Up the creek without a paddle
Stubborn as a mule
Like a child with a new toy
Cool as a cucumber

Worn-out words are overused or misused words that are nearly meaningless and smack of insincerity and shallowness. They include such words as "very good," "bad," "terrific," "somewhat," "great." President Clinton often uses worn out language when he speaks. In his 1995 State of the Union speech he said, "Let us put aside partisanship." "Our young people hold our future in their hands." "So I'm asking you that we work together." "I want to work together with all of you." "So let's work together on this." These are lifeless words that have no impact.[7] In the following example the speaker uses worn-out language to introduce a speaker:

> I'm really excited to introduce our speaker. He has a fabulous mind. I want to tell you you're going to get fabulous information that will really help you. This stuff is really powerful.

The language is trite and sounds insincere; the person talking sounds like a barker at a sideshow. Just be thankful this person wasn't introducing you.

Avoid Sexist Language Language that denigrates, stereotypes, or implies a second-class status for women should be avoided. Respect means treating people as they desire to be treated, beginning with names. References to a woman as a "gal," "chick," "broad," or "babe" are demeaning. Mix "he" and "she" throughout your speech or use "she/he" such as "A lawyer should present *his or her* case carefully." Or, use the plural and neutral pronoun "their" to describe gender such as "Lawyers should present their cases carefully." Use gender-neutral words such as "firefighter" instead of "fireman"; "chairperson" instead of "chairman"; and "congressperson" instead of "congressman."

ELIMINATE CLUTTER

Former President George Bush, when asked why he refused to support a ban on the sale of semi-automatic rifles, responded:

> I'll take a hard look. But I also want to have—be the President that protects the rights of, of people to, to have arms. And that—so you don't go so far that the legitimate rights on some legislation are, are, you know, impinges on.[8]

If you had problems understanding the president's response, so did a lot of other people. Why? Because it was cluttered.

Speaking concisely and directly to the point is a highly prized skill in the professional world. Streamlined messages are lean, focused, and clear. Important ideas stand out. Business is handled quickly and efficiently. At President Clinton's Economic Summit held in 1992, 300 business and professional leaders from around the country presented their views on the complex economic, environmental, and social issues facing America. Each speaker had fifteen minutes or less to present her or his ideas. The presentations were clear, direct, and to the point. There was little clutter because their points had to be made concisely and precisely.

"Excess baggage" in a speaker's language frustrates and bores audiences and obscures ideas. "Will he please get to the point?" is the question listeners ask. Cluttered language also indicates a lack of knowledge about a topic. In contrast, concise language makes ideas sparkle and listening a pleasure.

Three common types of clutter are redundancy, space fillers, and inflated language.

Redundancies Redundant language needlessly repeats a point. For example, "In my opinion, I think we should drop the plan," could be stated as "Let's drop the plan." Here are some other examples:

Redundant: His speech was brief in duration.

    Concise: His speech was brief.

Redundant: We should reduce the budget down.

    Concise: Let's reduce the budget.

Space Fillers   Often, people use three or four words to make a point when one will do. Look for ways to be concise. For example, a person might say, "We had a discussion about the problem," but could say "We discussed the problem." A seven-word sentence was reduced to four words. Here are some more examples:

Filler:	It is clear that the solution is impractical. *(8 words)*
Concise:	The solution is impractical. *(4 words)*
Filler:	I found it necessary to confer with the union officials with reference to the large number of complaints reported during the time I was away from the office. *(28 words)*
Concise:	I talked to the union about the many complaints made during my absence. *(13 words)*

Inflated Language   You have heard people use high-sounding or seemingly "sophisticated" words to make a point. This type of language is awkward and unnatural and smacks of a speaker trying to impress rather than be clear. Study the following examples. The inflated language obscures meaning. Clear language sparkles.

Inflated:	Ramifications of our performance shortfall included program discontinuation.
Clear:	The program failed and was terminated.
Inflated:	The committee acceded to the demands for additional compensation.
Clear:	The committee paid more.

Make your remarks clear and concise. You will be successful and impress others. One way to develop this skill is to practice shrinking your messages. Take a 2-minute speech, for example. Reduce it to a 30-second message you might leave on a voice-mail system. Then reduce that message to a single newspaper headline. You focus on the idea and conciseness simultaneously, pinpointing the idea and streamlining the message.

USE PERSONAL LANGUAGE

Personalize your language so your speech relates directly to the audience and creates a "we" environment versus an "I" and "you." Banquet speakers, for instance, personalize their speeches by naming the organization they are speaking to, the city they are in, identifying two or three people in the audience, and citing a special achievement of the group. When you refer to important issues, say "our problem" instead of "the problem," "our solution" instead of "the solution," and "your benefits," instead of "the benefits."

Use personal language when you speak.

When selecting examples, choose examples within the experience of the audience. If you're speaking to a group of financial advisors, for instance, use examples from their profession to illustrate points.

Former President Reagan had a special knack for speaking directly and intimately to his audiences. Here is an example of how he personalized his speeches by talking directly to his audience:

> My fellow citizens, those of you in this hall and those of you at home, I want you to know that I have always had the highest respect for you, for your common sense and intelligence and for your decency. I have always believed in you and what you could accomplish for yourselves and for others.
>
> And whatever history may say about me when I'm gone, I hope it will record that I appealed to your best hopes, not your worst fears, to your confidence rather than your doubts. My dream is that you will travel the road ahead with liberty's lamp guiding your steps and opportunity's steadying your way.[9]

A FINAL NOTE ABOUT USING LANGUAGE EFFECTIVELY

Read good writers and listen to good speakers. Read magazines, books, and newspapers that are well written by experts. These writers focus on ideas and reading them will help you think analytically and give you models for communicating information. They will help you become idea-oriented. Pick two or three columnists and read them on a regular basis. Commercial television is not a good source for ideas, reasoned analysis, or developing critical thinking skills. Television's primary emphasis is entertainment and personality—that is, how people look and act versus what they think or know. Issues are dramatized to induce emotional reactions.

Listen to good speakers, those who are experts and clearly communicate their ideas orally. They are sound models. C-SPAN televises speeches by people on the firing line of policy and ideas. Listen for their ideas and how they make them clear to their audiences. Read publications such as *Vital Speeches* that contain speeches by well-known people who communicate ideas, as well as anthologies of speeches by well-known people such as Winston Churchill, John F. Kennedy, Martin Luther King, and Ronald Reagan, all individuals who respected the power of language.

Finally, use language that is natural to you. Just as people can look funny when they dress "out of character," people can seem odd when they use language in an unnatural way. Practice the skills discussed in this chapter. Work at speaking to the point and using clear, specific, and descriptive language. Your ability to communicate verbally will increase steadily and so will the respect you receive from others.

SUMMARY

Language is the primary channel for communicating ideas. Methods for using language effectively include using language the audience will understand, being specific, using descriptive language, being appropriate, and personalizing your language for the audience. Eliminating clutter helps your ideas sparkle. Read good writers and listen to good speakers.

PROBES

1 Recall an occasion when you heard slang or profanity used in a speech. What was your reaction? Did it put you off? Was the language appropriate for the occasion and audience?

2 Recall an instance when a speaker used language, such as jargon, that you did not understand. How did it affect your listening? How did you react?

3 List some instances when a speaker used inflated language or fillers. How did it influence the speech? How did the audience react?

4 What does your language reveal about you?

5 How would you define clear language?

6 What are some ways of ensuring that your language is clear to the audience?

7 How does connotative language differ from denotative? Give some examples of each type of language.

8 Briefly describe two ways of making your language specific.

9 What are some ways of making your language vivid?

10 Describe four types of inappropriate language.

11 How does personal language help your speech?

12 Briefly describe three types of cluttered language.

APPLICATIONS

1 Make the following statements more specific:

    a I had a great summer vacation.

    b My political science class is really boring.

    c I like backpacking.

2 Give a vivid, concrete description of the following activities: (a) Bungee jumping. (b) Inline skating. (c) Surfing.

3 Take a brief excerpt (a couple of paragraphs will do) from a textbook or professional journal, and rewrite the material in a clear and specific manner that would be easily understood by the average person.

4 Find a speech or article that clearly describes a concept. What did the author do to make it clear?

5 Rewrite the following sentences to make them clear and concise:

    a The parts were shipped by means of air transportation for the purpose of meeting the delivery date for the simple reason that the railway workers were on strike.

    b A good manager must circulate around among her employees.

    c Studying, which can be extremely boring, is only learned by long hours of practice and a high degree of tolerance for frustration.

    d Our plan consists of presenting the information that you want distributed by effectively and substantially presenting said material in a new and original color brochure folder.

NOTES

1 Quoted in speech by Carl Wayne Hensley, "Speak With Style and Watch the Impact," *Vital Speeches,* Vol. 61, September 1, 1995, p. 701.

2 Quoted in speech by Ed Rubenstein, "The Economics of Crime," *Vital Speeches,* Vol. 62, October 15, 1995, p. 19.

3 Debbie S. Miller, "The Arctic National Wildlife Refuge: Petroleum or Preservation," *The Commonwealth,* Vol. 10, February 7, 1991, p. 175.

4 Arthur Miller, "Right of Privacy vs. Freedom of the Press," *The Commonwealth,* Vol. 45, November, 8, 1993, p. 645.

5 Chris Matthews, "Clinton Speech Raises Doubts," *The Contra Costa Times,* April 26, 1995, p. 12A.

6 Derrick Z. Jackson, "Ice Cube: Buckwheat with a Gutter Rap," *San Francisco Examiner,* December 11, 1992, p. A23.

7 Frank Rich, "Marathon Man," *The New York Times,* January 29, 1995, p. E15.

8 Tom Wicker, "Like Too Bad, Yeah," *The New York Times,* February 24, 1989, p. A33.

9 Ronald Reagan, speech before the Republican Convention, August 22, 1992; transcribed from videotape recording.

12

DELIVERY

CHAPTER OUTLINE

HOW TO DEAL WITH INTERFERENCE
ADAPTING TO AUDIENCE FEEDBACK
TEAM PRESENTATIONS

Time magazine described John F. Kennedy's speaking style this way:

> In appearance he is a slender man with a boyish face, an uncontrollable shock of hair, a dazzling smile. In manner he is alert, incisive, speaking in short, terse, sentences in a chowderish New England accent that he somehow makes attractive . . . reaching with no apparent effort into a first class mind for historical anecdotes or classical allusions . . . he projects a kind of conviction and vigor when talking of commonplace things in a commonplace way.[1]

Delivery gives life to your words and ideas. You want to stand before an audience, and, using your voice and body, present your speech clearly, confidently, and credibly. The more effectively you can deliver your speech, the more impact you and your message will have.

In this chapter we will discuss the substance of delivery, building confidence, methods of delivering a speech, communicating with your voice and body, dealing effectively with interference, and adapting to audience feedback.

SUBSTANCE OF DELIVERY

A Montana cowboy upon observing a rich city-slicker clinging onto a silver inlaid saddle atop a broken down horse remarked: "Ya have a thousand dollar saddle on a ten-dollar horse."

Some people take the narrow view that delivery—voice and body language—can be treated separately from character and conviction. They see public speaking as acting or learning to use techniques. Planned gestures and movement, carefully selected clothing and grooming, along with uttering fancy clichés and sound bytes, can sway an audience. They're putting a $1,000 saddle on a $10 horse. Delivery to have power and impact should spring from one's character and be in harmony with one's beliefs. General Colin Powell, for example, is admired by many people because of his character. According to Anthony Lewis of *The New York Times,* "Colin Powell's fundamental attraction for American voters is that he is a straight arrow who says what he thinks regardless of the consequences—'a plain blunt man,' in Shakespeare's phrase. He is admired not for his views on issues but for his steadfast character."[2] General Powell's communication flows from his principles.

You are the message and your delivery style is inseparable from your personality and character. Let's discuss the goals of effective delivery (Figure 12-1).

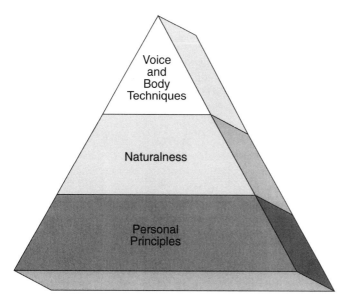

FIGURE 12-1
Substance of delivery.

Speak from Principle

A close examination of good speeches reveals conviction, a sincere desire by the speaker to communicate a message. The speaker has an important idea she wants the audience to grasp. Her enthusiasm and excitement about the idea fuel the voice and body and elevate delivery to new levels, giving the speech greater impact and the speaker greater credibility. Even when a speaker has average delivery skills, conviction gives impact to the speech. Michael Eisner, the well-known CEO of Disney Corporation, tells about the importance of conviction in presenting persuasive presentations:

> It's also interesting for me to watch my staff meetings every Friday to see which of the people in that group win the day. We make major decisions, hundreds of millions of dollars in new projects and new movies. It's always the person with a strong P.O.V. (point of view) that wins the day, that wins the argument. . . . Maybe it's just Hollywood, I don't know, but I'll tell you around here a strong P.O.V. is worth at least 80 IQ points.[3]

Build your delivery on your beliefs and convictions. Speak about topics on which you are knowledgeable. Speak in the best interests of the audience, even if your views are unpopular. Prepare thoroughly so you can deliver the best possible speech. Make a commitment to develop your knowledge and strengthen your values. Richard Dreyfuss, the movie actor, expressed his conviction about his subject during a presentation:

Well, my daughter Emily will be 17 in the year 2000; my sons, Benjamin and Harry, will be 14 and 11. I will be goddammed if I have to pass on to them the news that the American dream is over, that their ambitions have to be smaller than their parents', It is outrageous enough that they will have to make their way through a world made unnecessarily perilous by the expected mistakes of those who have held power. But to add to their burdens this attitude of defeatism or exhaustion disgusts and enrages me.[4]

Develop Your Natural Speaking Style

The most effective style is your own. Style is the way you most naturally like to speak. Some speakers like to stand stationary, others like to move. Some speakers are animated, energetic, and forceful. Others are more reserved and formal. Some are folksy; others, authoritative. One professional speaker had the habit of stroking and flipping out his necktie. It was folksy and unprofessional, but audiences loved it. It was a natural part of his personality. Jesse Jackson has a dynamic and emotional style of delivery. One observer describes it this way:

> Jesse Jackson doesn't use a Teleprompter. He memorizes set pieces that he has debuted elsewhere and weaves them together into a new whole. And he knows how to use fear. When he first comes out he stands back and sucks in the tension and high stakes in a great nostril-flaring inhalation; somewhere in his chest they turn into energy and the actor's art.[5]

That is Jesse Jackson's style. For others it would be inappropriate and unnatural.

Speakers are sometimes coached to behave or act in a certain way to build credibility: "Don't move around, gesture frequently, be assertive, never say 'I don't know' when answering a question, clear your throat before you begin to speak, point your finger when emphasizing an idea," and so forth. The idea is if you act this way you will be behaving in a "professional and powerful speaking manner." The problem is that this advice often doesn't match the speaker's natural style. The result is that the speaker appears phony and uncomfortable. Former President George Bush was often criticized for appearing insincere during his presentations. William Safire, former political speechwriter and now a syndicated columnist, described Bush's problem this way: "George Bush is a patrician, not folksy, and he clanks when he puts on Joe Sixpack nonairs."[6] Bush tried to be what he wasn't and appeared out of character.

One of your goals is to discover and develop your natural speaking style. As you give your speeches and receive feedback, keep a record of your performance. What did you feel comfortable doing? Did you speak with notes or an outline? Did you stand behind the podium or directly in front of the audience? What did the instructor and audience feedback tell you? Do you have an engaging smile? Pleasant demeanor? Natural gestures? Are you sincere? All this feedback can help you develop your natural style.

Eliminate Distracting Mannerisms

As you gain experience, eliminate verbal and nonverbal mannerisms that interfere with or draw attention away from your message. These are often little habits or unconscious gestures and movements. Or too many "ers," "ums," and "ahs" may distract the audience. You may have a habit of shifting from one leg to another frequently as if you were practicing a dance step. You may have your hands in your pockets, keeping you from gesturing naturally and freely. You should make a conscious effort to eliminate or replace these mannerisms. Here are some guidelines:

1 Identify and write down the habits you want to change.

2 Make a conscious effort to change one habit per speech. Work to eliminate it during rehearsal as well as during the speech. Record your speech on tape or video. Rehearse in front of a mirror.

3 Get feedback. During rehearsal ask someone to monitor and record your progress. Do the same during your speech. Tell the instructor your learning objective so that he or she can help you achieve it.

Learn what you do well naturally and work to expand those qualities.

BUILDING CONFIDENCE

Karl Wallenda once said, "Walking the tightrope is living, everything else is waiting." All speakers feel a sense of anxiety before presentations. In fact, all people who perform audience-centered activities—athletes, actors, rabbis, politicians, teachers, attorneys, and many others—report some degree of anxiety even after years of experience. They all handle anxiety effectively, just as you will in your speeches.

The easiest way to handle your anxiety is to follow class instruction. Learning how to give speeches—through discussion, preparation, and practice—significantly reduces nervousness. The solution is this simple for the great majority of speakers. It is okay to make mistakes as long as you prepared thoroughly and are doing the best you can at the moment. Nevertheless, let's discuss some other specific methods of building confidence.

Prepare Thoroughly

Bobby Knight, the famous Indiana University basketball coach, says the will to prepare to win is much more important than the will to win. Everyone wants to win, but few people are willing to pay the price—the long hours of practice, conditioning, and study it takes to excel at top levels. Roger Ailes, communication consultant to presidents and top executives, says preparation is the key to successful speaking.

Preparation predicts success. When you are prepared, you feel confident. You know you will succeed when your goal is clear, your ideas are etched in your mind, and you have rehearsed thoroughly with your notes and visuals. Shaky knees, sweaty palms, and dry throat disappear quickly when you are prepared. Conversely, knowing you are unprepared increases anxiety.

Rehearse Thoroughly

The goal of rehearsal is to become comfortable with your speech so you can deliver it in the most natural way. An actress practices her lines many times so that when she delivers them before the camera, she appears real and natural. You are not acting, but you want to rehearse a sufficient number of times so you are comfortable with your speech and can deliver it smoothly and naturally.

Your rehearsal should simulate speech conditions and be systematic, and you should get feedback so you can analyze your performance. Practice in front of a mirror to observe your movements. Practice with friends or classmates. Rehearse in an empty classroom, preferably your own. If you have the opportunity, record your rehearsal on video- and audiotape. Each of these methods gives you valuable feedback to strengthen your speech. Bill Clinton practiced for his acceptance speech at the 1992 Democratic Convention by rehearsing behind an exact replica of the podium he would be speaking from at the convention.[7]

The following steps can be helpful in rehearsing your speeches:

1 *Review the outline.* Being familiar with the organization and the main parts of the speech gives you direction and confidence. A speaker once said, "Memorize your ideas, not your words." Having the main ideas, and their order, etched in your mind facilitates delivery.

2 *Practice the speech.* Practice the speech as you would give it to an audience, including the notes, visuals, and other communication aids you would use in the speech. This helps you to simulate the experience and correct any problem. It also helps you see your progress as your performance improves with each rehearsal.

3 *Time each practice.* Check to see whether you are within the allotted time. If the speech is too long, you may need to eliminate a main point or reduce the amount of supporting material. You might time each section of the outline to ensure that there is a proper balance among the parts.

4 *Revise the speech.* Make the adjustments you need to strengthen the message. Maybe transitions are needed between main points. Perhaps a brief pause

Rehearsal improves delivery.

after stating main points. An analogy may be needed to clarify an idea. These small revisions are cumulative and will greatly improve your speech and your confidence in giving it.

5 *Repeat the rehearsal process.* Rehearse until the speech runs smoothly and you feel comfortable. There is no magic number of practices, but five or six would seem realistic. Record your speech on tape or video and play it back.

6 *Practice parts of the speech.* You might want to practice major parts of your speech separately. Maybe the introduction is choppy. Practice it alone. Perhaps the second major point lacks the clarity you would like. Practice it individually.

A six- to eight-minute speech is a series of two- or three-minute speeches linked together. Rehearsing your speech in sections—introduction, main points, conclusion—can improve delivery. Treat each part as a minispeech, which in fact it is. This ensures that each section will be given the attention it deserves. The following is an example of this approach.

Specific purpose:	To explain how to create an effective gymnastic floor exercise.
Central idea:	To create an effective gymnastic floor exercise, select the music and movement, and then coordinate them.

Body

Main points:
   I Select the music. *(2 minutes)*

   II Select the movements. *(2 minutes)*

   III Set the movements to the music. *(2 minutes)*

In this example, you would treat each part of the three-part structure as a minispeech. It is easier to deliver the message if you look at your speech as a series of short, linked speeches rather than one large one.

Gain Experience

Public speaking is a skill. The only way that skills can be nurtured and developed is through practice and experience. Each time you prepare, rehearse, and present a speech, you build competence and confidence. Not unlike playing golf, tennis, or skiing, each time you do it you get better.

One of the quickest ways to develop skills and confidence is to take every opportunity to speak in and out of class. If you belong to a social club, church group, or college organization, speak up. Give oral reports in your classes. All of these experiences will increase your skills and confidence. Barbara Jordan, the late congressperson from Texas, won numerous local and state oratorical contests as a student and was an outstanding college debater. She took every opportunity to speak and became a dynamic and persuasive presenter.

Make Speaking Effectiveness a Goal

Successful speakers make speaking effectiveness a goal. John F. Kennedy, acknowledged as one of our nation's most eloquent orators, was not an articulate and confident speaker until he made the commitment to become one. It wasn't until 1956, just four years before he became president, that Kennedy made effective public speaking a personal goal and he worked very hard to improve his skills. Kennedy's orations have inspired, and will continue to inspire, generations. John Sculley, the well-known CEO of several major corporations, in his autobiography *Odyssey,* described his obsession with becoming a top business presenter. He practiced hour after hour, day after day, to develop his style. He even overcame a serious stammer to become an effective speaker.

Tips for Handling Nervousness

Anxiety is part of giving a speech, but it is rarely an insurmountable obstacle. Here are a few quick tips for dealing with those pre-speech butterflies.

Give Extra Rehearsal to Your Introduction   When you first face an audience, you get a rush of anxiety. Having confidence in your introduction gets you through these rough spots. As your speech progresses, anxiety declines because your attention shifts from yourself to your audience and your message.[8] Figure 12-2 shows how anxiety diminishes in the course of a presentation.

Speak on Topics You Like and About Which You Are Knowledgeable
Enthusiasm means the "spirit within." When we speak on topics we like and care about, we unleash that spirit and we are more dynamic, entertaining, and articulate. This gives you confidence and naturally reduces tension.

Think in Terms of Communicating, Not Performing   Stay focused on the ideas you want to convey to the audience. Speaking is like an intense conversation in which you are describing important ideas to a group of friends. Your job is to get those ideas across, not to do a song-and-dance routine.

Loosen Up   There are a number of unobtrusive relaxation exercises you can use. Experienced presenters use them before their presentations. Here are some exercises you can do as you wait to present:

1 Slowly breathe in deeply; then slowly exhale. Do this a few times before you stand up to speak. Continue to breathe naturally and steadily as you speak. Proper breathing forces you to relax; it is used in meditation and natural childbirth, as well as by actors, musicians, and athletes.

2 Slowly clench and unclench your fists. This isometric exercise helps you release energy before you speak. You might also grab the sides of your chair or desk, clench, and release.

3 If you have a dry mouth and a tense throat, lightly chew your tongue; you'll have all the saliva you need to keep your mouth moist.

4 Let your tongue and jaw drop into a relaxed position. Relaxation of the jaw muscles reduces the physical sensation of tension. If you drink water or liquids before or during your speech, they should be warm or at room temperature. Cold liquids tighten the throat.

FIGURE 12-2
Stages of speech anxiety.

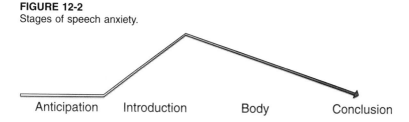

Anticipation   Introduction   Body   Conclusion

Maintain Your Daily Routine   Don't change your daily routine because you will be giving a presentation. For example, don't skip a breakfast or a lunch that you would normally have if you weren't giving a speech. Being hungry will only add to the stress you are feeling.

Think Positively   This may sound trite, but stay focused on your objective: speaking effectively. Nothing catastrophic is going to happen, and you will find yourself doing surprisingly well. Studies show that being positive and visualizing success significantly reduce nervousness.[9] Remember, you will be more critical of your performance than your peers. That's why you need feedback.

Finally, you may find consolation in the fact that anxiety is rarely detectable by the audience. Studies have shown that audiences, including trained observers (even speech professors), are unable to detect the degree of apprehension experienced by the speaker.[10] If you don't tell the audience that you are nervous, they are not going to know.

METHODS OF DELIVERING A SPEECH

How a speech is delivered is usually determined by the speaker's style and the occasion. Charles Osgood, the CBS news commentator, doesn't believe in scripts. He prefers speaking from scanty notes written on small cards so he can look at his audience while speaking. Another speaker may write out the speech word for word, rehearse extensively, and read from the manuscript.

Presidential speeches are often read because they are statements of national and international policy or negotiating tactics that require exact meaning. Ad-libbing or deviating from the prepared text could alter the meaning and confuse the target audience. In the tumultuous events leading to the Persian Gulf war, former President Bush's speeches were carefully crafted to reflect the U.S. negotiating strategy and meticulously read to ensure that they were not misinterpreted by the adversary.

There are four basic methods of delivering a speech: (1) You can speak extemporaneously. (2) You can read from a manuscript. (3) You can speak from memory. (4) You can speak impromptu. Let's discuss each method, although our primary focus will be on extemporaneous speaking.

Speaking Extemporaneously

Extemporaneous delivery is prepared speaking that is not memorized. The idea behind this type of speaking is to incorporate the feedback from the audience into the speech as it is being delivered. It would be used by a speaker who has extensive knowledge about a topic. The speaker would prepare a speech about the topic, rehearse extensively, and deliver the speech looking at the audience, only occasionally referring to notes. The result is a style of speaking that is highly prepared yet appears spontaneous because it is adapted to the audience during delivery. It is a formalized conversation between speaker and audience. Mary Louise Smith, a prominent speaker, describes the process this way, "Anyone who does any kind of public speaking will tell you that their (audience) response is a critical part of a good speech. . . . It doesn't just all flow out. There's an awful lot that flows back."[11]

When used effectively, extemporaneous delivery is a powerful way of speaking because it creates synergy between speaker and the audience. It demonstrates your knowledge about a subject, develops your natural speaking style, allows you to adjust to audience feedback, and personalizes your relationship with the audience. A product manager presenting a new line to a sales force, a drama coach describing acting technique to a group of students, or a learning specialist explaining educational tools for children to a group of parents would speak extemporaneously. These speakers want to speak naturally, adapt to their audience while speaking, and present a well-planned, carefully organized set of ideas.

In *My Life in Court,* renowned trial lawyer Louis Nizer described how he used the extemporaneous style in his opening remarks to the jury:

> I believe in an extensive opening statement. I speak without a note, but I have thought through my address very carefully. It is an early opportunity to look each juror in the eye and by sincerity and earnestness make contact with him. It is interesting to observe the bland look on a juror's face when you begin, perhaps even a cynical smile, and how he is caught up in the drama of your recital, his face responding properly with varying emotions of sympathy or resentment as the arguments make inroads upon him. Finally, when you walk up and back, and his eyes follow and are riveted upon you, the persuasive effort has begun successfully.[12]

An extemporaneous speech never unfolds exactly the way it is planned because you're speaking from notes, reading the audience's reaction, and adapting to it; the speech, while prepared, contains spontaneity. You may add or exclude information depending on how the audience responds. Here is how one person describes the process:

> A state-of-the-art presentation is the product of a person who knows where and how to lead an audience; one who can recognize landmarks, shortcuts, and unexpected delights along the road; and one who knows when the group has reached its destination.[13]

A good extemporaneous speech is well prepared and adapts to the audience.

Reading from Manuscript

A speech can be written word for word and read to an audience. Sometimes it appears this type of speech is not being read when a speaker uses a Teleprompter. A Teleprompter projects a manuscript onto special optical glass that is placed unobtrusively to the right and left in front of the speaker and allows the speaker to read the speech while appearing to be looking at the audience. Teleprompters are like the cue cards newscasters read from as they present the news while seemingly looking at the camera.

This method of speaking is used by speakers whose remarks will be published in whole or in part, or closely scrutinized by others, or are potentially controversial—for example, political figures. These speeches are often written by a professional speechwriter or by a committee in collaboration with the speaker. A CEO of a major corporation whose remarks influence thousands of employees and shareholders may read from a prepared text to ensure that the message is interpreted accurately and is consistent with company objectives.

Reading from manuscript is not recommended for inexperienced speakers. It ties you to a preset plan that may not adapt well to the audience and inhibits your natural enthusiasm for your topic. It also limits your ability to think on your feet, which is important as you attempt to adjust your ideas to an audience during delivery.

Speaking from Memory

Speaking from memory requires committing a manuscript, word for word, to memory before presenting it to an audience. This is a mechanical way of speaking, and it reduces a speaker's contact with the audience. Memorizing is a great deal of work and inhibits spontaneity and naturalness, and it always involves the danger of memory lapse—which can spell disaster.

Memorizing a speech requires great effort, and few people have the time to do it. Why memorize when you can read from a manuscript using a Teleprompter? What you should do is memorize your ideas, not your words, so that when you speak, your ideas sound fresh and natural.

Impromptu Speaking

Impromptu speaking, or spur-of-the-moment speaking, is the most common kind of speaking in daily life. You speak about a subject, but you haven't prepared a speech about it. Answering a question in class, expressing your opinion during a discussion, or giving directions are examples of impromptu speaking.

Impromptu speaking is the major type of communication in the workplace. According to John Kotter, executives, managers, supervisors, and professionals "spend the vast majority of their time with others . . . in short and disjointed conversations that are not planned in advance in any detail."[14] Another study of managers found that they may spend up to 78 percent of their time in verbal interaction. The ability to express your ideas spontaneously and at the same time clearly, concisely, and to the point is an important skill that influences performance and productivity. Impromptu speaking will be discussed in detail in Chapter 16.

COMMUNICATING WITH YOUR BODY

Someone once said you can have the greatest idea in the world but if it is presented in a dull or uninteresting way, no one will listen. Your voice and body can make or break the speech. A rigid posture and stiff or listless gestures may make an exciting idea lifeless and boring. A lively, fast-paced delivery may make a mediocre topic fascinating and memorable. This doesn't mean acting or performing. What it does mean is that learning how to communicate in a *natural and confident* manner increases your chances of success. The most powerful person you can be is yourself. Let's discuss four important types of body language: (1) eye contact, (2) facial expression, (3) gesture and movement, and (4) appearance.

Eye Contact

The saying "eyes are mirrors of the soul" reveals why eye contact is such an important part of delivery: it connects you to the audience. Eye contact communicates involvement, openness, and trust. Studies demonstrate that eye contact shows your interest in and builds rapport with the listeners.[14] Audiences like speakers who make good eye contact and rate them higher on integrity and expertise.[15] Picture for a moment a speaker who looks at the walls, her notes, the floor, everywhere but at the audience. What conclusions would you draw? Lack of confidence? Indifference? Disinterest? Here is how Gerry Spence, renowned trial attorney, describes the power of eye contact:

> The eyes of the credible convey a message consistent with the plain meaning of the spoken words. These eyes are in sync with the rest of the presentation. They are happy eyes, sad and sorrowful eyes, angry eyes, eyes that match the sounds, that support the feeling of the messenger and that are consistent with the message. And when the eyes do not have it, as it were, we know it.[16]

What is good eye contact? It is not gaping or gazing. Good eye contact is looking at individual members of the audience in a relaxed and natural manner for a few seconds. The idea is to hold your focus on each listener separately just as you would in a normal one-on-one conversation. This personalizes your delivery and helps each person feel you are talking directly to them.

If you are speaking to a large audience, select people in various parts of the room and make direct and extended eye contact with them. You might direct your eye contact in a right, middle, and left direction. What is important is to make direct eye contact with specific individuals and not scan the audience speaking to a blurred, undefined mass. That may increase your nervousness and give the wrong message to the audience.

Here are three exercises you can begin practicing to help you learn good eye contact.

1 Practice good eye contact in your one-on-one conversations.

2 In an empty classroom, tape paper to every third chair and practice eye contact at those designated spots.

3 When rehearsing in front of a live audience, have each person you make eye contact with silently count up to five seconds and signal you with a flick of their finger when time is up. Then make eye contact with another person in the audience for five seconds, and so on.

You can make rapid progress using these methods.

Practicing eye contact may seem awkward at first. Remember, it is a skill that turns into a natural part of communicating. But the benefits of making good eye contact are too great not to do it. You will impress your audiences, enhance your credibility, and have more control of the public-speaking process.

Facial Expressions

Your face is an expressive conveyor of your feelings, whether of anger, sadness, amusement, or excitement. If you're describing an exciting vacation experience, your face will light up and your eyes twinkle. Your face is naturally expressing the emotion you are describing in words, just as it should when you are speaking in public.

Your facial expression should naturally confirm the feelings expressed by your words. If you are describing a serious topic such as child abuse, your face sincerely expresses concern. If you are telling a humorous anecdote, you should be smiling. Jimmy Carter, former president and human rights activist, sometimes has problems matching his facial expressions to subject matter. When discussing a serious issue, his eyes would light up and he would convey a slight smile. He appeared insincere and at the very least, reduced the impact of his persuasion. Television journalist Sam Donaldson maintains a stone face when discussing issues whether the subject is incest, murder, bird calling, or obscene rap lyrics.

To demonstrate the importance of facial expressions matching your words, try the following exercise. Stand in front of a mirror and say "Hi, how are you?" Pretend you are saying these words to a person that you care for dearly. Say it first with a grim and serious facial expression. Then a neutral, deadpan expression. Last, say it with true enthusiasm.

Which salutation was most natural and authentic? The last one, of course. Communicate your natural feelings through your face.

Gestures

Gestures are expressive movements of some part or parts of the body, such as a hand or the arms, or of the whole body. A speaker may make a sweeping gesture of the hand when referring to the audience or jab a finger when emphasizing a point. We use gestures naturally in conversation. When giving directions we naturally point to a location; we wave good-bye when parting, or scratch our heads when thinking. Here is how one observer described one of former New York Governor Mario Cuomo's hand gestures:

> When Cuomo puts out his hand to maintain his command—that movement, that says, "Don't clap yet, the applause line is coming"—it is the short, blunt hand of a masseur. He's not only controlling the crowd, he's massaging them. He's touching the audience's shoulder and saying, "Like that? Wait'll I get to your back."[17]

Gestures highlight ideas and hold the attention of the audience. In a speech on motivation, a speaker said, "Never kick people when they are down," simultaneously making a kicking gesture with his leg. His gesture gave very powerful support to the point he was making.

Gestures should be purposeful and spontaneous, springing naturally from the message itself. Canned or scripted movements are often out of sync with the spoken word and smack of manipulation, offending audiences. Many television evangelists appear to lack sincerity because their gestures are staged.

One approach to letting gestures flow naturally is to assume a comfortable standing position when you speak. Stand straight but not stiff; you're not at attention. Your feet should be approximately shoulder-width apart. Maintain a good balance and place your hands at your sides or hold the sides of the lectern without clutching it. This way your body is free to gesture in a natural manner to reinforce your words.

Try this exercise as a way of understanding the importance of gestures and a comfortable standing position. Stand in front of a mirror. Try holding your hands in various positions such as behind your back, in front of you in a fig-leaf style, or with your arms crossed. In each position say enthusiastically, "I feel wonderful!" What is your body saying? Is it communicating another message? Now stand in a comfortable position, your hands at your sides and say, "I feel wonderful!" Your hands naturally move to support your words.

Gestures emphasize ideas and hold attention.

Appearance

How are you groomed? Whether or not the audience believes that you have made the effort to make yourself presentable can influence how they receive your message. Clothing should be appropriate to the situation and the audience. A finance officer of a bank addressing a group of businesspeople would be expected to dress in conservative business attire because a suit is a professional's uniform. John Molloy, dress consultant to businesspeople and professionals, suggests that a white blouse or shirt helps the wearer project a hardworking, sincere image. A dark suit is a symbol of power.

Dress should not only be appropriate for the audience, it should also be appropriate to you. Oliver North's decision to wear his U.S. Marines uniform with his chest full of medals and ribbons instead of a business suit during the Iran Contra hearings gained him much sympathy from viewers because it was a natural style for him. When a White House staffer once suggested that President Ronald Reagan take off his coat and roll up his sleeves as part of a national presentation, he was curtly told that the President doesn't take off his coat in public ceremonies or while working in the Oval Office.[18] Lawyers coach their clients to dress in a manner that favorably impresses a jury, but their dress must be in character. John Keker, a well-known defense attorney, in response to a question about dress in the courtroom, responded:

> It (dress) has an effect because jurors pay attention to everything and the suit has to be consistent with everything else you're trying to portray about yourself. If you're kind of flashy and wear five rings, that's OK, and if you're a more down-home person, to wear a rumpled suit with cigar burns and spaghetti all over it is fine. Your dress better *be* or at least *seem* authentic.[19]

Communicating with Your Voice

How you use your voice influences how an audience receives your message. A slow, monotonous voice will bore an audience and reduce the impact of your message and your credibility. A well-paced and lively vocal delivery holds attention and gives life to your ideas.

For most speakers special vocal training is unnecessary. A natural style, plus enthusiasm for your topic, is often sufficient to allow you to speak in an interesting and pleasant voice. Nevertheless, knowing how to use your voice can be helpful in practicing and delivering your presentation.

The key to using the voice effectively is practicing vocal variety, something most people naturally have in their daily conversations. They speed up at the beginning of a statement, pause briefly at the end of a sentence, and raise their voice to show enthusiasm. You should use your voice in a similar way when you deliver your speech. Let's discuss three important aspects of voice production that can help you attain vocal variety.

Rate   Rate is the speed at which you speak. The normal rate of speaking is about 140 to 150 words per minute. Listeners prefer a rate somewhere between 150 and 225 words per minute, with 175 the optimum. If you speak too slowly, you may bore the audience; too rapidly, and you may confuse them, especially if you are explaining complex data.

Varying your rate of speech holds attention and enhances understanding. You might pause before an important point or pause to focus the audience's attention on the statement. You might speed up or slow down at the beginning or ending of your presentation of an important idea. Some professional speakers mark their manuscripts with special symbols to signify when to speed up, slow down, and pause. Figure 12-3 shows a passage marked to vary rate: a slash / represents a pause, parentheses ( ) mean to speed up, an underline —— means to slow down. Read the passage at a normal rate. Then read the passage using the symbols. Can you tell the difference? Did following the symbols add vocal variety?

The gold medal process begins with a dream. / <u>A dream is wishful thinking</u>, the things we would like to see (happen in our lives.) <u>If they are honest</u>, / most achievers admit their dream begins with a feeling. (I wanted to feel like an Olympic champion.) We want to feel that we have the respect and admiration of the people who work for us and with us. <u>We want to feel in control of our lives</u>. / Its feelings that get us out of bed in the morning. / Its feelings that keep us going year after year.

FIGURE 12-3
Marked-up excerpt (From John Nabor, "The Gold Medal Performance: Eight Steps to Success," *The Commonwealth*, Vol. 52, Nov. 20, 1991, p 765.)

Pitch   Pitch refers to how high or low your voice sounds. For example, a tenor has a higher singing voice than a baritone. Whether your natural level is high or low, flexibility of pitch will give a natural tonal variety to your speech. It is not unusual to begin a sentence at a higher pitch and end at a lower pitch.

More important than the level of your voice is the need to vary it. An unvaried voice is monotonous and will affect the attitude of the audience toward you and your message. Try saying the following sentences in a monotone:

I think you are a liar.
I loved the movie.
I had a wonderful time.
One hundred people were saved from the flood.

Now say them expressively, as if you mean it. Notice how your pitch rises and falls naturally. Say what you mean and your voice will rise and fall naturally.

Volume   Volume refers to how loudly you speak. Naturally, you want to be heard easily and comfortably by the audience. For large audiences, microphones are used. When speaking to smaller groups adjust your volume by speaking to the person farthest away from you.

The most effective way to sustain good volume is to breathe from your diaphragm. The diaphragm is the area between your rib cage and navel. Think of it as a balloon inside your stomach. When you inhale, it expands; and when you exhale, it contracts. When you breathe properly the diaphragm forces air out of your lungs, giving you good and sustained volume. Breathing from the diaphragm also helps you relax.

To determine if you are breathing correctly, place your fingers on your belly and inhale. The breath pushes your fingers outward. Now exhale and your fingers move inward. Try this a number of times until you recognize the pattern. Practice this breathing technique each time you rehearse and when you deliver your speech. You will speak with good volume and be more relaxed.

HOW TO DEAL WITH INTERFERENCE

Public speaking, as much as we would like it to be, is never perfect. A speech is a moment-to-moment interaction of speaker, audience, and setting. Interference can occur at any moment. As you are showing a transparency, the overhead projector may blow a fuse. The tip of a felt pen used to illustrate a point may have dried out. Someone may have a coughing spell as you are discussing a critical point. A slide may stick in the tray. All of these things can happen, and most will.

When you encounter interference, treat it calmly and realistically. Don't throw up your hands, utter a profanity, and say "I quit." An old adage says, "Ride the horse in the direction it is going." Don't add to the problem or make a fool of yourself. Respond rationally. If the microphone malfunctions, put it aside, move closer to the audience or have them move closer to you, and speak louder. If someone is talking loudly outside the room, ask that person to stop. The following is an outstanding example of how interference can be handled with wit and grace.

> During a speech one evening, a power failure darkened the room. The speaker very calmly announced that this was not a problem because he had gone to "night school" and continued the presentation until the power was restored.

When interference occurs, concentrate on achieving your goal, even if it means altering the content of your speech. Audiences understand that interference happens and will respect you for handling it well. In fact, you will probably enhance your credibility if you manage the interference calmly. You have acted rationally in the face of the unexpected. What can be more revealing about your character? Some speeches appear not to have interference because the speaker handled it so skillfully. Instead of making an issue of the problem, the presenter incorporated it into the speech.

President Clinton did just that when he delivered his historic address on health care in 1993 before a joint session of congress and a national television audience. Few people knew that much of the speech was improvised. The speech that had been scrolled up on his Teleprompter was not the health care speech but an economic address he had given months before. The President stalled for time as his aids scrambled to find the speech. He fumbled and fudged. He waved to his wife, his Cabinet, the gallery. He began the speech reading from an emergency manuscript in front of him and improvising, all the while monitoring the Teleprompter from the corner of his eye until the correct text was found and downloaded, which came midway into the speech. Ironically, this speech was considered one of his best.[20] Don't make an issue of interference. Deal with it when it occurs and move on.

ADAPTING TO AUDIENCE FEEDBACK

In typical face-to-face communication, we use the verbal and nonverbal cues of others to guide our remarks. A nod of the head tells us the listener understands our comments. A grin shows agreement. A move forward shows interest. We observe these messages as we speak and adjust our comments accordingly.

We should do the same thing when we speak to an audience. That is why eye contact and extemporaneous delivery are important. We observe the feedback of the audience and adjust our message. A quizzical look indicates a need to explain a point more fully. By giving additional examples, an anecdote, or a definition, you help the audience understand the idea. You might even ask the audience if your additional explanation has helped them grasp the point.

Adapting to the audience's feedback shows your interest in them and your commitment to achieving your goal. You adjust your remarks as you would when talking to a good friend. This also increases the involvement of the audience. Audiences feel you are talking *with* them instead of *to* them when you respond to their feedback. Responding to feedback also increases your credibility.

TEAM PRESENTATIONS

Presenting in teams is becoming increasingly popular in the workplace. Many projects require the skills of professionals with diverse expertise. They work together as a team and communicate their results to audiences within and external to the organization. For instance, a company concerned about substance abuse in the workplace may team up a manager, a substance abuse expert, a psychologist, a consultant, and a project manager to develop and implement a plan. They work together as a group and give team presentations about their progress and results. Many high-tech companies have work groups made up of technicians, engineers, and support staff who give team presentations to customers.

Team presentations require planning and coordination. The process is similar to planning a symposium in which four or five people give separate presentations about a topic. The big difference is that in team presenting, each speaker is guided by the same specific purpose. It is one speech given by four or five people. Here are some tips for planning a group presentation:

Team members:	Joann Jones: Team Leader
	Manuel Gonzalez: Psychologist
	Bob White: Manager
	Robert Yee: Substance Abuse Expert
Audience:	Upper management
Specific purpose:	To adopt ABC plan for companywide substance abuse program.
Central idea:	ABC program will reduce the problem and is cost-effective.

Joann Jones
Introduction
A. Attention
B. Rapport
C. Orientation
    1. Audience expectations: needs, problems, objectives.
    2. Introduce team members.
    3. Lay out agenda.
D. Specific purposes.
E. Central idea.
Preview: Main points and presenters.

Body
Robert Yee
Substance Abuse
Expert
I. Scope of the problem.
   A.
   B.
Summary
Questions and answers
Transition to next speaker

Manuel
Gonzales
Psychologist
II. Rehabilitation.
   A.
   B.
Summary
Questions and answers
Transition to next speaker

Bob White
Manager
III. Implementation plan.
   A.
   B.
Summary
Questions and answers
Transition to team leader

Joann Jones
Conclusion
Summary
Questions and answers
Closing: Call for action

FIGURE 12-4
Team presentation outline.

1 The team must have a commonly understood goal, central idea, and strategy. Each person must understand the objectives and work to achieve them. Any misunderstandings and differences must be worked out and settled before the speech is delivered.

2 One person acts as the team leader and manages the preparation and presentation process.

3 An outline is prepared just as for an individual speech. Roles are assigned for specific main points or content based on a member's expertise: the manager may discuss costs, the psychologist may discuss rehabilitation, and the substance abuse expert may focus on the problem. Prepare summaries and transitions.

4 When not speaking, support the speaker with good listening behavior. Do not publicly disagree. Build on team members' comments if appropriate.

5 Have the group leader open and close the presentation and moderate questions directed to the group as a whole. Ensure that all major points and parts of the speech are presented.

Figure 12-4 shows a sample team presentation outline.

SUMMARY

Delivery is an important skill. The phrase "substance of delivery" refers to speaking from principle, developing your natural speaking style, and maximizing your intentional messages. Building confidence includes thorough preparation, rehearsing, gaining experience, and making a commitment to speak effectively. Four methods of delivering a speech are speaking extemporaneously, reading from a manuscript, speaking from memory, and impromptu speaking. You communicate with your body through eye contact, facial expression, gestures, and appearance. You communicate with your voice through rate, pitch, and volume. Don't call attention to interference; instead, learn to handle it intelligently. Adapt to the feedback from the audience. In team presenting, a number of people prepare and present the speech instead of just one person.

PROBES

1 You have been retained by your local congressperson as a communications consultant. She asks you what goals she should strive for in delivery. How do you respond?

2 You are running for president of the United States. What principles will be the basis of your delivery style when speaking to the American people?

3 You are auditioning to be the host of a new late night talk show. What elements of your own personal style would you try to sell the producers on?

4 It has been suggested that eye contact may be the most important aspect of nonverbal communication. Do you feel that assertion is correct? If so, why? If not, why not?

5 Why is character the foundation of a good delivery style?

6 Why is developing your natural speaking style so important?

7 Briefly list some guidelines for building confidence.

8 Briefly describe four ways of delivering a speech.

9 What are the advantages of speaking extemporaneously?

10 What is the best way to handle interference?

11 How does team presenting differ from giving a speech alone?

12 Identify three steps you can take immediately to gain public speaking experience.

APPLICATIONS

1 Analyze the nonverbal characteristics of a celebrity, someone like Jay Leno. How do the celebrity's appearance, movements, gestures, posture, facial expression, and voice convey meaning? Compare Jay Leno's nonverbal communication with that of David Letterman. How do they differ? Note the influence of nonverbal messages on the total communication.

2 You are giving a speech and observing the audience for nonverbal feedback on your message. How can you tell when they understand the message? How can you tell if they don't understand it? How can you tell when they are interested? Uninterested? What other kinds of feedback can you observe?

3 Tape an episode of *60 Minutes* and listen to the voices of the hosts without watching. Listen for rate, pitch, and volume. How do they use their voices to convey meaning?

4 Attend a speech and write down all the gestures that the speaker uses.

5 Keep a journal of your rehearsal habits. What can you do to improve them? How do they stack up against the criteria discussed in the book? What can you do to improve them?

6 Listen to some popular radio personalities such as Charles Osgood, Paul Harvey, Garrison Keillor. How do they use their voices to communicate?

NOTES

1 *Time* quote taken from Lloyd Rohler and Roger Cook, *Great American Speeches,* 2nd ed., (Alistair Press: Greenwood, IN, 1993), p. 291.

2 Anthony Lewis, "The General's Front Page in England," *San Francisco Chronicle,* October 24, 1995, p. A19.

3 Warren Bennis, "Reflections on Retirement,"*Vital Speeches* Vol. 61, October 1, 1995, p. 753.

4 Richard Dreyfuss, "Uncertain Times," *The Commonwealth,* Vol. 89, January 2, 1995, p. 1.

5 Peggy Noonan, "Behind Enemy Lines," *Newsweek,* July 27, 1992, p. 32.

6 William Safire, "Bush's Gamble," *The New York Times Magazine,* October 18, 1992, Sec. 6, p. 30.

7 Margret Carlson, "Bill's Big Bash," *Time,* July 27, 1992, p. 36.

8 Larry W. Carlile, Ralph R. Behnke, and James T. Kitchens, "A Physiological Pattern of Anxiety in Public Speaking," *Communication Quarterly,* Vol. 25, No. 4 (1977), pp. 44–46.

9 Joe Ayers, "Coping with Speech Anxiety: The Power of Positive Thinking," *Communication Education,* Vol. 37, October, 1988, pp. 289–298; and Joe Ayers and Theodore Hopf, "The Long-Term Effect of Visualization in the Classroom," *Communication Education,* Vol. 39, January, 1990, pp. 75–78.

10 Michael T. Motley, "Taking the Terror Out of Talk," *Psychology Today,* Vol. 22, January 1988, pp. 84.

11 Victoria L. DeFrancisco and Marvin D. Jensen, *Women's Voices in Our Time,* (Waveland Press: Prospect Heights, IL, 1994), p. 43.

12 Louis Nizer, *My Life in Court* (Pyramid Books: New York, 1967), pp. 40–41.

13 Susan E. Berry and Robert J. Garmston, "Become a State-of-the-Art Presenter," *Training and Development Journal,* January, 1987, p. 19.

14 John Kotter, *The General Manager* (The Free Press: New York, 1982), p. 133.

15 Stephen Glades, "Notes Are Not Enough," *Training and Development Journal,* Vol. 39, August 1985, p. 35.

16 Steven A. Beebe, "Eye Contact; A Nonverbal Determinant of Speaker Credibility," *Speech Teacher,* Vol. 23, January, 1974, pp. 21–25; B. F. Meeker, "Cooperation, Trust, and Reciprocity," *Human Relations,* Vol. 37, July, 1983, pp. 225–249.

17 Gerry Spence, *How to Argue and Win Every Time,* (St. Martins Press: New York, 1995), p. 50.

18 Peggy Noonan, "Behind Enemy Lines," *Newsweek,* July 27, 1992, p. 32.

19 Peggy Noonan, *What I Saw at the Revolution, A Political Life in the Reagan Era* (Ivy Books: New York, 1990), p. 125.

20 "This Lawyer Is No Joke," interview with John Keker in *San Francisco Examiner and Chronicle,* July 28, 1991, p. C-5.

21 Elizabeth Drew, *On the Edge: The Clinton Presidency* (Simon and Schuster: New York, 1994), p. 302.

22 Marie Flatley, "Team Presentation Skills: Essential Tools Today," *Business Education Forum,* Vol. 45, November 11, 1990, pp. 19–21.

PREPARING DIFFERENT TYPES OF SPEECHES

13

SPEAKING TO INFORM

We live in an information-oriented culture that places great emphasis on the dissemination of knowledge through the verbal medium, or speaking to inform. The United States spends 180 billion dollars annually on public education. American industry spends another 50 billion annually on training for its employees. The effectiveness of this education lies in our ability to communicate information effectively.

Think of all the places where information is communicated orally: in the classroom, on television, and on the playing field; in research centers, police academies, training seminars, boardrooms, community centers, hospitals, legislative bodies, religious gatherings, private homes, and on and on and on. Speaking to inform is an integral part of day-to-day communication.

Speaking to inform is the process of preparing and presenting information so an idea, process, or event is converted into useful and meaningful knowledge by an audience. A few examples are a corporate trainer explaining conflict resolution techniques to new managers, a basketball coach demonstrating how to shoot a free throw, a community leader describing plans for a fund-raising drive, and a supervisor in a factory describing the functions of a new machine to a team of employees. The specific purpose of an informative speech you might give in your class might be, for example:

To explain how a methanol engine works.
To explain ways of organic farming.
To explain the theory of self-esteem in children.
To describe the Internet.
To describe how to take a good photograph.

When you speak to inform, your objective is to have the audience understand and use the new knowledge. For example, if your purpose is to describe the basic process of applying a tourniquet to a wound, your goal is to have the audience be able to put the process to use in an emergency. A corporate trainer showing employees how to use new software expects them to employ it in their work.

The importance of speaking to inform cannot be overestimated. Knowledge empowers people. The communication of ideas helps people understand themselves and see the events surrounding them. Learning new skills enhances performance. The better educated a person, the greater his or her chances of success. President Clinton believes knowledge is tied directly to opportunity:

> . . . what you earn depends on what you learn. There's a direct relationship between high skills and high wages, and therefore, we have to educate our people better to compete. We will be as rich and strong and rife with opportunity as we are skilled and talented and trained. . . . We must invest in our people—their education, their training, and their skills—and take whatever steps we need to make sure every American has a chance to benefit.[1]

SELECTING SUBJECTS AND ORGANIZING MATERIAL FOR INFORMATIVE SPEECHES

Suppose you wanted to talk about South Africa, AIDS, stress, or how to safely lift heavy objects. How would you go about planning the speech? One way is to classify the topic.

Subjects for informative speeches may be divided into four broad categories. When you give an informative speech, you are (1) speaking about objects, (2) about processes, (3) about concepts, or (4) about issues and events.

1 Speeches about objects describe the physical qualities of the object.
2 Speeches about processes explain the relationships among events.
3 Speeches about concepts explain ideas, theories, or principles.
4 Speeches about issues and events describe contemporary and historical events.

Think of the subject of "democracy" in terms of these categories. "Democracy" could be approached as an object by describing its tangible symbols: the White House, the Capitol, the Supreme Court. Or it could be approached as a process and explained as a system of checks and balances operating in each branch of the government. Or it could also be approached as a concept and explained philosophically—that each person has inalienable rights, and so forth. A fourth approach would be to talk about democratic issues and historical events. For example, the Magna Carta was the first government document to validate the democratic principle.

These classifications give you a practical method for analyzing the preparation requirements of an informative speech. Again using the example of "democracy," if you choose to discuss the subject as a process, you would probably organize the speech around the three branches of government: executive, legislative, and judicial. Thus, approaching "democracy" as a process suggests the focus of the speech and organizing the body into a topical sequence. Let's discuss topics for informative speaking and how to plan these speeches.

Objects as Subjects

We are often called on to speak about tangible objects: about a "person, place, or thing." If you were discussing the life of Martin Luther King, Walt Disney World, a new sports car, or a new boyfriend or girlfriend, you would be describing an object.

Many speeches in professional, community, and social contexts are about objects. A product manager describing a new product to the sales force, a real estate agent showing a new house to a family, a park ranger conducting a tour of a national monument, and a town official showing plans for a new industrial park are all examples of people giving object speeches.

The goal of speeches on these types of subjects is to give a clear and vivid description of that object. If you were describing a dolphin, you would discuss its physical characteristics, habitat, intelligence, and behavior—a complete picture of the sea creature. Examples of subjects for an object speech:

Sharks	AIDS
The space shuttle	The ozone layer
Yosemite National Park	Steroids
The heart	Amelia Earhart

In an object speech the specific purpose reveals the subject, as the following examples show:

To describe the electric chair used in the execution of condemned prisoners.
To describe the Brazilian rain forest.
To describe a ten-speed racing bicycle used in competition.
To describe inline skates.
To describe a sumo wrestler.

The main points of an object speech are often organized in a spatial and topical manner. For example, if you want to describe a tennis racquet, you might arrange the main points in a spatial order according to three major parts of the racquet: (1) handle, (2) shaft, and (3) head.

Specific purpose:	To describe a tennis racquet.
Central idea:	Tennis racquets have three major parts.
Main points:	I The handle.
	II The shaft.
	III The head.

This spatial organization (bottom to top), which follows the natural divisions of the racquet, helps the audience visualize the subject. When preparing the main points, look for the natural divisions of the object and use them as your major divisions.

Main points for object speeches are often topical. If your subject is Albert Einstein, you could discuss him in terms of his significant contributions, in which case the main points would be topical, as shown below:

Specific purpose:	To describe the significant contributions of Albert Einstein.

Central idea:	Albert Einstein made significant contributions to humankind.
Main points:	I Einstein proposed the theory of relativity.
	II Einstein was an antiwar activist.
	III Einstein initiated work on momentous theories.

Or the sequence of your main points may be chronological. Using Albert Einstein again, you may choose to discuss his life from birth to his death, in which case your main points might look like this:

Specific purpose:	To describe the life of Albert Einstein.
Central idea:	Albert Einstein was a genius and a humanist.
Main points:	I Einstein's early years, 1879–1905.
	II Einstein's middle years, 1906–1934.
	III Einstein's later years, 1935–1955.

Processes as Subjects

Processes are an important type of subject. Much of our knowledge is a matter of learning a process. A doctor describing surgical procedures to a group of interns, a basketball coach showing team members how to shoot free throws, a nutritionist explaining proper dieting, all use descriptions of processes to help people achieve important goals.

A process is a particular method of doing something, usually a series of steps working together to produce a result. A tennis coach explaining how to hit a forehand shot would break down the stroke into three distinct steps: (1) assume the ready position, (2) pivot and turn, and (3) follow through. This approach helps the listener understand how to hit a ball effectively and then execute the stroke by practicing the steps. Some specific purposes for process speeches include:

To perform a magic trick.
To show how an actor creates a character.
To explain how to drill a water well.
To demonstrate how to stop severe bleeding.
To demonstrate how to juggle a soccer ball.

You could have one of two goals in explaining the process. You might want the audience to understand the process theoretically; that is, the audience should know the steps and their relationship to one another but not perform them. This speech might be called a "theory speech." Subjects for this category include:

How to secure a home from burglars.
How to prepare a résumé.
How to manage your time creatively.
How to reduce stress.

An alternative goal would be to explain a process so that the audience could perform it. If your purpose is to teach the audience to assemble a picture frame, you want the listeners to be able to reproduce the technique as a result of your message—or at least to have learned the process well enough to become skilled with practice. This might be called a "practice speech." Topics for this category include:

How to apply a tourniquet to a wound.
How to tune a guitar.
How to blow bubbles using sugarless gum.
How to draw freehand.
How to shell a lobster.

Discovering the main points of a process speech, be it a theory or a practical speech, is not difficult because the steps of the process convert easily into main points. The following are steps in the procedure for emergency evacuation of a commercial aircraft: (1) Listen to the instructions, (2) prepare for the landing, and (3) prepare for the evacuation. Observe how easily these three steps become the main points for a process speech:

Specific purpose:	To explain the process of emergency evacuation of a commercial aircraft.
Central idea:	The emergency evacuation of a commercial aircraft is a three-step process.
Main points:	I Listen to instructions. II Prepare for the landing. III Prepare for evacuation.

The steps in the procedure become the main points of the speech. This is characteristic of all process speeches.

The steps may fall into a time, topical, or spatial sequence. In the following example, the process follows a chronological pattern:

Specific purpose:	To describe to the audience how to bungee jump.
Central idea:	Bungee jumping is safe, fun, and exciting.
Main points:	I Listen to the instructions. II Wrap straps securely around ankles. III Hook bungee cords to straps. IV Jump into space screaming.

Concepts as Subjects

Thoreau once said that one sees the world more clearly if one sees it at an angle. Concepts could be defined as ideas in the abstract. Concepts include those ideas that form theories about what underlies events and/or behavior. A psychologist explaining the concept of preadolescent motivation to a group of parents may help them understand why their children behave in a certain way. A lawyer describing the concept of free speech to a group of students helps them understand the basic concept of constitutional government.

Subjects for concept speeches include ideas, theories, and values; a few examples are evolution, free will, socialism, affirmative action, justice, and insanity. Some examples of specific purposes for concept speeches are:

To explain the theory of method acting.
To explain the theory of supply and demand.
To explain the ideals of equality.
To explain the theory of global warming.
To explain the concept of Christianity.

The body of a concept speech is usually organized along topical lines. One approach is to define the concept in the first main point, explain the major elements in the next main point, and illustrate the concept through examples in the third main point. For example:

Specific purpose: To explain the concept of civil rights.

Central idea: Civil rights protect citizens from unreasonable government actions and are the basis of social change.

Main points:
I Civil rights are constitutional rights that protect individual citizens from arbitrary and irresponsible acts of the government.
II The significant elements of civil rights are "due process of law," "right to privacy," and "right to a fair trial and defense."
III Civil rights play a large role in promoting equal rights for minorities.

Another approach is first to define the concept and then to explain the major elements, as in this example:

Specific purpose: To explain the theory of learning.

Central idea: Learning theory is a theory that explains how people change.

Main points:
I Learning is a relatively permanent change in behavior that occurs as a result of experience.

> II Three important ways that people learn are through adjustment, association, and insight.

Some concepts may need only two main points—definition and examples—but definition should always be the first main point. Some concepts may also require the skillful use of subpoints.

Informing about Issues and Events

Issues and events are important topics; speeches on such topics can give people valuable insights and perspectives on historical and contemporary situations. A researcher explaining the causes of illiteracy or a doctor reporting on the status of the AIDS epidemic would be informing about issues and events.

Issues and events topics cover a wide range. You might explain an existing policy, such as the federal government's policy toward illegal aliens; you might analyze an important issue, such as the problems of foster care. You might delve into President Clinton's decision to send American troops to Bosnia or the early history of women's suffrage in America. Other examples of contemporary issues are:

Sexual harassment on the job	Grade inflation
Child care	Crime
Balanced federal budget	Television violence

Some specific purposes for issues and events speeches might be:

To explain how to save the Social Security system.
To explain the history of rock music.
To explain the spread of sexually transmitted diseases in the United States.

The sequence of your main points may be temporal, topical, or spatial, although a topical sequence offers a special flexibility when organizing these messages. The main points may be discovered by asking such questions as Who? What? Where? Why? When? and How? For example, if you wanted to give a speech about alcoholism, you might ask What? Who? and Why? The resulting main points would be:

(What?)   I Definition of alcoholism.
(Who?)   II Extent of the problem.
(Why?)   III Causes of the problem.

If you wanted to explain the depletion of the ozone layer, you might organize the main points in this way:

(Where?)   I The location of the holes in the ozone.

(What?)   II The extent of the depletion.

(How?)   III The causes of the depletion.

If you wanted to explain the theory of black holes, you might organize the main points of the speech this way:

(What?)   I Definition of the black hole.

(Where?)   II Their location in space.

(How?)   III How black holes come into existence.

A time sequence is useful for giving the history of a subject. For example, if your topic was the Statue of Liberty, you could divide its history into three major periods:

I 1874–1896: Construction.

II 1887–1983: Symbol of freedom.

III 1984–1986: Renovation.

PRINCIPLES OF INFORMATIVE SPEAKING

John Naisbitt said, "We are drowning in information but starving for knowledge." What he meant is that although we have the capability to communicate great quantities of information, little of it is being converted to knowledge that is meaningful and useful to people. That may partially explain why we have 24 million functional illiterates in America, 1 million high school dropouts every year, and SAT scores that continue to decline. Throwing information at people doesn't increase knowledge. Information must be presented in a way the audience finds valuable and engaging.

The goal of informative speaking is to prepare and deliver your speech in such a way that the audience finds it meaningful and useful. The keys to this process are building your speech on the principles that get the attention of the audience, presenting information clearly, and maintaining a high level of involvement. Figure 13-1 shows how an audience may respond to a speech that doesn't use the principles of informative speaking. Comprehension and retention dip significantly in the middle of the speech. Figure 13-2 shows how an audience responds to a speech based on sound communication principles.

We have already discussed some of these principles in previous chapters. Let's bring them all together and discuss the principles of informative speaking.

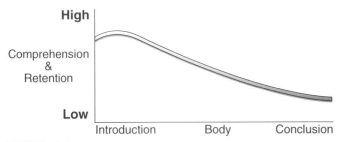

FIGURE 13-1
Not using principles of communication.

Set Realistic Goals

Audiences prefer highly focused single-idea topics they can easily grasp. Audiences have a limited capacity to absorb large amounts of information in public speaking settings, not to speak of short attention spans. If your goals are too ambitious, the audience will be overwhelmed and will tune out. A good teacher, for instance, will not present a whole subject area in a single lecture, but will break it up into several lectures so the students can easily understand the material. Limit your message to a single idea that can be supported in depth in the allotted time. (Review Chapter 4 on narrowing and phrasing the specific purpose.)

Integrate Your Topic with the Audience's Wants and Needs

If your topic is not relevant, the audience will not listen. People need to see value in the information you are presenting. How does your topic make their lives better? More efficient? More rewarding? How can your topic help them achieve important objectives? How will your topic improve their family, relationships, or performance? Identify specific issues and clearly show how your speech will help them.

FIGURE 13-2
Use principles of communication.

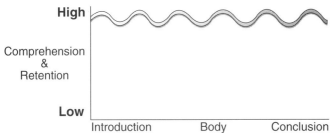

Making your topic entertaining increases comphrension.

Showing the value of your topic can be done in the introduction in the relevancy step that was discussed in Chapter 9. It can also be done in the body of the speech by relating specific information to audience expectations. For example, in a speech about building self-esteem in children before a group of parents, the speaker approached the concept this way:

> Building self-esteem in our children is one of our most important responsibilities as parents. Many of you listed this as one of your primary goals for the program today. In the next few minutes I'm going to describe a process that you can begin using right away.

Present Information in an Organized Manner

Deliver the speech in short, distinct units. People easily follow and remember information when it is divided into small parts and recognizable patterns. That is why good organization is so important. Audiences recognize each part of the speech and easily follow the message. Make your organizational plan stand out:

1 Use a preview, preferably a colorful chart listing the main points. This gives the audience "the big picture," a context in which to understand the whole before understanding the parts.

2 Identify the main points verbally: you might say "My first main point . . ." or "Now let's turn to my third and last major point." As you verbalize the main point, refer to it on the chart.

3 Use acronyms to make it easy for the audience to remember the main points. Acronyms are names formed from the first letters of a series of words that make it easier for the audience to remember a process or idea. They are usually short catchy words such as M*A*S*H* (Mobile Army Surgical Hospital). In a speech on motivation the speaker used the acronym GAAS to help the audience remember the main points:

G   I Goals.

A   II Assessment.

A   III Action.

S   IV Start.

4 Use transitions and summaries between main points because they refresh the memory and signal the introduction of new information. This renews the audience's interest. You are telling the audience you have completed an important point and are starting a new one.

Use your voice to break up information. Pacing refers to the rate at which you deliver your message. The ideal is to achieve variety—to speed up, slow down, and pause naturally at important junctures in the presentation (see Chapter 12).

Use a Multichannel Delivery

Using a multichannel delivery—telling, showing, and doing—increases your chances of having the audience understand and remember your speech. According to some learning authorities, people remember 10 percent of what they read; 20 percent of what they hear; 30 percent of what they see; 50 percent of what they hear and see; 70 percent of what they see, hear, and respond to; and 90 percent of what they see, hear, respond to, and do (Figure 13-3). Using all the channels also holds the audience's attention at high levels.

To improve retention, associate important ideas with entertaining devices such as stories, analogies, and visuals. For example, in a speech describing the importance of visualization to personal success, the speaker chose an entertaining and true story to demonstrate the importance of the concept:

People Remember...

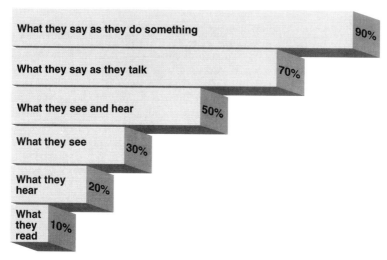

What they say as they do something — 90%

What they say as they talk — 70%

What they see and hear — 50%

What they see — 30%

What they hear — 20%

What they read — 10%

FIGURE 13-3
Knowledge retention.

Jim Thorpe has been hailed as one of America's greatest athletes. While on the ship that was heading for the 1912 Olympics, Jim leaned against the side of the cabin with his eyes closed, as the other track stars ran around the deck vigorously exercising. His coach came over and demanded to know why he wasn't exercising. "Just practicing," he replied. He was picturing himself competing and winning his event. History recorded his legendary feats and record-breaking performances. Jim Thorpe was using a technique called visualization. He was winning before it actually happened.

Use colorful drawings with word charts so audiences can visualize the ideas as they read and hear the words. Visual information stimulates the mind in a way the spoken word never can. Create simple exercises the audience can perform that illustrate important points. In a speech explaining the concept of potential energy, the speaker gave the audience rubber bands and had them stretch them out. He had them release them and observe how the concept of potential energy worked in action. A simple but dramatic and entertaining way of explaining an abstract concept.

Use humor. Humor increases interest and retention of information. It also enhances your image.[2] Humor may take the form of stories, jokes, or self-disparaging remarks made in good taste.

Tie humor to important points you want the audience to understand and remember. Groucho Marx once said, "Before I speak, I have something important to say." His point was that humor won't save a speech if the speaker has nothing meaningful to say. Here is an example of how one speaker used a humorous story to reinforce an important political principle:

> Then Senator Bill Bradley of New Jersey was at a luncheon when the waiter came by and put a pat of butter on his plate. The senator said, "Excuse me, I'll have two." The waiter replied, "Sorry, one to a customer," and moved on to the next diner. The senator called the waiter back and said, "Excuse me, waiter, I don't think you know who I am. I played basketball at Princeton, I was an All-American for three years, I was a Rhodes Scholar at Oxford, I played for the New York Knicks, I was a six-time all-star, and I am now a United States Senator from New Jersey." The waiter paused and said, "I don't think you know who I am." The senator said, "Well, who are you?" The waiter replied, "I'm the guy in charge of the butter."
>
> That is what politics is all about, who's in charge of the butter. You have to deal with that person.[3]

Link New Information to the Audience's Experience

Audiences bring important resources to a speech—expectations, education, occupations, common experiences—that you should use in the speech through examples, ancedotes, and so forth. An audience will grasp new information faster when you make these associations. For example, a manager explains a new procedure for reporting expenses by showing how the new procedure is similar to the old one and how it is different. If she is explaining the procedure to a new employee, she might compare it to the procedure she knows the employee used in his last job. Linking new information to the audience's experience is a valuable principle of informative speaking and a key to effective communication. In the following example, the speaker relates professional political handlers to the management of Walt Disney World:

> From the day a political campaign begins professional handlers—pollsters, media consultants, scriptwriters—control every sound, song, and word you hear about a candidate. They are like the people who run the city of [Walt] Disney World, where they teach everyone to smile and how to say hello. They create and control the mood of a fantasy city.[4]

Keep Your Language and Visuals Simple and Concrete

People understand and remember concrete words better than abstract words. Kick, slash, blood red, tennis shoe, and bubble gum are understood quicker and retained longer than truth, justice, government, society, or welfare. In the following example, see how concrete language brings alive the experience of bungee jumping:

Demonstration helps audiences grasp information.

I was plummeting through space. The bridge rails shot past me and the water rushed up at me as if I were looking through a zoom lens. After a few seconds the cord stiffened and cracked like a whip. I blanked out. A second later my head dunked in the frigid water. I rocketed back up, almost to the top and began to free fall again. I bounced up and down and the straps bit into my ankles. Finally, I was lowered into a boat.

Avoid excessive detail in both language and visuals. Audiences can't remember it. It is best to condense complex data into simple steps or charts the audience can easily understand. Put complex information in handouts and distribute the handouts after the presentation.

Adapt information from other sources for oral presentations. Much printed information is designed to be understood in that context and needs modification to be presented orally. A complex chart may work well in a book, but it would have to be simplified to be used in a speech.

Emphasize Concrete Results

Audiences feel satisfied when they walk away with useful information. Show the audience how your speech has helped them achieve important goals. This gives them a sense of achievement and you, high credibility. Be specific. For example, a speaker explaining the concept of deficit financing told the audience how knowledge of that concept would help them understand whether government spending policies were financially sound. Or, after explaining the steps for applying an emergency splint to a wound, the speaker reiterates that the audience members, in an emergency, would be able to perform the technique by following the process described in the speech.

OUTLINE OF AN INFORMATIVE SPEECH: CARDIOPULMONARY RESUSCITATION

Study the following outline for a speech about cardiopulmonary resuscitation (CPR). As you read, note how the speech is organized and how an acronym is used to help the audience remember the main points. The speaker uses this device throughout the message.

CARDIOPULMONARY RESUSCITATION

Introduction

A Attention material: You are faced with an emergency situation. Do you know what to do?

B Relevancy material: Cardiopulmonary resuscitation is a lifesaving skill that can artificially maintain the breathing and circulation of a victim.

C Credentials: I hold certification in CPR and have saved lives.

D Specific purpose: To demonstrate cardiopulmonary resuscitation.

E Central idea: Cardiopulmonary resuscitation is a simple and easy-to-learn first-aid technique.

Body

(*Preview:* (1) A = airway, (2) B = breathing, (3) C = circulation.)

I Clear the airway.
  A Remove obstacles from the mouth.
  B Tilt the head back to adjust the tongue.

II Maintain the breathing.
  A Inflate the lungs.
    1 Prepare to give mouth-to-mouth resuscitation.
    2 Blow two bursts of air into the lungs.
  B Be gentle with infants.
    1 Cover child's nose with your mouth.
    2 Blow less air.

III Sustain the circulation.
  A Lay the victim on a firm surface.

B Place palm on chest.
C Press firmly, then release.
D Repeat fifteen times.
E Maintain the proper ratio.

Conclusion

CPR can save your life and others' lives. Remember your ABC's.

TEXT OF A PROCESS SPEECH: CARDIOPULMONARY RESUSCITATION

Study the following informative speech about cardiopulmonary resuscitation. As you read it, note how the speaker uses the principles of informative speaking. The goal is clear and realistic. The speech establishes relevance. It presents the information in small units. The speaker uses demonstrations, charts, and simple and concrete language. The speech moves crisply. The conclusion summarizes the steps and demonstrates concrete results. Note that the style is crisp and simple, that the dialogue is maintained throughout the message, and that the conclusion reinforces the main points.

CARDIOPULMONARY RESUSCITATION

1 Picture yourself at a baseball game, and the person sitting in front of you slumps to the ground. He is unconscious. He stops breathing. A human being is dying in front of you. What do you do? Would you know what to do?

2 This is not an uncommon situation. This kind of emergency happens to thousands of people. In fact, over 1 million people are stricken by heart attacks every year; 650,000 die. Over half of these deaths can be prevented with proper first aid. Cardiopulmonary resuscitation, commonly known as CPR, is a first-aid skill that can save a person's life in such an emergency. CPR is a simple and easy-to-learn process that can artificially maintain breathing and circulation until the victim can resume these functions normally or until help arrives.

3 I first became interested in CPR when my grandfather was stricken in a restaurant. He was saved by a stranger who knew CPR. I have since become certified in CPR and have applied it in two emergencies. It can help you save lives and reduce serious injury.

4 My purpose is to demonstrate to you cardiopulmonary resuscitation. My goal is to have you learn this lifesaving technique so that you can use it in an emergency situation.

5 If you know your ABC's, you can learn CPR. CPR is divided into three steps: (1) opening the airway, (2) maintaining the breathing, and (3) sustaining the circulation. The sequence can be easily remembered by thinking of ABC: **A** stands for airway, **B** stands for breathing, and **C** stands for circulation. Remember ABC.

6 The first step is to clear and open the airway. Remove any obstacles, such as food, by reaching into the victim's mouth with your index and middle finger, like pliers, and pulling the object out. The tongue is also an obstruction and must be tilted back out of the way. This is achieved by placing one hand under the neck and the other hand on the forehead and gently lifting the neck up and pushing the head back. Maintain the victim's head in that position. This opens the airway and completes **A,** the first part of the process.

7 The second step of the process is to maintain the breathing of the victim. If the human brain is denied oxygen for 4 to 6 minutes, it will be damaged beyond restoration. Pinch the victim's nostrils together, and inflate the lungs through mouth-to-mouth breathing. Blow air into the lungs with two quick, full-sized breaths. (For an infant, cover the child's mouth and nose with your mouth and blow gently once, just enough to make the chest rise. Excessive air will cause the lungs to explode and cause death. You cover the infant's nose to prevent the air from escaping as you blow it.) This completes the **B** part of the process, but unless the heart is beating to circulate the blood and oxygen, the victim will not survive.

8 The third step is to maintain the circulation by pumping the heart manually. Prior to this step, make sure the victim is lying on a hard surface. The heart must be compressed, and a soft surface such as a mattress will absorb the pressure instead of the heart.

9 Kneel down next to the person and with your arms stiff and one hand superimposed on the other, place your palm on the victim's chest at the bottom of their rib cage. Make sure your fingers are up and your palm is down. Press down slowly but firmly, then release. Do this fifteen times, yes, fifteen times, and then again blow into the mouth two times. Maintain this ratio of fifteen to two until the victim is revived or medical help arrives. This completes the **C** part of the process.

10 Cardiopulmonary resuscitation is a simple process that can save your life and the lives of others. Remember your ABC: **A,** open the airway; **B,** maintain the breathing; and **C,** sustain the circulation. You now have the steps for saving a life and can use them in an emergency. CPR may take five minutes or five hours, but you have a life in the palm of your hands. *(Used with the permission of Brett Holbrook.)*

Commentary

A paragraph-by-paragraph analysis of this speech shows how the speaker manages to make the CPR process clear to the audience.

1 The speaker opens the speech with a dramatic story and question, an effective way of capturing the attention of the audience.

2 The speaker orients the audience and gives them statistical data showing the relevance of CPR: it saves lives. The central idea is revealed: CPR is an easy-to-learn process that maintains life in an emergency.

3 The speaker reveals his credentials. He also reinforces relevancy.

4 The specific purpose is revealed as the speaker tells the audience what he wants them to know. Note the clarity of the statement.

5 Excellent preview: CPR is as easy to learn as ABC. The audience can easily follow the sequence of the speech as the speech progresses.

6 The first step is clearly stated. Note the analogy "like pliers." Clear transition follows the explanation of the first main step.

7 The second step is identified. Study how clearly and carefully the speaker leads the audience through the process. Again a transition is used to lead the audience from one main point to another.

8 The third step is stated.

9 The third main point is explained. Again the language is kept simple and the information is easy to follow. The repetition will help the audience remember that fifteen is the number of times to press down on the chest.

10 The conclusion summarizes the process. ABC is restated. Concrete results are shown. The entire speech achieves unity.

SUMMARY

Speaking to inform is a major type of public speaking whose goal is understanding and retention of information. The subjects for informative speaking include objects, processes, concepts, and issues and events. Seven important principles of communication include (1) setting realistic objectives, (2) integrating your topic with the needs and wants of your audience, (3) presenting information in an organized manner, (4) using a multichannel delivery, (5) linking new information to the audience's past experience, (6) keeping your language and visuals simple and concrete, and (7) emphasizing concrete results.

PROBES

1 Answer the following questions about the CPR speech:
  a Do you now have a clear understanding of CPR? Could you perform CPR based on the material presented in the speech?
  b How was the body of the speech organized? Were the main points easy to follow?
  c Were the main points adequately developed?
  d Were the main types of clarifying information used?
  e What could the speaker have done to improve the message?
2 What is the goal of speaking to inform? Why is it important?
3 In what ways do the subjects of objects; processes; concepts; issues and events differ?
4 List seven principles for presenting information.

APPLICATIONS

1 Classify the following subjects as objects, processes, concepts, or issues and events: (a) Surfboard. (b) Bungee jumping. (c) How to buy stock. (d) Gravity. (e) Rush Limbaugh. (f) Multiculturalism. (g) Beauty. (h) Recycling paper. (i) Yosemite National Park. (j) Insanity.

2 Using the discussion of objects, processes, concepts, or issues and events as subjects, convert the following topics into speech subjects that conform to those classifications. (For example, the subject of solar energy could be treated as a concept, "The theory of solar energy"; as a process, "How solar energy generates power"; or as an object, "What a solar machine looks like.") (a) Crime. (b) Balanced budget. (c) The atom. (d) Love.

3 Using your understanding of the principles of informative speaking, describe how the following people would use those principles: (a) A minister. (b) A basketball coach. (c) A sales manager.

4 Suppose you were a communications consultant, and a business executive asked your advice on how to prepare an informative speech for a group of employees. What advice would you give the executive?

5 Using the classification of subjects as objects, processes, concepts, and issues and events, classify the following speech objectives:
a You want to tell about your summer vacation.
b You want to give a report on animal cruelty in laboratories.
c You want to talk about class registration procedures.
d You want to talk about student attitudes on campus.

ASSIGNMENT

Prepare a five-minute speech about a process. Your goal is to explain the process clearly so that the audience will understand and retain the message. Select a topic you are interested in and feel will be of interest to the audience. Prepare an outline using the example in this chapter as a model. Limit the main points to four; condense the information if the process has more than four steps. All the channels—telling, showing, and doing—should be used. Give special attention to reinforcing the message. Look for ways to use visual aids. Charts may be useful.

Your message will be evaluated on the clarity of your outline, the explanation of the process, and your delivery. The following checklist should be helpful as you prepare your message.

1 Is my audience likely to be interested in my topic?
2 Is my specific purpose clear and realistic?
3 Is the central idea clearly phrased?
4 Are my main points clear?
5 Are there transitions between the main points?
6 Are the channels of telling, showing, and doing used effectively?

    a Can visual aids be used?

    b Are the main points adequately reinforced?

7 Do the introduction and the conclusion fulfill these objectives?

8 Have I rehearsed my message a sufficient number of times?

What are your personal objectives for the speech? List them. Be specific.

A final note: You might practice for this assignment by recalling a past experience when you organized an event.

NOTES

1 Bill Clinton, opening remarks at Economic Conference Opening Session, Little Rock, Arkansas, December 14, 1992, p. 3.

2 Ron Zemke, "Humor in Training," *Training,* Vol. 28, August 1991, pp. 26–29.

3 Christopher Matthews, "Hardball: How Politics Is Played," *The Commonwealth,* Vol. 45, November 7, 1988, p. 478.

4 Christopher Matthews, "Hardball: How Politics Is Played," *The Commonwealth,* Vol. 45, Nov. 7, 1988, p. 479.

ARLES
CHES

GEORGE
MILLER

14

SPEAKING TO PERSUADE

Effectively persuading others is one of our most important skills. Emerson said, "Speech is power: speech is to persuade, to convert, to compel." What he means is that persuasion is the way we exercise our personal influence. It is how we communicate to get things done and is a strong measure of our success both personally and professionally.

Persuasion is the way we get people to adopt new ideas and change their behavior. You may have a better solution to a problem, or an idea that changes perception. You may believe in the principle of personal responsibility and urge others to adopt that concept as a personal value and basis for personal behavior. A manager faced with rising health costs may urge subordinates to adopt healthier lifestyles as a means of reducing medical costs. Tom Peters, the well-known business consultant, describes how managers persuade:

> Management . . . involves energizing people, often large numbers of people, to do new things they previously had not thought important. . . . It requires . . . managers to get people to share our sense of urgency in new priorities; to develop personal, soul-deep animosity toward things as they are; to get up the nerve and energy to take on the forces of inertia that bog down any significant change program.[1]

As a persuader you want people to change their actions or thinking. You take a position on a subject and advocate it. You are not impartial as you might be if you're speaking to inform. You want to change behavior or the way an audience perceives an issue or event. Take the subject of abortion, for example. If you were informing, your goal might be to help the audience understand the arguments, both pro and con, about such a controversial subject. As a persuader, you take a position, for or against it, and attempt to convince the audience to accept your point of view. Here are some examples of topics for persuasive speeches:

The Internet should be regulated.
Practice safe sex.
Ban advertising aimed at children.
Become an organ donor.
"Gangsta rap" encourages violence.

Persuasion is a challenging process. People do not change easily and often only grudgingly. Your proposal may be risky. Asking people to give up a valuable program, habit, or perk for a new untried approach involves risk. President Clinton's 1993 health care reform proposal died after extensive national debate. Many people considered it too radical and complex and were unwilling to jeopardize their existing coverage, in which they had confidence, for an untested and confusing government-controlled alternative.

To be an effective persuader places important demands on a speaker. You must speak clearly so people understand your arguments. You must understand what motivates people to change their thinking and actions and apply those principles in an ethical manner. You must learn to think strategically and use logical arguments and evidence to convince the audience. Most important, you must present yourself and the message honestly and substantively so the audience sees your true character.

THE ETHICS OF PERSUASION

Ethics are standards of right and wrong that guide our behavior and communication. At its core is our integrity and our willingness to communicate honestly and openly when we speak to advance our cause. We speak ethically when we sincerely believe our topic benefits the audience equally or in greater proportion than ourselves. Respect for the audience is the basis of your persuasion. Ethics breaks down when integrity breaks down, when we seek advantage over the audience or when our cause becomes greater than the audience. Then, people will use deceit to justify their case.

That is what happened in 1992 when *Dateline,* an NBC News magazine program, aired a segment showing a General Motors pickup truck bursting into flames after being hit from the side by a sedan. The graphic demonstration was used to support the storyline that GM pickups were unsafely designed and engineered. General Motors sued, claiming the crash was rigged. In an on-the-air apology, NBC admitted the crash was staged: Incendiary rockets were ignited by remote control to ensure that an explosion and fire would occur upon impact after two previously staged crashes did not cause an explosion. The gas tanks were also filled to overflowing and nonstandard gas caps were used to seal the tanks to insure the hoax would work as planned. *Dateline* lied to the audience. The cause was more important than the truth.

Lapses in ethics are costly to individuals and institutions because they lose their prestige and people stop listening. Political communication is held in very low esteem. The great majority of people believe politicians will say or do anything to stay in office and make promises they have no intention of keeping. As a result, people turn off and become cynical. It is not any wonder that term limits and third parties have become popular movements. People want honest communication in public life.

What can you do to insure you persuade ethically? The following guidelines can assist in making ethical decisions when speaking.

Accept the Burden of Proof

Winston Churchill once said, "What the people really want to hear is the truth—it is the exciting thing—to speak the truth." As the speaker you carry the burden of proof, the responsibility to prove that the audience should change its actions and behavior. Select the strongest evidence from the most credible sources to build your arguments and deliver your speech with conviction. That is the obligation you owe the audience when you seek change. You will not always be successful when you persuade, but you must make the strongest effort to prove your case.

Put Your Cards on the Table

Tell the audience clearly and specifically what you want them to believe or do. The issue here is integrity. Max De Pree once said, "The first responsibility of a leader is to define reality." What he means is tell the truth, then you will have the audience's trust even if they disagree or dislike what you say. Avoid hidden agendas or the appearance of one. Washington journalist Christopher Matthews criticizes President Clinton on this very point. Instead of answering questions directly about potentially embarrassing issues, he responds with what Matthews calls "rolling disclosures," partial or indirect answers that suggest hidden agendas and only lead later to more questions.[2]

Do Not Put Cause Before Honesty

Resist the temptation to fabricate or hype information to support your case. In the long run it will backfire and you will lose your credibility and support for your cause. Pat Stevens, a guest on CNN's *Crossfire,* claimed that 60 million women were battered by their husbands or male friends. Yet there are only about 55 million women married or living with a male.[3] The statement was a gross exaggeration and simply not believable. The serious and tragic problem of domestic violence was ill served and probably set back by these and other remarks that hype the issue.

Respect Your Audience

Speak in the best interests of the audience. Treat them with respect and dignity. When General Colin Powell withdrew his name from consideration for the Republican nomination for president in 1996, he told the nation, who overwhelmingly supported his candidacy, that he lacked the "passion" at that time to run. In his heart he wasn't ready to do it. If he did run, he would be betraying the special "bond" he had with the American people which was to be true himself and tell the truth.[4] General Powell respected his audience. He would not compromise his integrity and deceive the audience.

SUBJECTS FOR PERSUASIVE SPEAKING

A helpful way for learning how to prepare persuasive speeches is to categorize them according to their objective or goal. For example, persuading an audience to take a particular action may require a motivational strategy, whereas attempting to change their thinking may require evidence and reasoning. Persuasive speeches may be divided into three categories: (1) speaking to influence perceptions or thinking, (2) speaking to influence actions, and (3) speaking to influence policy.

Changing Perceptions

One of the important reasons we persuade is to change people's thinking about themselves, others, events, and issues. You may want them to adopt a new belief, modify an existing belief, or give up a belief. Suppose you believe that a flat tax is a more equitable and fair method of taxation and the audience thinks differently. Then you would be attempting to modify their beliefs about the subject. A manager discussing the advantage of a new corporate strategy with her employees would be attempting to establish a positive attitude toward the plan. Here are some examples of subjects for speeches to influence thinking:

Age discrimination is wrong.
UFOs exist.
Animal experimentation is cruel.
Build your life on moral principles.
Voter apathy threatens democracy.
Child abuse is rampant.

The main points for a speech to change perception are often arranged topically. You give the audience reasons why they should accept your point of view. In the following example, the speaker wants the audience to believe that drugs should not be legalized:

Specific purpose:	To persuade the audience that drugs should not be legalized.
Central idea:	Legalization of drugs will lead to worse problems.
Main points:	I It will lead to more addiction. (Reason)
	II It will expand the illegal drug trade. (Reason)
	III It will compromise the morality of our culture. (Reason)

When you arrange the main points topically, you should put the strongest reasons first based on your audience analysis. There are exceptions to this rule but, generally speaking, the arguments should be in descending order. The idea is to gain agreement quickly by presenting the most convincing argument first. Time is also a factor. If you leave your strongest argument last, you may not be able to fully develop it or even present it because your allotted time has expired.

Another way of arranging main points is the cause/effect sequence. The specific purpose states the cause and the main points, the effects. In the following example, the speaker wants the audience to believe that television is harmful to children.

Specific purpose: To persuade the audience that TV is detrimental to children. (What does TV do that is detrimental to children?)

Central idea: TV has a detrimental effect on the growth and feelings of children.

Main points:
I TV retards the learning capacity of children.
II TV exposes children to extensive violence.
III TV distorts reality.

Changing Actions

One of the important reasons we persuade is to get people to change behaviors that may be detrimental to them or to others or to introduce new actions that improve their lives and increase their well-being. A dietitian may persuade a group of at-risk patients to reduce the amount of fat in their diet by 40 percent. A sports celebrity may try to persuade a youth group not to use drugs. A manager may exhort employees to cut costs to meet expense targets.

The goal of this type of persuasion is to get people to change their actions. The action may be a one-time act; for example, you may urge a group to write a letter to their local congressperson to protest about a specific issue. The action may be long-term—for example, a nutritionist might urge a group of parents to feed their children more fruits and vegetables and fewer sweets.

The specific purpose states the action you want the audience to take. Whatever the subject, the goal is to persuade the audience to do something. The following are examples of specific purposes for speeches of action:

To persuade audience members to take a course in self-defense.
To persuade audience members to donate time to a convalescent hospital.
To persuade the audience to recycle household waste.
To persuade audience members to donate their organs in the event of accidental death.

Remember, the specific purpose must be stated clearly, and the action must be one the audience can realistically achieve.

The main points for a speech about changing actions are often motivational appeals and are arranged in the cause/effect sequence. You show the audience how taking the action will result in achieving important personal

Emphasize the key points.

goals—having enough money for college, getting a high-paying job, or having more satisfying relationships. If the audience strongly desires these objectives, they will act favorably on your specific purpose.

In the body of the speech you select the most compelling benefits to be the main points—that is, the reasons you use to persuade the target audience.

Specific purpose:	To persuade the audience to exercise on a regular basis.
Central idea:	Regular exercise has many benefits.
Main points:	I Exercise improves your health.
	II Exercise improves your appearance.
	III Exercise increases your self-confidence.

Another strategy for moving people to action is Monroe's motivated sequence, a process of persuasion based on psychological principles. Instead of persuading using positive motivators, you show the audience how your topic will eliminate undesirable conditions harmful to them. If you want to persuade the audience that the purchase of a smoke alarm reduces the chances of injury or death by fire, you would begin by alerting them to the ever-present danger of fire and then presenting the solution, the installation of alarms. Monroe's motivated sequence is often used by salespeople and advertisers. They create a need and then show how their product will fill it.

The motivated sequence has five steps:

I Attention step:	Introduction captures the attention of the audience.
II Need step:	Demonstrates the presence of the undesirable condition.
III Satisfaction step:	Presents solution (the specific purpose) that removes the undesirable condition.
IV Visualization step:	Describes the benefits of the solution in vivid detail.
V Action step:	Tells the audience how to execute solution.

Give special emphasis to Step II, the "need step" because it is the crucial point in the sequence. If the audience does not feel harm or concludes there is not a compelling problem, they will not be motivated to act or listen to the remainder of the speech.

Let's apply the motivated sequence to the same goal discussed above, persuading the audience to exercise on a regular basis, so you can see how the motivated sequence compares to the organizational pattern based on benefits.

Specific purpose:	To persuade the audience to exercise on a regular basis.
Central idea:	Exercising on a regular basis improves health.
I Attention step:	Over 300,000 Americans die of heart attacks every year. (Startling statement)
II Need step:	Americans are unhealthy due to lack of exercise.
III Satisfaction step:	Exercise on a regular basis.
IV Visualization step:	Exercising on a regular basis increases your performance, self-esteem, and energy.
V Action step:	Exercising on a regular basis is simple and easy. Let's discuss some options.

The benefits approach and Monroe's motivated sequence are effective strategies for moving people to action. One approach focuses on the benefits of taking action, the other on removing an undesirable condition.

Changing Policies

An important goal of persuasive speaking is to propose solutions when existing policies and programs falter. Life sentences without parole for repeat offenders has been proposed as a solution for reducing violent crimes. A manager may propose a more flexible work schedule as a means of boosting morale and productivity. In both instances, speakers are seeking changes in policy.

The specific purpose states the solution you are proposing, as the following examples show:

To persuade the audience that all health care professionals should be tested for HIV.

To persuade the audience that more stringent laws are needed for foster care homes.

To persuade the audience that prison sentences for pornographers who exploit children should be more severe.

To persuade the audience that the president of the United States should be limited to one six-year term.

The body of a policy speech is organized in a problem/solution sequence, as discussed in Chapter 6. The first main point identifies the problem and points out the deficiencies in the current policy. The second main point states the solution and how it would correct the problem. A third, optional main point may show the extra benefits from adopting the solution. The following is a typical problem/solution sequence.

Specific purpose:	Junk food should not be sold in the school cafeteria.
Central idea:	Banning junk food would reinforce sound nutritional principles.
Main points:	**I** Junk food impairs the health of students. (Problem)
	II Junk food should not be sold in the school cafeteria. (Solution)
	III Benefits (Advantages)
	A Would eliminate a source of bad nutrition.
	B Would establish an educational principle about nutrition.

Please note that the specific purpose and main point II are both the statement of solution.

The problem/solution relationship must be logical. The solution must represent a carefully thought-out answer to the issues presented in the problem step. Either it eliminates the problem or significantly reduces it. For example, some people advocate the legalization of drugs, such as cocaine and marijuana, as a way of eliminating the drug trade. However, the solution doesn't address a significant part of the problem, that the majority of drug users are minors. There would still be a large illegal drug trade selling to youth. The solution doesn't solve the problem unless the speaker can show it would significantly reduce the problem and not create a host of other ones.

One of the ways of ensuring that your analysis is sound is to use subpoints that answer important questions about the problem and solution. Some questions about the problem include:

1 What is the extent of the problem? Is it widespread and sufficient in scope to justify change? Tell who is affected, where, and how they are affected.

2 What is the harm? How are people being hurt by the existence of the problem? The audience must feel involvement or injured by the problem or they will not entertain the solution.

3 How is the current policy causing the problem? How is the current program obsolete, flawed, etc.?

The following example shows subpoints for a problem/solution sequence.

Specific purpose:	To persuade the audience that a system of charter schools should be adopted for public schools.
Central idea:	Charter schools will increase student performance.
Problem:	**I** The public school system has not been educating students effectively.
(Extent)	**A** Low achievement and high dropout rates. **1** SAT scores unchanged for years. **2** U.S. twelfth graders rank near bottom in performance standards in fifteen-nation survey. **3** 1 million dropouts every year.
(Harm)	**B** High unemployment and inefficiency. **1** 6 of 10 job applicants fail entry-level tests. **2** 25 million illiterates. **3** Remedial courses necessary in college.
(Cause)	**C** No standards and accountability in public schools. **1** No measurable learning goals. **2** Contradictory government regulations. **3** Administrative bureaucracy. **4** No connection between results and rewards.

The subpoints break down the problem into component parts that make it easier to analyze and communicate the message.

The solution portion of the sequence should answer the following questions about a potential solution to the problem:

1 Will the solution reduce or eliminate the problem? What will the solution do?

2 How will the plan work?

3 Will the plan work efficiently?

The following example shows the subpoints for a solution; it continues the "charter schools" example above.

Solution: **II** Adopt a charter system for public school education.

    A Charter schools would be based on clear and measurable standards of performance.

      1 Schools set standards of performance.

      2 If they fail to meet standards, they are dissolved.

(Plan) **B** How plan works.

      1 Group applies for charter school.

      2 They would be funded by the state at the average level of per-pupil expenditures.

      3 Open admissions policy.

(Efficiency) **C** Plan will work smoothly.

      1 Focus on learning.

      2 Parents, students, teachers work for common goal.

      3 Eliminate waste and bureaucracy.

The subpoints break down the solution into parts so the audience can understand how it solves the problem and how it works. This is an effective approach to persuasion and will work if well applied.

PRINCIPLES OF PERSUASIVE SPEAKING

Speaking to persuade places important demands upon a speaker. Unlike speaking to inform which has an instructional theme, persuasion seeks change and that means overcoming some degree of resistance. The audience may have a long-held attitude about the topic. The audience may be indifferent toward your subject. The audience may be reluctant to give up a habit you consider harmful.

How do you get an audience to change? There is no formula but the following principles can help you be successful. Your presentation must not only be clear and well organized, but you must also convince the audience in three specific ways: (1) you must show them you are worthy of belief, (2) you must emotionally draw them into the topic, and (3) you must convince them your proposal is intellectually sound. Let's discuss each of the principles.

Convince the Audience You Are Credible

Consider these audience reactions to a speaker:

"You know, I like the speaker's arguments, but there was something about his personality I didn't like."

"The speaker's arguments didn't impress me. I knew more about the subject than she did."

"The speaker didn't put all his cards on the table. He wasn't telling the truth."

Each of these statements expresses a serious reservation about the speaker: He wasn't sincere, she seemed to lack knowledge or she didn't do her homework about the topic, or maybe he is dishonest. These types of observations about a speaker damage persuasion.

Credibility comes from the Greek word *credo* meaning "to believe." It means the speaker has presented the speech in such a way that the audience concludes she is a truthful and exemplary person. This principle has endured since ancient times when Quintilian defined the orator as "the good man speaking well." Aristotle considered the speaker's credibility the most persuasive part of a speech. All contemporary studies verify the central role of credibility in persuasion.

The audience believes a person is credible when they possess three important qualities when they speak: (1) integrity, (2) knowledge, and (3) sincerity:

Integrity: The audience believes the speaker is an honest and truthful person.

Knowledge: The audience believes the speaker understands the subject in depth and speaks with authority.

Sincerity: The audience believes the speaker is genuinely interested in and concerned about them.

If the audience believes you have these qualities, you will be persuasive. Former President Bush's reputation for being unprincipled plagued his presidency. His famous pledge in the 1988 presidential campaign, "Read my lips, no new taxes," came back to haunt him in 1991, when he agreed to increase taxes. He misused the voters' trust and lost many supporters. President Clinton's integrity has been questioned throughout his presidency by reneging on campaign appeals to cut middle-class taxes and government spending and by shifting positions and ideology based on public opinion polls.

What can you do to build your credibility? First and foremost, speak from conviction. Your delivery will naturally convey the intensity and sincerity you feel about your subject. If you are acting or pretending, your body language will reveal the make-believe. Television evangelist Jimmy Swaggert preached virtue but practiced vice and it showed in his delivery.

Be yourself. A person once said, "The most powerful person you can be is yourself." When you speak naturally, you are confident and relaxed. You make good eye contact. Your posture is relaxed, and your gestures and movement are spontaneous and in harmony with your words. Your facial expression conveys your internal emotions. Audiences want authenticity.

There are techniques you can, and sometimes must, use to establish your credibility with an audience. If an audience knows little or nothing about you, you may need to give them your credentials in the introduction to build your expertise. You cite extensive experience or training you have about the subject. If your topic is controversial, you may need to acknowledge the differences between you and the audience in an honest and straightforward way. This demonstrates empathy and respect for the audience's concerns or opposition to the topic. Here are some ways of building your credibility:

1 Demonstrate your competence. Prepare thoroughly using quality information and authoritative testimony. Present your ideas logically and clearly. Cite any special knowledge, experience, or personal achievements you have about the topic. Refer to experts respected by the audience. Do not exaggerate claims about the topic.

2 Demonstrate your interest in the audience. Show empathy for the needs and concerns of the audience. Establish rapport and common ground if necessary. Tie appeals directly to the audience's needs. Make direct eye contact and dress appropriately. Do not pander to or patronize the audience.

3 Maintain your composure. Treat interference calmly and logically. Avoid overly serious behavior. Don't belittle others. Respect the views of others even when they disagree with or are hostile toward your cause. Speaker of the House of Representatives, Newt Gingrich, has been criticized for making excessively harsh statements about his opponents.

Convince the Audience Emotionally

Audiences must be emotionally involved to be persuaded. It is naive to think that logic alone can move an audience. Just as a topic must be relevant to an audience, logical arguments must have emotional energy—fear, anger, compassion, sorrow, and indignation—to be persuasive. How could anyone not be emotionally affected by issues such as rape, child abuse, violent crime, AIDS, racism, substance abuse, unemployment, or abortion? It is the emotions that drive the discussion. Mary Fisher, in her famous speech to the 1992 Republican convention and a national television audience, eloquently and movingly, addressed the scourge of AIDS:

> The lesson history teaches is this: If you believe you are safe, you are at risk. If you do not see this killer stalking your children, look again. There is no family or community, no race or religion, no place left in America that is safe. Until we genuinely embrace this message, we are a nation at risk.
>
> Tonight, HIV marches resolutely toward AIDS in more than a million American homes, littering its pathway with the bodies of the young. Young men. Young women. Young parents, and children. One of the families is mine. If it is true that HIV inevitably turns to AIDS, then my children will inevitably turn to orphans.[5]

Emotionally involve the audience.

Mary Fisher, herself a victim, wanted to shake the audience from its apathy about AIDS by appealing to fear: No one is safe! Your family and loved ones, indeed you, are at risk. Her appeal was dignified and moving and many in the audience quietly sobbed as she told her story.

How do you determine the emotional impact of your speech and how do you plan emotional appeals if you feel they are needed? First, examine your speech for its emotional appeals. Some topics will have a high emotional content and some will not. Child pornography is an emotionally explosive issue and even rational arguments will be highly charged. Planning emotional appeals for this type of topic could be overkill and perceived as manipulative. On the other hand, if your topic is reforming college registration procedures, some emotional appeals may be needed to capture the reality of the problem such as describing the frustration of getting required classes, the inconvenience of standing in long lines, and the humiliation of begging instructors to let you into a class that is full.

Emotional appeals can be made in a number of ways, including: examples, vivid description, single words or phrases, or genuine expressions of feeling by the speaker. "Gash," "rape," "decapitation," "bashing," and "bloody" are words that can evoke strong reactions. The word "homeless" has a powerful connotation. The images evoked by this word are moving: desperate men, women, and children without shelter, roots, food, or hope.

President Clinton and his advisors used the word "security" during the health care reform debate to describe his program. The word was carefully chosen after polls and focus groups felt it had strong emotional appeal—the fear of losing health benefits.

In a speech on violent crime, this speaker gives a frightening description of two criminals' callous disregard for human life:

> A young mother and her two-year-old daughter stopped at a stop sign in their neighborhood when two young hoods opened the door and pulled her out of the car. Her daughter was still in the car. The two hoods jumped in and sped away. The woman, tangled in the seat belt, was dragged for a mile-and-a-half while the perpetrators kept knocking the car against obstacles to strip her off. After a mile-and-a-half, she died. Then the hoods threw the baby, still in a car seat, out the window. The two suspects, while being booked in the local precinct, were laughing and blowing kisses at the female officers, showing no remorse whatsoever.[6]

How could anyone not be outraged by such shocking acts.

Gestures and movements can have emotional impact. A reformed alcoholic addressing a group of parents described how his addiction led to his violent behavior and attacks on his wife. As he spoke a snarl formed on his face, sweat poured from his brow, and the veins in his neck protruded as he described how one evening he crashed his fist into his wife's face, while simultaneously smashing his fist into the palm of his hand with a loud smacking thump. The gesture was a powerful act of violent behavior.

Planning emotional appeals requires sensitivity to human feelings and values. You should not attempt to fabricate the appeal, manipulate the feelings of the audience, or act in an inappropriate manner. If the audience believes you are insincere, they will turn off. During a speech on censorship and television before an audience of company executives and dignitaries, Steven Chao, president of the Fox television network, had a male model come on stage and strip to illustrate a point about censorship. The audience was stunned. The ploy backfired; it angered and insulted the audience. Chao's boss, who was in the audience, fired him on the spot.[7] The following guidelines can help you in using emotional appeals:

1 Identify what emotions might be at work in the speech and how the audience will react to them.

2 If you plan to use emotional evidence, determine if it will be perceived as a natural and appropriate part of the topic.

3 Ask yourself if the appeal can be made with integrity. Does the appeal meet your standards of ethics, sincerity, and taste?

4 Will the appeal meet the values of the audience and dignify your presentation? Is the appeal appropriate to the listener?

Convince the Audience Intellectually

Before people will change their thinking and actions, you must convince them that your proposal has a strong rational basis. You must carefully select your reasons and evidence and prove your case is justified by the facts. If you want the audience to believe that excessive fat in the diet is harmful, then you must supply evidence to support that assertion. You must cite studies that show the high intake of fat clogs the arteries, reduces the flow of blood to heart, and impairs the heart's ability to function properly. You cite experts who have studied the problem and have concluded that fat is a major cause of illness and death.

Convincing the audience intellectually is called reasoning, sometimes referred to as the logical basis of persuasion. You use evidence to prove your case. A prosecutor presents fingerprints, bloodstains, eyewitnesses, forensic experts, and ballistics reports to prove a defendant guilty of the crime. We believe smoking is harmful because a myriad of scientific studies have proven beyond a doubt that smoking is linked to many serious and often fatal diseases.

Evidence is persuasive when it is logical and clearly presented and comes from highly qualified sources. The conclusions must be accurate interpretations of the facts. There must be a sufficient amount of evidence to justify the assertion. The arguments must be clearly presented so the audience easily understands the argument. Fallacies or erroneous thinking patterns that damage credibility must be avoided. Reasoning is such an important part of persuasion that learning how to use reasoning effectively will be discussed in Chapter 15, "Argument and Rational Analysis."

Convincing the audience intellectually, emotionally, and with your credibility are important principles of persuasion. Let's now apply the principles to a persuasive speech.

OUTLINE OF A PERSUASIVE SPEECH: BEYOND THE FREEDOM OF SPEECH

Study the following outline for a speech about weapons literature. As you read, note how the topic is organized. Three major reasons are presented and supported with evidence. *(Example used with the permission of Donna Murdock)*

BEYOND THE FREEDOM OF SPEECH
Introduction

A Attention Material:	Imagine yourself a passenger on a subway train and nerve gas is released.

B Relevancy Material: We are all potential victims. 169 innocent people killed in Oklahoma City bombing.

C Specific Purpose: To persuade the audience to support ban on how-to weapons literature.

D Central Idea: Banning weapons literature will save lives.

Body

I Weapons literature teaches people how to commit mass murder.
  A Paladin Press publishes how-to-make bombs books.
    1 *Homemade C-4*
      a Companion video
    2 *Homemade Semtex*
    3 *Deadly Brew: Advanced Improvised Explosives*
  B Desert Publications
    1 *Poor Man's Nuclear Bomb & Other Homemade Weapons of Mass Destruction*
  C Delta Press
    1 *Assorted Nasties: the Ultimate Handbook on Poisons & Applications Devices*
II Literature and videos are used by bombers.
  A FBI Bomb Data Center
    1 1993, 1,880 bombings.
      a 500% increase in 10 years
    2 43 people killed
    3 81 injured
    4 World Trade Center bombing
      a 6 people killed
      b 1,042 injured
  B John Farley
    1 Distribution of bombing literature a major cause.
  C Books found in libraries of serial killers and bombers.
  D Al Gleason, AFT investigator
    1 People who want to make bombs now have information
  E High school students downloaded bomb blueprints from Internet.
III Weapons literature teaches how to murder and maim.
  A *Deathtrap! Improvised Booby-Trap Devices*
    1 Make your own booby-traps
  B *Kill Without Joy*
    1 Slit throats of victims expertly and decapitation
  C *Black Medicine: The Dark Art of Death*
    1 Use martial arts to kill

D *Be Your Own Undertaker*

    1 Hide the bodies of your victims.

E Thomas Lavy made deadliest poison from handbook.

F Husband and mistress plot murder.

    1 *The Original Poor Man's James Bond, Volume 1*

G Hired killer uses *Hit Man* as guide for murder.

Conclusion

A Support a ban on books and videos that glorify and teach violence.

B We are living in fear and losing our freedom.

C Save your life and that of innocent people.

TEXT OF PERSUASIVE SPEECH: BEYOND THE FREEDOM OF SPEECH

1 Imagine yourself riding the subway. It could be in San Francisco or New York, or any subway in the world. And as your train speeds ahead at 90 miles an hour underground, your car begins to fill with gas. Your breath becomes shorter as you struggle to breathe. The air is thick and people around you begin to panic. Passengers are screaming and hysterically crash against closed doors in a desperate attempt to escape. Your lungs are about to burst.

2 Does this story sound like the latest action movie? Well, it shouldn't because that is what happened in the Tokyo subway. Five thousand five-hundred innocent people were injured and ten died in the subway when members of a fanatical religious cult planted nerve gas in one of the cars. How could this have happened? Really quite simply. The chemicals they needed could be purchased legally and the information for constructing the nerve gas was readily available. They had access to information and the ingredients to make the gas, just as individuals and groups in our country have access to this type of information and more.

3 Who can forget the mass murder of 169 innocent adults and children in Oklahoma City just a short time ago? A small group of individuals purchased the lethal ingredients, built the bomb, and detonated it, causing the worse terrorist attack in American History.

4 I'm not here to discuss the motivation of these terrorists and fanatics or even their pathology. I'm here to discuss a problem just as insidious—the sale and distribution of the books, manuals, and videotapes that teach people how to make bombs, booby-traps, and other weapons of death and destruction. This literature is being used by individuals and groups to carry out their evil fantasies. I want you to join me in seeking a ban on the sale and distribution of this information that includes declassified military manuals.

5 This isn't a matter of freedom of speech but of public safety and common sense. Today, anyone can walk into a bookstore, call an 800 number, surf the Internet, or order books and videos by mail that will teach them how to make and use the most terrifying and destructible weapons imaginable—bombs, booby-traps, sniper rifles, blasting caps, poison. Even manuals on murder are part of this lethal literature. The audience for this information is not you or me but the radical, the fanatic, the mentally deranged, the emotionally disturbed or the gang member. But we are the target. Let's sample some of these books and videos.

6 These books encourage and teach people how to commit mass murder. Paladin Press, one of the leading publishers of weapons literature, proudly advertises the destructive power of its books and videos. Their book *Homemade C-4* tells the reader how to make C-4, an explosive of immense destructive capability. It is illegal to buy C-4, but that doesn't stop Paladin from teaching readers how to make it. They proudly say *Homemade C-4* ". . . takes you step-by-step through everything you need to know to assemble, prepare and use improvised C-4 at home." A companion video shows live footage of C-4 blowing up cars and buildings. You can also purchase *Homemade Semtex*. Semtex is an internationally banned substance that looks like play dough and has been used to blow up passenger planes. It is a favorite of terrorists.

7 If *Homemade C-4* doesn't turn you on, try *Deadly Brew: Advanced Improvised Explosives*. It teaches ". . . how to construct explosive devices which provide detonation through an immediate mixture of . . . simple acid and a common industrial chemical." These publications are available by calling 1-800-392-2400, 24 hours a day, and you can use your credit card. You can purchase the *Poor Man's Nuclear Bomb & Other Homemade Weapons of Mass Destruction* from Desert Publications. From Delta Press you can purchase *Assorted Nasties: the Ultimate Handbook on Poisons & Application Devices.*

8 These books and videos are being used to kill and terrorize people. In 1993, according to the FBI Bomb Data Center, there were 1,880 bombings that killed 43 people and injured 81. That excludes the six people killed and 1,042 injured in the World Trade Center bombing. The number of bombings has increased 500% in ten years. One of the causes, according to journalist John Farley who has studied the problem, is the bombmaking literature. He states, "A significant factor in the increase in bombing is that the dissemination of bomb know-how has become a minor industry."

9 Police and federal agents find these books in the libraries of serial killers and bombers. The bombs that blew up the Federal office building in Oklahoma City and severely damaged the World Trade Center in New York City were made from materials legally purchased and the perpetrators knew how to combine the ingredients to create these weapons of mass destruction. Al Gleason, a retired ATF agent who has spent fifty years investigating bombings, says, "People who feel that the bomb might be their weapon of choice now have the information to make one."

10 Recently, three New Jersey teenagers sent two bomb threats to their high school in an attempt to extort 1.3 million dollars. At their home, the police found a bomb-making manual, *Jolly Rogers Cookbook,* that had been downloaded from the Internet. Bomb making is not the only subject of these publications. They instruct on how to maim and murder people.

11 *Deathtrap! Improvised Booby-Trap Devices* teaches readers how to make booby-traps from commonly available material. You can booby-trap doors, telephones, tape decks, door latches, and more. The author calls these "nasty surprises." Other books and videos teach you how to conceal weapons, build sniper rifles, make silencers, homemade gunpowder, conceal weapons, pick locks, and harass people. *Kill Without Joy* is a 500-page how-to murder book, including how to efficiently slit a victim's throat and tips on decapitation. *Black Medicine: The Dark Art of Death* teaches how to use martial arts to kill people. *Be Your Own Undertaker* teaches you how to hide the body of your victim and any incriminating evidence. The list goes on.

12 Recently the FBI arrested Thomas Lavy for attempting to smuggle 130 grams of ricin, one of the deadliest poisons known to humankind. It is 6,000 times more poisonous than cyanide and 12,000 times more poisonous than rattlesnake venom. A mere speck of ricin can lead to an agonizing death. He made the poison at home using several "recipe books" including *The Poisoner's Handbook* and *Silent Death.* He had enough poison to kill thousands of people.

13 Last year at one of our local shopping centers a pregnant woman, Rebecca Martin, was waiting in her car to pick up her husband and son who were attending a movie. As she waited alone twenty rounds from a semi-automatic rifle smashed into the car striking her three times. She survived. The attackers were first thought to be gangs involved in a drive-by shooting or a case of mistaken identity. The perpetrators of this shocking attack turned out to be her husband and his mistress, who fired the shots. The plan for their deadly scheme was based on the manual *The Original Poor Man's James Bond, Volume 1* that describes in detail how to assassinate people without getting caught. The husband purchased the book at a local bookstore.

14 One of the most shocking examples of the use of these books is the case of James Perry, convicted of triple murder and sentenced to death. He ordered through the mail and had sent directly to his home, *Hit Man: A Technical Manual for Independent Contractors.* The book written by Rex Feral, a professional killer, spells out in minute detail how to murder people for profit. It tells aspiring contract killers which weapons are most effective, what part of the body to shoot when using a gun, and how to avoid getting splattered with blood.

15 Perry followed the instructions to the letter in murdering his victims. He shot two of them in the eye just as the manual advised. The survivors of Perry's rampage are suing Paladin Press, publishers of *Hit Man,* for complicity in the crime. They believe the book aided in the commission of the murders and that Paladin Press should be held accountable.

16 In conclusion, I ask you to join with me in seeking a ban on these books and videos that glorify and teach violence, mayham, and mass murder. Clearly the target audience, no pun intended, for this information is not you or me, but terrorists, fanatics, criminals, sociopaths, and impressionable children. Each day we read in the newspaper about plots to blow up buildings, passenger airplanes, and trains that would kill hundreds of innocent victims. Today, Americans can no longer drive by the White House in our nation's capital. The street has been blocked off for fear of a bombing attack.

17 I have prepared individual letters for you to sign urging your local representative to seek a ban on this literature of murder and mayham. The life you save may be your own. Thank you. *(Used with the permission of Donna Murdoch)*

BIBLIOGRAPHY

1 Erik Larson, "Libraries of Killers," *The Wall Street Journal,* January 6, 1993, p. A1.
2 Robert Burnson, "After Pittsburg Attack, A Run on Heinous How-to Book," *The Contra Costa Times,* April 4, 10, 1994, p. 1A.
3 John Kifner, "Antiterrorism Law Used in Poison Smuggling Case," *The New York Times,* December 23, 1995, p. L7.
4 Christopher John Farley, "America's Bomb Culture," *Time,* July 31, 1995, p. 56.
5 Richard A. Serrano, "Deadly Mixture of Fertilizer, Oil Detailed by FBI," *Los Angeles Times,* April 21, 1995, p. A1.
6 Charles G. Brown, "Murder by the Book: Is the Publisher Responsible," *The Wall Street Journal,* March 6, 1996, p. A19.

COMMENTARY

A paragraph-by-paragraph analysis shows how the speaker developed the speech using reasoning and evidence.

1 The speaker opens with a hypothetical situation based on a real-life event.

2 Speaker lays groundwork for specific purpose and central idea.

3 Speaker refers to worst terrorist attack in American history to set stage for presentation.

4 Speaker narrows topic to weapons literature and claims it is partially responsible for acts of violence. Speaker clearly states specific purpose; banning how-to-make-weapons literature. It is being used by individuals and fringe groups to build bombs and to commit acts of violence.

5 Speaker talks about how easy it is to obtain the weapons literature.

6 Speaker presents her first major argument: Books and videos encourage and teach people how to build bombs. She then begins to describe individual publications that do just that.

7 Speaker continues her inductive argument by giving more examples of bomb-making manuals. She shows how easy it is to obtain the publications and video by giving the 800 number to place an order.

8 Speaker gives statistical evidence to show the increase in bombing and testimony to draw a cause/effect relationship between access to the literature and the violence associated with it.

9 The speaker gives more evidence to support the association between the bombing and literature on how to make explosives.

10 Speaker gives example of how three teens easily obtained bomb-building information through the Internet and used it in an attempt to extort money.

11 Speaker presents third major argument, that publications show how to kill and maim people. She describes the horrible acts these books show people how to perform.

12 Speaker gives factual example of person who made one of the most deadliest poisons known in his home using a how-to book. The poison, if used, could have killed thousands.

13 Speaker gives example of plot to kill woman that was taken from a book on assassination.

14 Speaker gives factual example of hired killer who uses manual to carry out murders.

15 Speaker argues that book was instrumental in carrying out gruesome crimes.

16 The speaker summarizes her arguments and gives examples to show the problem persists. Even the nation's capital is not safe.

17 The speaker exorts the audience to sign the letter she has prepared for each of them. She ends with word of caution about personal safety.

SUMMARY

Persuasion is the way we get people to adopt new ideas and change their actions. Your persuasion should be ethical. Being ethical includes accepting the burden of proof, avoiding hidden agendas, not putting cause before integrity, and respecting the audience. Persuasive topics seek to influence thinking, actions, and policies. Methods of persuasion include establishing your credibility, convincing the audience intellectually, and convincing them emotionally.

PROBES

1 How would you define persuasion?

2 Do you agree with the chapter's discussion of ethics in persuasion? What areas of a speech are most vulnerable to unethical practices?

3 What are four ways to demonstrate your ethics?

4 What are the different types of persuasive speeches? How are they different?

5 How does speaking to persuade differ from speaking to inform?

6 How would you describe credibility? What are three important elements of credibility?

7 What are some guidelines for developing your credibility in a speech?

8 What is reasoning? Why is it important?

9 Why are emotional appeals important? Describe three ways of using emotional evidence.

10 Was the speech "Beyond the Freedom of Speech" persuasive to you? How was the speech organized? How were the subpoints organized? What kinds of appeals did the speaker use? Were you persuaded? Why? Why not?

APPLICATIONS

1 You want the audience to donate time to a homeless shelter. How would you persuade them to take that action?

2 Give three examples when a speaker you know acted unethically.

3 Select a persuasive speech in *Vital Speeches* and analyze how it was organized.

4 Think of a person who is very credible to you. What qualities of character does he or she possess? Does he or she parallel the characteristics of knowledge, integrity, and goodwill discussed in the text?

5 Think of a speech in which you were emotionally moved. What feelings did you experience? Anger? Sadness? Compassion?

6 You have been hired as President Clinton's communications consultant. What advice would you give him to help him be more persuasive using the principles discussed in the chapter?

7 Formulate a persuasive goal for each of the following topics: (a) Space exploration. (b) Illiteracy. (c) Animal experimentation. (d) Television.

8 What main points would you select for the following topics?

    a Stop the spread of venereal disease.

    b Become a vegetarian.

    c Conserve water.

    d Support gun control laws.

ASSIGNMENT

Prepare a five-minute persuasive speech in which you attempt to motivate the audience to act in a certain way, influence thinking, or change a policy. Select a topic you are interested in or have conviction about and feel will be of interest to the audience. Use the principles of persuasion discussed in the chapter to build the speech.

Your speech will be evaluated on the clarity of the body of the speech, your reasoning process, the evidence you use in support, the overall outline, and your delivery style. The following checklist should help you prepare your speech:

1 Have I analyzed the audience effectively?
2 Will my topic be of interest to the audience?
3 Are my specific purpose and central idea clearly stated?
4 Are my main points clearly phrased and do they reveal a clear strategy?
5 Will the introduction and conclusion achieve their objective?
6 Have I prepared an effective speaking outline and notes?
7 Have I rehearsed my speech a sufficient number of times?

NOTES

1 Tom Peters, "Take Symbolic Action," *Contra Costa Times,* June 5, 1993, p. 20.
2 Christopher Matthews, "Clinton's Nasty Habit of Rolling Disclosure," *San Francisco Examiner,* March 24, 1994, p. A21.
3 Armin Brott, "Hyped Stats on Wife Abuse Only Worsen Problem," *San Ramon Valley Times,* August 17, 1994, p. 19A.
4 Christopher Matthews, "Four Years From Now, Look for Colin Powell," *San Francisco Examiner,* Nov 12, 1995, p. B13.
5 Mary Fisher, "We Are All Victims of AIDS," speech delivered before 1992 Republican convention. Taken from videotape recording.
6 William Barr, "Combatting Violent Crime," *The Commonwealth,* Vol. 42, September 29, 1992, p. 622.
7 "Murdoch Fires New Fox TV Chief," *San Francisco Chronicle,* May 22, 1992, p. A5.

15

REASONING AND CRITICAL ANALYSIS

Convincing an audience intellectually is called reasoning. Reasoning is the process of using evidence to prove a point. It is very similar to using telling, showing, and doing to explain or describe a main point and, indeed, you still use these channels when reasoning. But now you are using them to prove a main point and ultimately persuade an audience.

The importance of using sound reasoning in persuasion cannot be underestimated. People cannot be told what to do or how to think. They cannot be coerced into acting a certain way. They must be persuaded and convinced that a particular idea or decision is the logical and intelligent course of action. They must understand why an idea is important.

Logic and evidence is the way we make decisions, solve problems, take actions, and form beliefs. Suppose you're a prosecutor and are presented with the evidence against a suspect. You analyze the facts to determine if they lead to the conclusion the suspect committed the crime or to some other scenario(s). If the evidence points to the suspect, then you use it to build your case and present it to the jury. The expectation is they will draw the same conclusion as you. A business, too, desiring to expand will gather all the facts about the new venture, analyze them and then decide whether it is a good investment. You follow the same process when you reason with an audience.

If your reasoning is sloppy, you will not be persuasive. You may have had insufficient or weak evidence. The conclusions you reach from the evidence may be erroneous or contradictory. If this occurs, you will be disbelieved and your credibility may be damaged. The audience will conclude you didn't do your homework, you are deceitful, or you lack knowledge about the topic. Remember, your reasoning is your thought process communicated to an audience. Let's discuss how you can use logic and evidence effectively.

THE ELEMENTS OF REASONING

Aristotle said, "A speech has two parts. Necessarily, you state your case, and you prove it." Reasoning has two major elements: (1) evidence and (2) conclusions (sometimes called inferences, generalizations, and main points). Together they form a unit of proof called an argument. The evidence is the facts, statistics, and testimony you use to prove a conclusion (See Figure 15-1). The strength and believability of the conclusion are based on the evidence. This relationship is fundamental to every argument, regardless of its form. In the following argument, Susan Blumenthal, M.D., wants the audience to believe that breast cancer is a serious problem and uses evidence to prove the assertion:

> The incidence of breast cancer has been escalating in the last several years. In the 1950s, the rates were 1 in 20 women in her lifetime. Today, breast cancer will affect 1 in 8 women over her lifetime. This year, 182,000 cases of breast cancer will be diagnosed, and 46,000 women will die of the disease.[1]

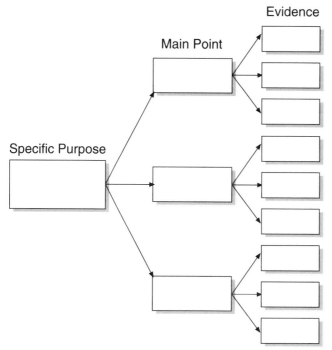

FIGURE 15-1
Outlining logical arguments in a speech.

The argument can be outlined in the following manner:

I Breast cancer is increasing in women.
  A In 1950, 1 in 20 women had breast cancer.
  B Today, 1 in 8 women have breast cancer.
  C This year, 182,000 have breast cancer.
  D This year, 46,000 women will die from breast cancer.

The speaker wants the audience to believe that breast cancer is increasing in women. Assuming the statistics are true, that could be a reasonable interpretation of the evidence.

Types of Evidence

You can use illustrations, examples, descriptions, visual aids, and even demonstration as evidence to support a conclusion. However, we will focus on three specific types of evidence: (1) facts, (2) statistics, and (3) expert testimony.

Facts   Facts are concrete types of evidence that in many instances have physical properties and can therefore be measured and verified. Blood found at the scene of a crime can be scientifically tested and can be linked to a specific person by type and DNA. Fingerprints can also identify a suspect. This is powerful evidence because it links a suspect to the scene of a crime. Evidence may also be events that happened, scientific studies, or new discoveries. The Persian Gulf War, the hazards of smoking, and the discovery of polio vaccine are all facts. Their concreteness makes them persuasive. In the following example, the speaker uses factual examples to prove the hazards of smoking tobacco:

> Smoking is also the single greatest cause of cancer mortality. It is a major cause of emphysema and a major contributor to oral, esophageal and many other kinds cancers. It also turns out that cigarettes are not only a major contributor to heart disease, but that 3,000 individuals a year die of the consequences of second hand smoke.[2]

Statistics   How to select and communicate statistics were extensively discussed in Chapter 7 and you should review that section now. Keep your statistics simple, accurate, and meaningful. Here is an example of how a speaker uses statistics to convince the audience that AIDS is reaching adolescents:

> HIV is targeting adolescents. The largest number of new infections is occurring in the 15- to 25-year-old age group, and this is true in both developed and developing countries.
>
> And children are targeted by the disease, both directly and indirectly. By the year 2000, there could be as many as 10 million children orphaned as a result of AIDS deaths. Within 15 years, projected life expectancy will decline by more than 25 years in Thailand, Kenya, and Zimbabwe. In Uganda, where HIV prevalence currently is the highest, life expectancy has already declined to 17 years.[3]

Expert Opinion   How to select and present testimony was extensively discussed in Chapter 7 and you should review that section now. Expert opinion is the use of recognized authority to prove a point. Sometimes facts and statistics are insufficient to prove a point or clarify an issue, and expert opinion is necessary to enhance believability. In these instances, the opinion of an individual with broad experience, extensive knowledge, and established reputation can serve as evidence. For instance, Carl Sagan, author, scholar, astronomer, is often called upon to give his opinion on outer space. In the following example, the speaker uses the research of a noted scholar to support a new approach to criminal behavior:

About 25 years ago, economists began developing a new model of criminal activity. The major breakthrough was the work of Gary Becker, a University of Chicago economist and now a Nobel laureate. In Becker's model, criminals are rational individuals acting in their own best interest. In deciding to commit a crime, criminals weigh the expected costs against the expected benefits.[4]

In the following example the speaker directly quotes the expert to support his point that the greater the segregation, the higher the crime:

> The greater the racial segregation in an area, the higher the crime rate. Sociologist Doug Massey argues that urban poverty and urban crime are consequences of extremely high levels of black residential segregation and racial discrimination. Massey says, "Take a group of people, segregate them, cut off their capital and guess what? The neighborhoods go downhill. There's no other outcome possible."[5]

Enhancing Your Reasoning

Evidence, used ethically and skillfully, increases your credibility and persuasiveness. Let's discuss specific ways for using evidence effectively.

Deliver evidence with conviction.

Document Your Sources   If you do not have expertise about your subject, citing sources enhances your believability. However, your sources must be credible to the audience or can be made credible. For instance, if your sources are highly qualified but unknown to the audience, then cite the credentials of your sources. In the infamous O.J. Simpson murder trial, the defense successfully challenged the credibility of the evidence by attacking the competence of the criminalist and detectives. They showed that the evidence was sloppily collected and stored. The evidence could therefore not be considered reliable.

Select objective sources, those that have no self-interest in the subjects you are discussing and have a reputation for accuracy. Cite your sources by name and date, not in a general or vague terms. For example, you might say "According to the June, 1996 issue of the *New England Journal of Medicine*." Network news, on the other hand, is fond of saying "according to informed sources," in reference to the origin of important facts for its stories. This reduces believability. In the following example, Doctor David Smith cites sources for his point that drug addiction is the nation's biggest health problem:

> Drug abuse represents our biggest national public health problem. The two most widely used surveys of drug use in the U.S. are the National Household Survey on Drug Use and the High School Senior Survey. They provide information on drug and alcohol patterns among 8th, 9th, and 10th graders in the U.S. and give an idea of drug use trends in society. Based on these surveys, in 1992, 98 million Americans reported using alcohol in the last month, and 10 million were problem drinkers. 54 million smoked cigarettes; 11 million used illicit drugs, and 2.6 million reported non-medical use of the prescription drugs.[6]

Do not document all your sources because that becomes repetitive and boring and possibly dilutes the quality of the evidence. However, documenting key evidence can increase your persuasiveness.

Present Evidence With Conviction and Clarity   Presenting evidence in a dull or monotonous manner diminishes its impact. Present evidence in a lively and natural fashion using multiple channels. Good rehearsal techniques can help you present citations and testimony with force. Use striking visuals. Review Chapter 7 for communicating statistics and testimony.

Use the Most Recent Evidence   New facts and expert opinion previously unknown to the audience are very persuasive. Old facts or arguments are unlikely to sway listeners. For example, timeless issues such as abortion and capital punishment remain unresolved because the arguments and evidence about them are antiquated. In contrast, much new evidence is emerging about the relationship between television violence and behavior, especially in children, that is changing perceptions and leading to reforms in programming.

Select the Strongest Evidence No argument can contain all the relevant evidence. To attempt to do so would bore and turn off the audience. Therefore, select the strongest and most convincing evidence and feature it in your presentation. That is the evidence that most directly supports the main point and comes from the most credible source. See Chapter 5 on selecting information and Figure 5-7 on the "Differences Between Magazines and Periodicals."

TYPES OF ARGUMENTS

There are many ways that evidence can be used to prove a point. A manager may use statistics to prove that production costs are increasing. A researcher may use facts to show the relationship between airbags and a reduction in deaths in highway accidents. Let's discuss four common types of reasoning patterns: (1) reasoning with facts, (2) reasoning from premises, (3) reasoning from cause, and (4) reasoning by analogy.

Reasoning with Facts

You have been stopped by a highway patrol officer for speeding. You plead your case by telling the officer you are a victim of extenuating circumstances. Your speedometer is broken, the speed limit sign was poorly lit and obscured by a tree, and you were observing the flow of traffic. You are using facts to sway the officer to believe you are not guilty.

Reasoning with facts, often called inductive reasoning, uses specific instances to lead people to a belief. (See Figure 15-2.) Typically with this type of argument you want the audience to change their way of thinking about a topic or issue. For example, a store manager trying to persuade her employees to improve customer relations might cite several customer complaints as the basis of her belief that friendlier service would result in more business. Similarly, a speaker trying to persuade a group of high school students not to drink might cite statistics that show alcohol is present in 70 percent of drivers involved in car accidents, and conclude that drinking is a major contributor to traffic accidents. In the following example Lee Brown, Director, Office of National Drug Control Policy, uses induction to convince the audience that drugs are easy to get and their use is widespread:

> Drugs are easy to obtain. In fact, they are readily available to anyone who wants to buy them. Cocaine and heroin street prices are low and the purity is high. Marijuana, the choice of many in the younger generation, is increasingly more available, more potent, and cheaper than ever. The problem is also widespread. About 11.7 million Americans currently use drugs. One in three Americans has used an illicit drug, and one-half of high school seniors have tried an illegal drug.[7]

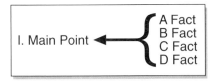

FIGURE 15-2
Reasoning with facts.

If the argument was outlined it would look like this:

I Drugs are easy to obtain.
  A Cocaine and heroin street prices are low and the purity is high.
  B Marijuana, the choice of many in the younger generation, is increasingly more available, more potent, and cheaper than ever.
II The problem is widespread.
  A About 11.7 million Americans currently use drugs.
  B One in three Americans has used an illicit drug.
  C One-half of high school seniors have tried illegal drugs.

How much evidence is sufficient to prove a point using facts? There is no formula. In a court of law the test is "beyond a reasonable doubt"; however, in an oral presentation you cannot possibly present all the evidence. The best guide is to use the strongest facts, statistics, or expert opinion. For some presentations that may be three or four, while another issue may require more evidence. What is important is that the audience conclude your argument is logically sound and strongly grounded in fact. Make a determination as to the quantity of facts needed to prove your point, but don't bore your audience with excessive facts or engage in overkill.

Reasoning from Premises

Reasoning from premises, often called deduction, doesn't use facts to persuade but generally accepted beliefs, attitudes, and values. As a speaker, you prove your point by associating it with accepted ways of thinking or acting. A politician might argue that new legislation should be opposed because it increases the size of government and we all know that big government is bad (premise). The premise acts as the evidence to prove the point. If you accept that premise, then you belief the argument. Deductive arguments are shown graphically in Figure 15-3. In each instance the conclusion is derived from the premise. Note that premises are conceptual rather than evidential.

To be effective, the premise must be believed by the audience. For example, equality of opportunity is a cherished American value and one you can be sure will be held in high regard by the audience. Using that value as a

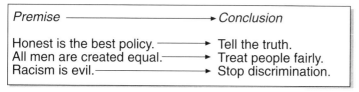

FIGURE 15-3
Reasoning with premises.

premise in arguing for equal opportunity for people would probably be accepted by the audience. In the following argument, the speaker uses a premise to support his argument:

> Sometimes it seems hopeless, that our representatives will always be compromised by the professional politicians, lobbyists, and inside-the-beltway hangers-on. Inevitably it seems, the voter message sent on election day gets diluted, distorted, or simply sidetracked and what triumphs is not the will of the people but business as usual.[8]

The above argument would be outlined and paraphrased as follows:

I The will of the people is thwarted.
   A Special interests run the federal government.

The evidence for the argument is the premise "Special interests run the federal government." If the audience believes that statement, then they will believe the main point.

Reasoning from Cause

Reasoning from cause attempts to lead people to belief by showing that one event has the power, means, or ability to produce another event. (See Figure 15-4.) For example, a candidate for political office might try to show how the incumbent has created the current economic problems by increasing taxes. A sales representative trying to convince a small business owner to buy a copy machine might try to show that owning the copy machine will save money.

In the following example, the speaker draws a cause-effect relationship between drug use and crime:

> Evidence supports a clear link between alcohol and illicit drug use and crime. In 1990 there were more than 1 million arrests for drug offenses and more than 3 million arrests for alcohol-related offenses. It has been estimated that one-third to one-half of all criminal justice costs are related to alcohol and other types of drug abuse. Up to 80 percent of those in the criminal justice system have substance abuse problems.[9]

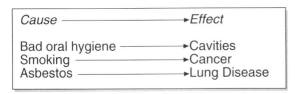

FIGURE 15-4
Reasoning from cause.

If the above argument is outlined, it would look like the following example:

I Evidence supports a clear link between alcohol and illicit drug use and crime.
   A It has been estimated that one-third to one-half of all criminal justice costs are related to alcohol and other types of drug abuse.
   B Up to 80% of those in the criminal justice system have substance-abuse problems.

Causal reasoning can be powerful but proving causal association is challenging because there are many related factors that assist in producing a given effect. A shrewd lawyer may argue, "Yes, my client robbed that store. Yes, he beat up the proprietor. Yes, he fired at the police. But he is not really a bad person. He is a victim of society. He was abused as a child." The cause is not the actions of the perpetrator of the crime but the society that caused him to be that way. The notorious Menendez brothers who brutally shot-gunned their parents to death claimed they were victims of sexual and physical abuse and shot their parents in self-defense.

Or, consider the case of the arson investigator who was sent to determine the cause of a suspicious fire. Following his investigation he reports that the fire was caused by the presence of oxygen in the atmosphere. His boss fired him on the spot for incompetence. Why? Because, while oxygen is necessary for fire to burn, it is not sufficient to cause the fire.

To be convincing the cause/effect analysis must show that the cause by itself is capable of producing the effect. If other causes can produce the effect, or if an accidental or a single-instance phenomenon occurred, your reasoning will be significantly weakened. Smoking has been proven to cause lung cancer and a myriad of other diseases. If every smoker stopped smoking and the prevalence of lung cancer remained the same, then smoking could not be considered a major cause of lung cancer. Demonstrate clearly the cause/effect relationship.

Reasoning by Analogy

Reasoning by analogy attempts to prove a point by showing how two things are similar. A convenience store manager trying to persuade her supervisor to install a coffee machine in her store, for instance, might compare her store with a similar store in town and point out how the other store's profits increased when it added a coffee machine.

Reasoning by analogy is less an argument than a means of clarifying an argument. The comparison may make the objects better understood, but it doesn't mean they are logically related. The fact that a horse and a car can both transport people doesn't make them logically related. Nor does the fact that rats can develop cancer after being injected with saccharin necessarily mean the same fate will befall humans. Nevertheless, reasoning by analogy can be effective. In the following example, the speaker draws an analogy between nuclear waste and commonly used products to prove that the concerns about nuclear waste may be unfounded:

> Radioactive waste is a serious problem, but an extreme degree of concern is not warranted. Nuclear waste is extremely toxic and the waste from a single reactor is enough to poison the world's population several times over. Also nuclear waste will persist for thousands and perhaps millions of years. But, don't confuse toxicity with hazard. The existence of a toxic substance is not a hazard unless assimilated into the human body.
>
> There are many comparable hazards that we live with daily. The average supermarket has enough toxic chemicals in the form of bleaches, cleaning compounds, and insecticides to poison everyone in the community, if not the state. Lead used in the manufacture of automobile batteries each year is sufficient to poison the world population many times over. In addition, lead, being a stable element, will exist forever. Nuclear waste has a limited life span.

The argument, when outlined, looks like this:

I Radioactive waste is a serious problem, but a high degree of concern is not warranted.
  A Nuclear waste, although extremely toxic, is not a hazard unless digested.
  B Common household and automobile products are equally hazardous unless digested.

For the analogy to be logical and believable—and therefore effective—the two events being compared must be similar in important ways. To say that gun control works in England and would therefore work in the United States overlooks vast differences in culture, population size, and geography. Don't mix apples and oranges. If significant differences are found between the things you claim are similar, your reasoning will be disproved.

ERRONEOUS REASONING

Erroneous reasoning occurs when evidence and main points are weakly, falsely, or deceptively connected. They occur when a speaker out of igno-

Present your arguments clearly.

rance or sloppiness doesn't do his or her homework or uses superficial or insufficient evidence to prove a point. Or, the speaker is attempting to evade or oversimplify an issue. How many times have you heard the statement, "A vote for the Democrats is a vote for big government" or "The criminal justice system is corrupt because innocent people are convicted of crimes"? These are oversimplifications. The first statement is false because not every Democrat supports expanded government; the second statement is erroneous because imperfection doesn't warrant condemning an entire system. The conclusion doesn't follow from the evidence.

Fallacies are very common in public speaking, especially in the media and in political statements. They are sometimes hard to detect and often convincing to uncritical listeners. In a professional or on-the-job setting, fallacious reasoning is usually less convincing and often challenged and exposed. Weak analysis is not tolerated because important decisions involving performance, productivity, and investments are at stake. That doesn't mean every decision will be correct but your chances of success are increased because the issues are extensively debated.

You should learn to avoid fallacies in your own thinking and listen for them in the messages of others. Let's discuss some common types of fallacies.

Faulty Generalization

This is a very common type of fallacy. A speaker presents conclusions based on insufficient data. (See Figure 15-5.) Have you heard this argument: "Professor Smith is a hard teacher because two of my friends got D's in her class"? The conclusion is overstated. The fact that two students out of the many graded by Professor Smith received poor grades doesn't mean she is a "hard" teacher. The D's may have been exceptions and given because the students earned them. More information is needed about Professor Smith's grading habits before such a conclusion can be reached. Make sure you have sufficient facts before jumping to conclusions.

False Cause

This fallacy, often called non sequitur, happens when a speaker links two unrelated events. While John is strolling across the lawn, a black cat crosses his path; he stumbles, breaking his big toe. He concludes the black cat caused him to break his toe.

A cat crossing his path before he stumbled did not cause John to fall and break his toe. The two events were coincidental. (See Figure 15-6.) "Poverty breeds crime" is a popularly held belief. Yet, the great majority of poor people never commit crimes. Several years ago a man blamed his wife's death from brain cancer on her use of a cellular telephone. He sued and the resulting lawsuit drew wide media coverage, fear on the part of many cellular phone users, and a decline in the stock prices of cellular phone companies. Analysis showed that the incidence of brain cancer is six people per 100,000 annually. There are over 10,000,000 users of cellular phones. Based on those figures it would be expected there would be about 600 cases of brain cancer among cellular phone users.[10]

Under close examination, many conditions that appear to be logically related are only superficially connected. Beware of false associations.

Attacking the Person

A speaker using this type of fallacy, called an ad hominem argument, attacks the character of the opposition. This is usually an evasive tactic used to

FIGURE 15-5
The fallacy of faulty generalization.

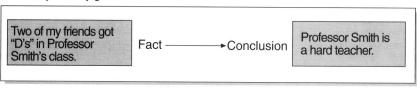

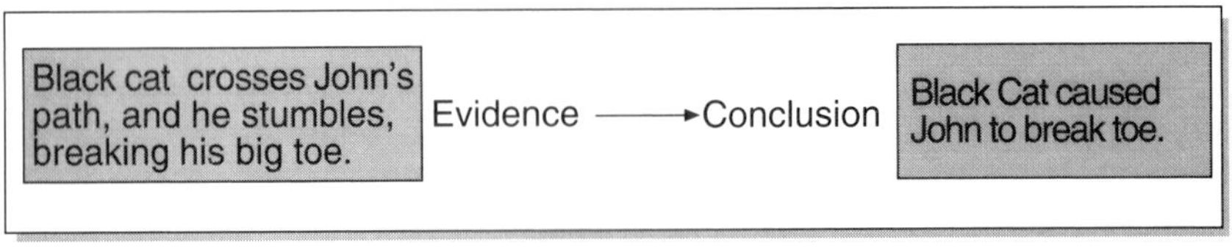

FIGURE 15-6
Fallacy of false cause.

deflect attention away from the merits of an opponent's arguments or the weakness of their own. Politically correct communication is sometimes ad hominem. People who challenge or disagree with these beliefs are labeled "racist," "homophobic," "sexist," "angry white males," or "the good-old boys club." First Lady Hillary Rodham Clinton used ad hominem argument in response to an interviewer's question as to why some people are criticizing her role in the White House:

> People are not really often reacting to me so much as they are reacting to their own lives. . . . If somebody has a female boss for the first time, and they've never experienced that—well, maybe they can't take out their hostility against her so they turn it on me.[11]

Rather than address her role as a policy and decision maker in the White House, including her leadership in the health care reform effort, the First Lady suggested people who disagree with her are threatened by women with power.

Politicians often use ad hominem arguments and audiences are not sympathetic to it. Richard Reeves, syndicated columnist, describes how this fallacy is damaging political communication:

> "Dirty politics" is, in fact, destroying all politics these days. Candidates and officeholders seem to be so stupid that they do not understand that their endless, hypocritical and sanctimonious smearing of each other is the reason people distrust and don't want to vote for them.
>
> Politicians don't seem to know what they're doing to themselves. Two candidates spend the better part of a year calling each other the most vile things they can imagine—beginning with liar, thief, pervert—and then when it's over, bravely shake hands. For them it's all over on election day; the people have spoken. But the people, the rest of us, remember what they said about each other. The winner is damaged goods to begin with.[12]

Either/Or Reasoning

The either/or fallacy asserts there are only two solutions to a problem. Speakers who use this fallacy usually make one of the solutions so undesirable that the one they want will be accepted. Consider the statement "Either we raise taxes, or the city will go bankrupt." The issue is framed so the audience is limited to choosing between two options. And since no one wants bankruptcy, taxes must be raised. Of course, there are other options: reduce expenses, float a bond, borrow money, cut services, to name but a few. Either/or reasoning attempts to exclude alternative solutions.

Arguing in a Circle

A speaker using this fallacy employs one unproved statement to prove another statement. The statement "Anyone with knowledge about prison operations knows that rehabilitation doesn't work" is attempting to prove that "rehabilitation doesn't work" because people "with knowledge about prison operations" know it doesn't. Thus, the speaker is arguing in a circle. Speakers use this fallacy as a way to avoid supplying evidence for their claims. "Bill Clinton will solve the nation's problems because he has vision." How do we know Bill Clinton will solve our problems? We know because he has "vision." The speaker is arguing in a circle.

Appeal to False Authority

Speakers use this fallacy when they employ the name of a popular but unqualified individual who has no special expertise to support their argument. Rush Limbaugh may be a well-known radio commentator, but to quote him as an expert on economics, foreign policy, or political philosophy would be to appeal to false authority.

In summary, fallacies are false reasoning. Avoid them when you are speaking and learn to detect them in the speech of others.

SUMMARY

Reasoning is the process of using evidence to prove a point. Key types of evidence are facts, expert opinion, and statistics. Important ways of enhancing include documenting sources, presenting it with conviction, presenting new evidence, and presenting the strongest evidence. Important types of reasoning include reasoning with facts (inductive), reasoning from premises (deductive), reasoning from cause, and reasoning by analogy. A fallacy is erroneous reasoning. Common fallacies include faulty generalization, false cause, attacking the person, either/or reasoning, arguing in a circle, and appeal to false authority.

PROBES

1 How would you describe reasoning?
2 How would you describe evidence?
3 What are the different types of evidence?
4 Describe four ways of making your evidence more persuasive.
5 Describe six types of logical fallacies and give examples.

APPLICATIONS

1 Identify the type of argument used in the following arguments:

> One of the benefits of legalizing gambling will be the increase in employment opportunities. People will be needed in casinos, hotels, motels, construction, maintenance, and management positions.
>
> Legalizing prostitution would have a corrupting influence by attracting seedy, corrupt, and generally undesirable people to our town. It would be just like the porno movie house across the tracks that draws all the bums in town.
>
> If capital punishment is a deterrent to crime, then the crime rate should decline where the death penalty is legal. In Florida, where capital punishment is the law, crime continues to rise. The death penalty doesn't work.
>
> The total cost of alcohol, illicit drugs, and tobacco to the U.S. economy exceeded $250 billion. Alcohol costs were about $100 billion, illicit drugs about $70 billion, and tobacco smoking costs about $80 billion. This is a major drain on our economic resources.

2 Identify the following fallacies:
  a The new governor took office last January and crime has already gone up 15%.
  b Either we pass the bill or fail the people.
  c Michael Jordan says this is the best car, so we should buy it.
  d Patrick Buchanan is a fascist!
  e Don't shop at that store. The clothing is lousy. I bought a dress there and it shrunk.
  f The stories about welfare cheaters show the welfare system only supports people who lie.

NOTES

1 Susan Blumenthal, M.D. "Making Sense of Women's Health," *The Commonwealth,* Vol. 89, September 4, 1995, p. 2.
2 David Smith, M.D. "Social and Economic Consequences of Addiction in America," *The Commonwealth,* Vol. 90, January 29, 1996, p. 4.
3 J. Brian Atwood, "1990's: The Decade of AIDS Mortality," *Vital Speeches,* September 15, 1995, p. 716.
4 Ed Rubenstein, "The Economics of Crime: The Rational Criminal," *Vital Speeches,* Vol. 62, October 15, 1995, p. 20.
5 D. Stanley Eitzen, "Violent Crime: Myths, Facts, and Solutions," *Vital Speeches,* Vol. 61, May 15, 1995, p. 470.

6 Smith, p. 3.

7 Lee Brown, "President Clinton's National Drug Control Policy," *The Commonwealth,* Vol. 89, April 17, 1995, p. 2.

8 Mark Draper, "The Bells of Freedom Ring," *Vital Speeches,* Vol. 62, November 1, 1995, p. 58.

9 Smith, p. 3.

10 John Allen Paulos, "Reading News With Our Math Lenses On," *The Christian Science Monitor,* June 7, 1995, p. 19.

11 Charles Krauthammer, "Angry, White Male Is Just a Myth," *San Ramon Valley Times,* May 30, 1995, p. 10A.

12 Richard Reeves, "Dirty Politics, Old and New," *The San Francisco Chronicle,* Nov 15, 1993, p. A21.

16

SPEAKING FOR SPECIAL OCCASIONS

"I have a dream" and . . . "that government of the people, by the people, and for the people shall not perish from this earth" are timeless statements inspired by special occasions. In the last three chapters we have focused on speaking to inform and persuade. However, there are many other occasions when we are called on to speak. We may be asked to spontaneously express our views on a subject in a meeting or discussion. We may be called upon to give a special presentation or award. Let's discuss some of these important types of special occasion speeches. They include impromptu speaking, answering questions, introductions, after-dinner speeches, presentations, acceptance speeches, and commemorative speaking.

IMPROMPTU SPEAKING

Impromptu speaking is the most common type of public speaking. It is spontaneous and unrehearsed. You draw on your experience and knowledge to present a short speech. Examples of impromptu speaking are answering questions, expressing your opinion, and giving a status report or short briefing. Your goal is to be clear, concise, and to the point. Long-winded answers and vague generalities are not desirable, especially in professional settings, where succinctness and precision are highly valued. People are busy and want communication they can immediately understand. Here are some tips for speaking effectively in an impromptu manner:

1 *Focus on a central idea.* What is the major conclusion you want the audience to reach about the subject? If you begin your presentation with a straightforward statement of the central idea—such as "Computer System FXL will raise company profits by streamlining bookkeeping procedures and thus increasing productivity"—your audience will grasp the central idea quickly and follow the details of your speech more easily. Plus your delivery is more likely to be smooth, logical, and easy to follow because you have an idea to focus on.

2 *Identify the main points.* Make a quick and simple short-sentence outline. If your central idea is clearly phrased, the main points should emerge easily. In the previous example "higher profits," "streamlined procedures," and "increased productivity" were the benefits cited for the system. They become your main points.

    I   Higher profits.
   II   Streamlined procedures.
 III   Increased productivity.

3 *Briefly explain the main points.* Give enough supporting information to clarify the main ideas. Clear examples and statistics should work just fine. Your goal is to clarify issues and ideas, not give a fully developed speech.

Here is an example of an impromptu speech delivered by a student in response to the topic "Should smoking be banned in public places?" He states the central idea and follows with two main points and supporting material:

I believe smoking should be banned in public places such as restaurants, super-markets, and athletic events. *(Central idea)* Smoking is discourteous and harmful to nonsmokers. *(First main point)* Smokers don't understand how their habit affects others. *(Supporting material)* The smoke gets in their hair and clothing, leaving a strong odor. When I've been around smokers, my eyes water and I experience shortness of breath. Other nonsmokers I've talked to have had similar experiences. *(Second main point)* Most important, exposure to secondhand smoke is harmful. *(Supporting material)* Studies show that nonsmokers in the presence of smokers for long periods can suffer the same diseases as smokers. I believe smoking should be banned in public places.

Your delivery should be natural. Use good eye contact whether you are standing or sitting.

ANSWERING QUESTIONS

A question-and-answer period frequently follows a speech. Occasionally, a question-and-answer period may be strategically placed within the presentation itself. Questions give you the opportunity to clarify and reinforce points made earlier in the speech and possibly to make new points, further strengthening your arguments. Answering questions effectively also enhances your credibility. Conversely, evasion, ambiguity, or emotional responses may hurt your case and lead the audience to question your motives, knowledge, and confidence. Here are some general guidelines for answering questions:

1 Make sure you understand the question. If you are unsure of the meaning, ask the questioner to repeat it, rephrase it, or give an example so you understand the question.

2 Be direct. Respond directly to the question. Make sure your answer is complete but concise. Avoid ambiguous or technical language.

3 Check back to make sure your response is satisfactory. Saying "Does that answer your question?" or "Do you need more information?" helps ensure that your response is complete.

4 If you don't know the answer, say so. Tell the questioner you don't know, and offer to get the answer and pass it on. Don't fake it. The audience will know. You might respond by saying, "I am not familiar with those facts, but I will follow up on it and get back to you with the specific information."

5 Maintain a relaxed posture and good eye contact with the questioner. You might even step toward the questioner to acknowledge your interest during the question. As you answer the question, make eye contact with other members of the audience as well.

6 Maintain your composure and control of the situation. If you get rattled or emotional, you will lose credibility and reverse the gains made in your speech.

Types of Questions

There are many types of questions. You want to be able to identify the type of question so you can respond to it effectively. Questions may be divided into two broad categories: informative questions and challenging questions. Let's discuss each category.

Informative Questions   Informative questions are easier to identify and answer because the questioner is interested in clarifying what was said or wants more information about the subject. Informative questions include:

1 *Clarifying questions.* The questioner wants to verify the meaning of an idea, fact, or statement in the speech. Examples might include:

"Would you give me an example of what you mean by extraterrestrial?"
"Would you please define for me one more time what you mean by obscenity?"

2 *Probing questions.* These questions seek to clarify the underlying thinking or premise of an idea or program. The questioner might ask:

"Is the idea behind capital punishment that society must take a strong stand against crime?"

3 *Additional information.* The questioner wants more information about some part of the speech and asks the speaker where to get more.

"Where can I get more information about how AIDS is contracted?"

4 *Peripheral questions.* This type of question has only marginal relevance to the subject and is often asked by someone who was not listening attentively. Handle it politely and steer the questioner back to the subject. You might respond this way:

"That is a good question but it's beyond the realm of this discussion. Maybe it will be addressed by one of the next speakers. Who has the next question?"

Challenging Questions   Challenging questions are usually asked when your speech is persuasive, especially when your topic is controversial. The questioner's goal may be to ferret out weaknesses and refute your arguments. Challenging questions may also be asked to test your confidence and coolness under fire. Good speakers anticipate these questions and practice responding to them. Here are some examples of challenging questions.

1 *Either/or dilemma.* The speaker is given two options, both of which are undesirable. The questioner's goal is to get the speaker to commit to a bad option and then later attack the speaker for adopting the position. For example, the questioner might ask, "Do we raise taxes or increase the deficit?" Neither action may be desirable and there may be other options. Skilled speakers immediately recognize this kind of question and defuse it. The speaker might respond this way:

> "The issue isn't a matter of choosing between two options. There are other options as well, such as cutting costs and expanding production. We favor a combination of these approaches."

2 *Putting words in your mouth.* The questioner intentionally or unintentionally misstates the speaker's position. For example, the questioner says, "So you're saying you think the program has been a catastrophe?" If you answer the question in that context, you will be misstating your own position. You might respond this way:

> "That's not an accurate statement of my position. We have had problems with the program but they are correctable and the program will succeed."

3 *Direct disagreement.* When this occurs, acknowledge the differences and move on. Do not debate the issue because you will give the opposition a platform and you may lose control of the situation. Here is how to handle this kind of objection:

> "We have an honest disagreement on this point and I appreciate your bringing it up, but my experience and research have led me to a different conclusion. I'll be happy to discuss it further with you after my presentation."

4 *Being set up.* This is a two-part strategy. The questioner gets you to take a position, setting you up, and then asks a second question knocking you down. For example, a questioner might ask, "Are you satisfied with the progress of the child abuse prevention programs?" If you say "Yes," the questioner follows up by asking, "Do you think the child who was beaten last week is satisfied?" You have egg on your face. The proper response to the first question is, "No, we are not satisfied and we are working diligently to improve our prevention efforts." That defuses the bomb.

5 *False conclusion.* The listener draws a conclusion that is false or erroneous. For example, the questioner might ask, "So, after these cost-cutting procedures, there will be more layoffs, right?" You defuse by contradicting the false conclusion and scoring a point for your proposal:

> "I wouldn't draw that conclusion. In fact, as I stated early in the speech, these cost cuts should lead to higher profits and expansion, which mean more jobs."

There are many other types of challenging questions. We covered only a sample of them here.

SPEECH OF INTRODUCTION

Speeches of introduction are given for most formal and banquet speaking events. Their purpose is to get the attention of the audience and create interest in the speaker and the topic. Speeches of introduction should be organized in a short introduction, body, and conclusion format. Give interesting and relevant facts about the speaker and why she or he has been invited to speak. Build the speaker's credibility and give biographical data and an anecdote that personalizes the speech. Conclude by making a transition into the speech.

You can get information about speakers in a number of ways. Often speakers have résumés you can obtain in advance that list their backgrounds and relevant education and experience. That and a personal interview should give you all the information you need to build an entertaining and solid introduction. Here is an example of a speech of introduction:

> Good evening and welcome. It's gratifying to see so many of you brave the inclement weather to be here. Winter has arrived with a vengeance and that means our consumption of energy will increase, not to speak of the demands for oil or the accompanying higher utility bills, which have more than doubled in the last several years.
>
> All of us here practice some form of energy conservation. Many of us are considering the use of solar energy and our guest speaker, Mr. Jerry Johnson, will give us important information on the potential of this and other renewable energy.
>
> Mr. Johnson heads the state agency on solar energy, called SolarCal, and was director of the state Solar Energy Task Force. He has been a consultant in environment planning, energy sources, and urban affairs since 1981. He holds a B.S. degree in civil engineering from Cal Tech and an M.A. in engineering and economics from Harvard, and he has done further graduate work in environmental engineering at Cal Tech.
>
> He not only knows something about energy, he is doing something about it too. He is building his own adobe house, which will utilize solar energy. The house, incidentally, was designed by his wife. I give you Jerry Johnson.

This is a very good speech of introduction. The emcee begins by greeting the audience and establishing rapport and empathy regarding the need for energy. He leads into the subject and then gives the speaker's credentials and education. He concludes with a brief personal note about the speaker, which reveals more about the speaker's personality.

AFTER-DINNER SPEAKING

You've been called upon to be the after-dinner speaker. The audience has just completed a full three-course dinner with wine, preceded by a two-hour cocktail party. Some members are rubbing their stomachs, others are yawning, and some people's eyes are half closed. What do you talk about? Cer-

After-dinner speaking should be fun and entertaining.

tainly not the implications of Plato's Dialogues for moral development. No, your remarks had better be light, humorous, and entertaining.

Humor Is Important in After-Dinner Speaking

After-dinner speaking offers the opportunity to use a rich variety of techniques to entertain the audience. Witticisms, epigrams, humorous anecdotes, satire, exaggeration, wordplay, and jokes are all candidates for after-dinner speaking. You may build the speech around a humorous theme, talk about a serious subject in a humorous way, or tell a series of funny stories. Here are some examples of ways to use humor in a speech.

Satire   Satire pokes fun at social customs, manners, and behavior. Satire uncovers the facade of myths and public roles for a closer look at the reality of our behavior. There is a fine line between *satire* and *ridicule or sarcasm* that you should be careful to observe. Ridicule and sarcasm are not funny. In the following example, the speaker uses satire in talking about lying:

> The first question you may have is, "Why lie?" Well, for many reasons. First of all, nobody wants to hear that their conversation is boring, that their children are obnoxious, or that their New Year's Eve party was a flop. And it doesn't exactly bring a glow to your eyes to hear that your loved one no longer turns dizzy with

desire every time you walk into the room. Silence is not always golden in these matters either. If you've just done a room in a silk print or had your hair done, you want it admired—a quick "very nice" simply will not suffice. The truth is plain—the very least you can do is dress it up a little, add some color here and there. Now, you may feel that lying is against your morals and upbringing. But didn't your parents lie when you asked where you came from and they told you the stork brought you? What about Santa Claus and the Tooth Fairy? And were you ever told that for each lie you told, your nose would grow a little longer?

Exaggeration   Exaggeration is used when you want to overstate an experience or event. You take a typical or common experience and relate it from a new perspective, as in the following example:

I was pulled from the womb by my head. The next thing I knew a masked man grabbed me by the legs, turned me upside down, and began to spank me. I was terrified. I started to scream. I looked over at my mother for help, and she had a big smile on her face.

Incongruity   Incongruity arises from two statements that are inconsistent with each other, such as a serious story or comment quickly capped off with a funny conclusion. Benno Schmidt, former president of Yale University, used incongruity to explain to an audience why he left Yale to become president and CEO of an ambitious and innovative private school system called The Edison Project:

I have often been asked why I left Yale to head up The Edison Project. When Woodrow Wilson was asked why he left the presidency of Princeton University to run for Governor of New Jersey, he replied, "I got tired of the politics." I left Yale to get involved in education.[1]

Guidelines for Using Humor in a Speech

You want to choose your humor carefully and learn how to use it effectively in a presentation. Here are some guidelines for using humor in a speech.

1 Use only stories, jokes, or quotes that are funny to you. Your enthusiasm will give you confidence telling the joke; it will heighten the audience's anticipation of your next remark and increase their involvement in the speech.

2 Understand the punchline and know why the story is funny. Practice the timing. Everything you say builds to that one climactic moment. Knowing the punchline will also make your delivery crisp and concise. Remember, comedians tell the same stories hundreds of times, but each time sounds like the first. They know the story.

3 Tell the stories in your own style. Don't tell it as your favorite comic or storyteller would. Robin Williams and Eddie Murphy have their own styles. Use your words, your voice, your gestures. Incorporate unique aspects of the audience and occasion to personalize the humor.

4 Use humor consistent with your beliefs. Avoid off-color jokes that may offend others and diminish your credibility. If you feel uncomfortable about the story, don't tell it.

5 Evaluate the humor from the audience's point of view. You won't know if the joke's funny until they laugh. However, you might ask: If I were sitting in the audience, would I laugh at it? Would I be offended? Would I understand the point?

Where do you find humor for your speeches? First, from your own experience. Think back on humorous personal experiences, even embarrassing ones, that you can tell publicly. They are often funny and have important morals and lessons. The basis of most comedians' humor are their life experiences. As you hear funny stories, write them down. Sift through the many books on humor in the bookstores. They contain one-liners, humorous anecdotes, and short stories. Watch stand-up comics on cable television. Attend some live comedy shows. Rent videotapes of stand-up comics. These sources can all give you ideas for humor as well as stories.

If you are going to be speaking to a group in the same profession or occupation, find out from the master of ceremonies what humor or jokes might be appropriate to those groups. Accountants, engineers, salespeople, lawyers, managers all have inside humor. You might tell an accountant's or lawyer's story. For instance, you might ask, "Why do they bury lawyers 24 feet underground? Because deep down they are good people."

PRESENTATION SPEECH

Presentation speeches are very common. We give awards for special achievements: for example, to the best athlete, the most inspirational player, the outstanding student, the top salesperson, the employee of the month, and the championship team.

The presentation speech has two main parts. First, give a brief history of the award—how it originated—along with a clear explanation of what the award is for. Next, describe what the recipient(s) did to earn the honor. Go into detail here so the audience fully appreciates the effort that went into the achievement. Here is an example of how one speaker presented an award:

> Each year, the Kennedy-King scholarship is given to that student who through his or her actions and achievements exemplifies the spirit and values of John Kennedy and Martin Luther King, Jr. The recipient is judged on three criteria: (1) financial need, (2) community involvement, and (3) scholarship. The committee

is proud to give this year's award to Cynthia Hernandez. This is a very special young woman and when I hear about all her activities, I don't know how she fits them into a single day. She works part time. She tutors high school students and supervises activities at the Pine Street neighborhood center. Her grade point average is 4.0. She plans to major in special education and her ultimate goal is to run a school for mentally retarded children. Congratulations, Cynthia.

ACCEPTANCE SPEECH

Be gracious. Thank the person or organization sponsoring the award and the people who helped you. Rarely is a personal achievement the act of a single individual. Usually it is the result of many people working together, culminating in the recognition of one or a few. The Oscar-winning actress thanks the director, screenwriter, costume designer, and producer for making her award possible. When you achieve an award, acknowledge the role that others played in helping you achieve it. Here is an example of an acceptance speech.

I want to thank the College Booster's Club for the Outstanding Swimmer Award. It is a real honor and I deeply appreciate it. Being very honest, I never expected

Be gracious when accepting an award.

to receive it and it never occurred to me that I would even be considered, let alone win it. I have some people to thank. Mary Jo, my roommate, who got me to practices on time when my car wouldn't start. But most of all, a big thanks to Coach Johnson. He boosted my spirits when they were low, and when my head got too big, he made me swim extra laps. A big thank you to all of you and my teammates.

COMMEMORATIVE SPEECH

Commemorative speeches are speeches of tribute. They praise the achievements of individuals, groups, or institutions, or they celebrate historical milestones connected to important events or ideas. The Gettysburg Address by Abraham Lincoln may have been the greatest commemorative speech ever given. Veterans Day, Memorial Day, Labor Day, and Martin Luther King, Jr. Day all represent occasions for speeches of tribute.

Speeches of tribute are uplifting and inspiring. They should focus on deeds and accomplishments, qualities of character (bravery, courage, sacrifice, virtue), and preserved cherished principles and institutions. The language should be lofty and eloquent. The audience should be moved and inspired by the presentation. Ronald Reagan's speech to commemorate the Normandy Invasion has been called "Churchillian eloquence." Here are some excerpts from that speech, given June 6, 1984, on the fortieth anniversary of the Normandy Invasion:

> We're here to mark that day in history when Allied armies joined in battle to reclaim this continent to liberty. For four long years, much of Europe had been under a terrible shadow. Free nations had fallen, Jews cried out in the camps, millions cried out for liberation. Europe was enslaved, and the world prayed for its rescue. Here in Normandy the rescue began. Here the allies stood and fought against a tyranny in a giant undertaking unparalleled in human history.
>
> We stand on a lonely, windswept point on the northern shore of France. The air is soft, but forty years ago at this moment, the air was dense with smoke and the cries of men, and the air was filled with the crack of rifle fire and the roar of cannon. . . .
>
> The men of Normandy had faith that what they were doing was right, faith that they fought for all humanity, faith that a just God would grant them mercy on this beachhead or on the next. It was the deep knowledge—and pray God we have not lost it—that there is a profound, moral difference between the use of force for liberation and the use of force for conquest. . . .
>
> Strengthened by their courage, heartened by their valor, and borne by their memory, let us continue to stand for the ideals for which they lived and died.[2]

The speech is filled with lofty language and themes of courage and greatness. Note how the writer sets the stage with the task, "liberation," and sets the scene of battle, "air filled with the crack of rifle fire and the roar of cannon," against a backdrop of "soft" air.

SUMMARY

There are many kinds of speaking for special occasions, including (1) impromptu speaking, (2) answering questions, (3) speeches of introduction, (4) after-dinner speeches, (5) presentation speeches, (6) acceptance speeches, and (7) commemorative speeches.

PROBES

1 List three steps for planning an impromptu speech.
2 Briefly describe four types of informational questions.
3 Briefly describe four types of challenging questions.
4 What is the difference between informational questions and challenging questions?
5 Why are questions important to a speaker?
6 Briefly list some guidelines for answering questions.
7 Briefly list some guidelines for using humor in a speech.
8 Briefly describe the steps for preparing a speech of introduction.
9 What are the two major parts of a presentation speech?
10 Briefly describe the qualities of a commemorative speech.

APPLICATIONS

1 Your instructor will organize an impromptu speaking assignment. You will be evaluated on how well you organize and develop the topic and your delivery.
2 Prepare a speech of introduction about a student in your class using the steps discussed in the chapter.
3 Watch a presidential news conference or a news program, such as *This Week with David Brinkley,* and record the kind of questions asked. What kind of informational and challenging questions were asked? How effectively did the interviewee respond?
4 Prepare a short speech of presentation using the steps in the chapter.
5 Find a humorous anecdote you consider very funny. Practice telling it so it has your voice and mannerisms and you have the punchline and timing down pat. Use it in a speech or at some special occasion and monitor the reaction.
6 Practice telling the following story using the "Guidelines for Using Humor in a Speech" discussed in the chapter until you can tell it with impact using your style:

A women planning a special luncheon for her bible reading club admonished her children to be courteous and polite to all the guests. One guest in particular would be a gentleman who had a nose of unusual length and curvature that was always a focal point of discussion, out of earshot, of course. The woman was particularly concerned that her children not gawk or make mention of the man's elephantine nose and reminded them several times to be polite and avoid looking or mentioning the nose. At the luncheon everything progressed smoothly as the happy hostess moved from group to group pouring more coffee and tea. She spied her children talking quietly to the man in question, walked over to them and joined the conversation to insure the children were behaving appropriately. Reassured, she was about to turn and leave when she noticed his cup was empty. She inquired if the gentleman would like "coffee or tea with his nose."

NOTES

1 Benno Schmidt, speech before The Commonwealth Club of California, February 10, 1993. Excerpt taken from personal notes of presentation.
2 Remarks at a ceremony commemorating the fortieth anniversary of the Normandy Invasion, D-Day, June 6, 1984, taken from *Public Papers of the Presidents of the United States,* Ronald Reagan, 1984, U.S. Government Printing Office, Washington, D.C., 1986, pp. 817–819.

SPEECHES BY PROFESSIONALS

The three speeches printed here were delivered by a diverse group of professionals: Larry King, the well-known television and radio personality; Ruth Bader Ginsburg, a justice of the Supreme Court; and General Colin Powell, former chairman of the Joint Chiefs of Staff. Each of the presentations are both personal and public statements and the last two are rich in history. King's speech will make you laugh. Ginsburg's will inspire. Powell's speech will give you confidence. What do the speeches reveal about the character of the speakers and American culture?

How to Talk to Anyone, Anytime, Anywhere*

Larry King

Larry King is the host of "Larry King Live" and one of the best-known interviewers on television and radio. The speech is entertaining and a good example of after-dinner speaking. King is a good storyteller and strings a number of them together to make a very funny presentation. King does not pre-interview guests nor pre-plan his questions. "Everything is off the top of his head" he says. It is believed he does not rehearse his speeches. The speech was delivered before The Commonwealth Club of California in San Francisco on January 30, 1995. Did you like the stories? Did you find them entertaining? Is this a good example of humorous speaking?

Last year I was in Israel for the first time. I had always wanted to go. My mother and father, of course, were Jewish. My father died when I was very young, and my mother always wanted to go there. Finally, I went with my brother. I'm standing at the Western Wall, and although I'm not very religious, I was very spiritually moved. There was this old Rabbi on the ground, praying fiercely. He looks up at me and asks, "What's with Perot?" That taught me something about impact.

I want to tell you a story that almost curtailed my speaking career. It happened in Miami. This guy calls me in January, and says, "Mr. King, I'm the speaker's chairman. In June, six months from now, we have our annual Miami Shores Rotary Get Together. Wives are invited. We're the oldest club in Florida. Ponce De Leon was the first member. We'd love to have you speak." I said, "Fine, I'm free then." He said, "Wonderful; what's your topic?" I said, "I don't have a topic." He said, "You must have a topic. This is Rotary. From Mr. Eisenhower we would demand a topic." I said, "Call him," and hung up.

THE SPEAKER'S CHAIRMAN

The next night as I'm about to go on the radio, station WIOD, the producer comes in and says, "Emergency call on line one." It's the speaker's chairman. He says, "This is the speaker's chairman from the Rotary. I'm at the print shop. We're printing the flyer for your meeting. What is your topic?" To this day I have no idea why, but I told him my topic was "The Future of the Merchant Marine."

It's six months later, and I drive to the Miami Shores Country Club. The parking lot's full. I park a block away, and my ego is going berserk. I packed the joint. I mean, I drew this crowd.

I walk to the building—God's truth—and there's a sign that says, "Tonight! The Future of the Merchant Marine." I thought to myself, "Jesus Christ! They've got two speakers!" I don't remember the conversation. Now, the speaker's chairman comes running out, beside himself with excitement. He tells me that my topic, "The Future of the Merchant Marine," broke their all-time attendance record!

*Reprinted from the *Commonwealth* Jan. 30, 1995, Issue 50.

Inside, it's a mob scene. I'm up on a dais, and it's a dreary place—old country club, very conservative. Trust me; on the wall, there was a big picture of Barry Goldwater with the word "Pinko." They were handing out baby pictures of Rush Limbaugh that said, "He is born." They were in another league.

The speaker's chairman gets up and says, "Ladies and Gentlemen, since this guy is going to tell you about the future of the merchant marine, I'll tell you about the past." It was the dullest 20 minutes of my life. This guy was talking about tonnage and harbor sizes. The audience is enraptured; their mouths are hanging open. Finally, he says, "And now, ladies and gentlemen, here is Larry King."

I was in a panic. I don't know a cotton pickin' thing about the Merchant Marine. I made a decision; I didn't say a word about the merchant marine. I talked for half an hour about politics, baseball—everything else I could think of. I finished, there was no applause—nothing. I ran out. I get to my car and start it. I've got the air conditioner on—it's humid in Miami. I'm sweating and thinking, "I'll never speak in public again."

All of a sudden someone bangs on the window. It's the speaker's chairman. He'd followed me to my car. I hit the button, the window rolls down, and he sticks his head in. This is a precious moment; I've got my hand on the button, and he's got his head in the window. For a little Jewish boy from Brooklyn, this was power. He pulls out his head and starts to scream. "You never talked about the merchant marine! We got the largest turnout in our history, and you never once mention the merchant marine!" I said, "They have no future" and drove away.

SAGA OF BOOM BOOM JOURNO

Like most of you, I used to think that all the Mafia did all day was commit crime. But how many crimes can you commit? There's got to be some space in between, and in that space, they shop, they clean their houses, send their kids to school, travel, and get involved with charity. How do I know they get involved with charity? I got booked by the Mafia.

I was working for Channel 4 in Miami. The director came in one day and said, "Larry, pick up line two; it's for you. It's a Mr. Boom Boom Journo." That's the truth. I picked up the phone, and this voice says, "November 7. War Memorial Auditorium. Fort Lauderdale. Boy's Town of Italy. It's a charity. You're the emcee. Eight o'clock. Black tie." Then he hung up. Something told me I should go.

The evening arrives. I put on my tuxedo and drive to the War Memorial Auditorium. There's a big sign that says "Tonight, Boy's Town of Italy. Master of Ceremonies: Larry King." I park my car and get out. There's this guy, double-breasted suit, cigarette dangling from his mouth. He says, "My name is Boom Boom Journo; we are very glad you came."

We were both glad. They had a cardinal flown in from Italy. They had a huge band; it was incredible. Boom Boom gives me my instructions. "Here's what we want," he says. "Go up, take 20 minutes. Kid us all you want. Then introduce Sergio. Go ahead; tell all the jokes you want. Make fun of us, but don't turn up the house lights." I said, "I gotta ask, Boom Boom, why?" He said, "There are people in the olive oil business, people in the jukebox business, a whole section of FBI agents. Leave the lights dark." I said, "O.K."

I get on stage and have a wonderful time. Then I bring on Sergio. He sings for an hour and just murders them. They give the cardinal a $500,000 check for Boy's Town of Italy. The crowd is on its feet, stomping and cheering. It was an unbelievable night.

Boom Boom walks me to my car. He's got his arms around my shoulders, and says, "Hey, kid, thanks." I said, "It was my pleasure." He says, "No; we really appreciate it. We owe you a favor." I said, "Nah, Boom Boom. I was happy to do it. I had a great time." Boom Boom turns and says, "We don't like to owe favors."

I had to say something, right? So I said the logical thing: "What do you have in mind?"

I still remember the chill that went up my spine. I remember how my arms felt and how the wind hit my face. He said five words: "Got anybody you don't like?" I'll tell you the truth—when somebody says that, all that you think of are names. I saved the life of the general manager at Channel 4 that night. "To tell you the truth, I can't do that, Boom Boom," I told him. Finally, as we're saying goodbye, he asks, "Do you like horse racing?" I said "Yeah." He said, "We'll be in touch."

About three weeks later, I pick up the phone and a voice says, "Apple Tree in the third at Hialeah." I had $800 to my name. I borrowed another $500, went to Hialeah, and in the third race, bet $300 to win on Apple Tree. As I watched the horses go into the gate, I was thinking: there are three sure things in life—death, taxes, and Apple Tree in the third.

HIGH NOTE

There are times when you take an audience, and through the power of words, change its mind. It happened to me once.

Dick Gerstein was district attorney of Miami at the time; he was the fellow who hired Janet Reno, right out of Harvard. I must have been 25 years old at the time.

Gerstein had heard me speak before. He calls me up, and says, "Larry, I got a real problem. There are two conventions going on in Miami Beach at the same time, the National District Attorneys and the National Chiefs of Police. The conventions are Sunday night. They decided since they're both here, they are going to take the Grand Ballroom of the Fountainbleu for a combined dinner. And they made me chairman.

"My problem is that I have a seminar scheduled for Sunday at two o'clock with Frank Sullivan, chairman of the Florida Crime Commission. We had to cancel it to make room for the dinner. So, anyway, I had to invite Frank Sullivan to speak." I said, "So what do you need me for?" He said, "Frank Sullivan is a boring speaker. Could you follow him? We want to end the convention on a high note." I said, "But nobody knows me." He said, "I'll give you a big introduction."

So I'm sitting up on this dais with district attorneys and chiefs of police, some of them in uniforms. Frank Sullivan gets up to speak. He came with charts and graphs, and he spoke in a monotone. The first person to fall asleep was his wife. He went on and on about crime, and you could see the audience getting more and more bored. Finally, he finishes, and everybody gets up and starts to leave.

Gerstein gets up, and here's his introduction: "Before you go, my friend Larry King." He hasn't said a thing about me. Everybody is standing up; they've just heard the world's most boring speaker, and they're ready to get out of there. I run to the microphone, and say, "Ladies and gentlemen, in broadcasting, we have an equal time doctrine. We have just heard Frank Sullivan speak against crime. I am here to speak on behalf of crime." You could have heard a pin drop. They all sat down—boom—dead silence. I had to think of something to say.

"How many people would like to live in Butte, Montana?" I ask the audience. Nobody raises a hand—not even the guy from Butte. I said, "Okay; nobody wants to go to Butte, Montana, the lowest crime city in the U.S. But what are the top five tourist cities in America? Chicago, Las Vegas, Los Angeles, Miami, New York. What are the top crime cities? Chicago, Las Vegas, Los Angeles, Miami, and New York. Yes, folks, crime is a tourist attraction. People go where crime is."

"Another benefit of crime is that the money stays local. No federal government, no taxes. The local bookmaker goes to the local restaurant, and the money funnels around the community. If we all listen to Frank Sullivan, and if we all do what he says, then yes—we wipe out crime in America. Then what? Everyone in this room is out of work. The police chief of Louisville, Kentucky jumps up and says, "What can we do to help?"

CHUTZPAH

Hadassah is another group that you have to speak if they invite you. My late mother was a member of Hadassah. There are 68,000 of them, and they are all 72-year-old Jewish women. They all have blue hair, and they are all widows. When you meet them, you understand why. Every man went out smiling. Hadassah invented the word "Chutzpah." They have only one goal: get every last dollar out of America and give it to Israel. They stare straight ahead. Hadassah women don't blink; a dollar could drop and they'd miss it. I love the word; it means "gall," but it's beyond gall. The best example of chutzpah that I can give you is Hadassah has a fundraising office in Libya.

Acceptance Speech
Ruth Bader Ginsburg

Ruth Bader Ginsburg is the second woman appointed to the United States Supreme Court. Her presentation is a good example of an acceptance speech. She had been nominated by President Bill Clinton and delivered her acceptance speech from the White House lawn on June 14, 1993. Note how she tells her life story as a student, lawyer, and court of appeals judge. She conveys the importance and dignity of the law. She then thanks her family for their support and love. Did you like her presentation? Did she include all the important parts of an acceptance speech? What impressions did you make about her character?

Mr. President, I am grateful beyond measure for the confidence you have placed in me. And I will strive, with all that I have, to live up to your expectations in making this appointment. I appreciate, too, the special caring of Senator Daniel Patrick Moynihan, the more so because I do not actually know the Senator. I was born and brought up in New York, the state Senator Moynihan represents, and he was the very first person to call with good wishes when President Carter nominated me, in 1980, to serve on the U.S. Court of Appeals for the District of Columbia Circuit. Senator Moynihan has offered the same encouragement on this occasion.

The announcement the President just made is significant, I believe, because it contributes to the end of the days when women, at least half the talent pool in our society, appear in high places only as one at a time performers. Recall that when President Carter took office in 1976, no woman had ever served on the Supreme Court, and only one woman—Shirley Hufstedler of California—then served at the next federal court level, the United States Courts of Appeals. Today, Justice Sandra Day O'Connor graces the Supreme Court bench, and 23 women serve at the federal court of appeals level, two as Chief Judges. I am confident many more will soon join them.

That seems to me inevitable, given the change in law school enrollment. My law school class in the late 1950s numbered over 500; that class included less than 10 women. Not a law firm in the entire city of New York bid for my employment as a lawyer when I earned my degree. Today, few law schools have a female enrollment under 40 percent, and several have reached or passed the 50 percent mark. And, thanks to Title VII, no entry doors are barred.

My daughter, Jane, reminded me a few hours ago, in a good luck call from Australia, of a sign of the change we have had the good fortune to experience. In her high school yearbook on her graduation in 1973, the listing for Jane Ginsburg under "Ambition" was: To see her mother appointed to the Supreme Court. The next line read: If necessary, Jane will appoint her. Jane is so pleased, Mr. President, that you did it instead. Her brother James is too.

I expect to be asked, in some detail, about my views of the work of a good judge on a high court bench. This afternoon is not the moment for extended remarks on that subject, but I might state a few prime guides. Chief Justice Rehnquist offered one I keep in the front of my mind: A judge is bound to decide each case fairly, in accord with the relevant facts and the applicable law, even when the decision is, as he put it, not the one the home crowd wants.

Next, I know no better summary than the one Justice O'Connor recently provided, drawn from a paper by NYU Law Professor Burt Neuborne. The remarks concern the enduring influence of Justice Oliver Wendell Holmes. They read:

When a modern constitutional judge is confronted with a "hard" case, Holmes is at her side with three gentle reminders: (1) intellectual honesty about the available policy choices; (2) disciplined self-restraint in respecting the majority's policy choice; (3) principled commitment to defense of individual autonomy, even in the face of majority action.

To that I can only say "Amen."

I am indebted to so many for this extraordinary chance and challenge, to a revived women's movement in the 1970s that opened doors for people like me, to the civil rights movement of the 1960s from which the women's movement drew inspiration, to my teaching colleagues at Rutgers and Columbia, and for 13 years, my D.C. Circuit colleagues, who shaped and heightened my appreciation of the value of collegiality. Most closely, I have been aided by my life's partner, Martin D. Ginsburg, who has been since our teenage days, my best friend and biggest booster; by my mother-in-law, Evelyn Ginsburg, the most supportive parent a person could have; and by a daughter and son with the taste to appreciate that Daddy cooks ever so much better than Mommy, and so phased me out of the kitchen at a relatively early age.

Finally, I know Hillary Rodham Clinton has encouraged and supported the President's decision to utilize the skills and talent of all the people of the United States. I did not until today know Mrs. Clinton. But, I hasten to add that I am not the first member of my family to stand close to her. There is another I love dearly to whom the First Lady is already an old friend—my wonderful granddaughter, Clara, witness this super, unposed photograph taken last October when Mrs. Clinton visited a nursery school in New York City and led the small people in the toothbrush song. The little one right in front is Clara.

I have a last thank you. It is to my mother, Celia Amster Bader, the bravest, strongest person I have known, who was taken from me much too soon. I pray that I may be all that she would have been, had she lived in an age when women could aspire and achieve, and daughters are cherished as much as sons.

I look forward to stimulating weeks this summer and, if I am confirmed, to working at a neighboring Court, to the best of my ability, for the advancement of the law in the service of society.

I Am Not a Candidate
General Colin Powell

General Colin Powell served as Chairman of the Joint Chiefs of Staff and on the National Security Council. He became a national figure during the Persian Gulf War and, to many, a hero. He was mentioned prominently as a president candidate and in public opinion polls he was favored by 71% of the electorate. After much consideration General Powell declared he was not a candidate and made the announcement on November 8, 1995. Did you like the presentation? Were you moved? What qualities of character did General Powell demonstrate? What does his speech reveal about the history of America?

Good afternoon. For 35 years of my life, I served my nation as a soldier proudly and to the best of my ability. Since my retirement two years ago, I have written my life story and traveled across the country speaking and listening to my fellow Americans. What I saw and heard renewed my faith in our country, its people and its promise.

I also came away with a deeper understanding of the challenges we face, of the problems we must solve to reach the dreams of our founders. All of us have a role to play, and I have been giving the most prayerful consideration to the role I should play. The question I faced was: Should I enter politics and seek the presidency of the United States?

Many of you have encouraged me to do so. I have been deeply honored by the hundreds of letters I have received and by the hard work of grass-roots organizing committees. I thank all of you for the faith and confidence you had in me.

For the past few weeks, I have been consulting with friends and advisers. I have spent long hours talking with my wife and children, the most important people in my life, about the impact an entry into political life would have on us. It would require sacrifices and changes in our lives that would be difficult for us to make at this time.

The welfare of my family had to be uppermost in my mind. Ultimately, however, I had to look deep into my own soul, standing aside from the expectations and enthusiasms of others, because I have a bond of trust with the American people, and to offer myself as a candidate for president requires a commitment and a passion to run the race and to succeed in the quest—the kind of passion and the kind of commitment that I felt every day of my 35 years as a soldier, a passion and commitment that despite my every effort I do not have for political life, because such a life requires a calling that I do not yet hear.

And for me to pretend otherwise would not be honest to myself, it would not be honest to the American people, and I would break that bond of trust. And therefore I cannot go forward. I will not be a candidate for president or for any other elective office in 1996.

I know that this is the right decision for me. It was not reached easily or without a great deal of personal anguish. For me and my family, saying no was even harder than saying yes. I will remain in private life and seek other ways to serve. I have a deep love for this country that has no bounds. I will find other ways to contribute to the important work needed to keep us moving forward.

I know my decision will disappoint many who have supported me. I thank them once again from the bottom of my heart, and I ask for their understanding. I also know that my actions in taking the time to reach this decision has created an enormous level of expectation and anticipation. But I needed the time to give this the most careful study.

I will continue to speak out forcefully in the future on the issues of the day, as I have been doing in recent weeks. I will do so as a member of the Republican Party and try to assist the party in broadening its appeal. I believe I can help the party of Lincoln move once again close to the spirit of Lincoln.

I will give my talent and energy to charitable and educational activities. I will also try to find ways for me to help heal the racial divides that still exist within our society.

Finally, let me say how honored I am that so many of you thought me worthy of your support. It says more about America than it says about me. In one generation, we have moved from denying a black man service at a lunch counter to elevating one to the highest military office in the nation and to being a serious contender for the presidency. This is a magnificent country, and I am proud to be one of its sons.

Thank you very much.

INDEX